THE FESTIVE SUTRAS
A YOGI'S GUIDE TO SHABBAT & JEWISH FESTIVALS

by Marcus J Freed

www.marcusjfreed.com

Freedthinker Books
8829 Alcott Street, Suite #5, Los Angeles, CA 90035
www.marcusjfreed.com

Copyright© 2017 by Marcus J Freed
All rights reserved. No part of this publication may be reproduced or transmitted in any form or by any means, electronic or mechanical, including photocopying, recording or any information storage or retrieval system, without permission in writing from the publishers.

Original version printed in the United States of America.

First edition, February, 2017.

Library of Congress Control Number: 2016911475

ISBN: 978-0-9963506-8-6 (Print Edition). ISBN: 978-0-9963506-5-5 (Electronic Book).

Cover Design & Chapter Logo: Joshua Rudolph
Page Layout: Ann Steer
Proof Reading: Gillian Freed
Additional Cover Photographs: Tom Levy & stock images
Author Portrait Photograph: Timothy Fielding
Yoga Photographs: Timothy Riese
Consulting Rabbi on Yoga: Rabbi Dovid Ebner

LANGUAGE AND FONTS

We have followed UK English spellings and punctuation styles throughout the book. The primary font is Adobe Caslon, originally designed by William Caslon (1692-1766) in London. I chose this font because of its good readability, workability and the connection to my native England. Hebrew and Hebrew transliterations are usually in italics, titles are in Trilogy Sans. The footnote font is Candara.

The Hebrew transliterations are generally written with the modern Sephardic pronunciation, e.g. Shabbat rather than Shabbes, Shabbos or Shobbos.
To represent the guttural 'Chet' sound (as in Chanukah or L'Chayim), we have written a 'Ch'. The 'chet' sound is hard to accurately pronounce by the written word alone, without vocal instruction. You will know it is being said incorrectly when somebody articulates 'chutzpah' (or hutzpah) with a soft ch that is not coming from the back of the throat. It is a mix between clearing your throat and blowing a smoke ring (and the latter practice is definitely not recommended as part of any yogic healthcare plan). You can get decent pronunciation samples of the sound in any Broadway or West End cast recording of Fiddler on the Roof singing "To Life/ L'Chayim" (although it is a bit hit-or-miss with the amateur productions).

DISCLAIMER

Please consult your health care provider and obtain full medical clearance before practicing yoga or any exercise programme. Practising under the direct supervision and careful guidance of a qualified instructor will reduce risk of injuries. The information in this book is strictly for reference only and not in any manner a substitute for medical advice or the direct teaching of a qualified yoga teacher. The author, illustrators, photographers and publishers assume no responsibility for injuries or losses that may result from following any of the advice contained herein. If, whilst practicing, you find the room suddenly filling with light, angels are singing and your skin is glowing, you are on the right track. Now, practice in safety and good health! L'Chayim!

BOOKS BY MARCUS J FREED

The Kosher Sutras: The Jewish Way in Yoga & Meditation

The Kabbalah Sutras: 49 Steps to Enlightenment

The Festive Sutras: A Yogi's Guide to Shabbat & Festivals

DEDICATION

For Luca and Justin.

*May your spiritual journeys be accompanied
with peace, joy, light and truth.*

ACKNOWLEDGEMENTS

Thank you to everyone who helped with the project: Dr Adam Silver, Aharon Varady & the Open Siddur Project, Amanda Van Dyk, Barry Freed, Beverly Hills Chiropractic & Orthopedic Centre, Boris Kievsky, Chaya Shira Sheaks, Danny Knust, Debora Gianonne, Dr Farzad Rabbany, Elissa Krycer, Eric Rosen, Evanna Lynch, Gillian Freed, Isabelle Loeb, Eli Doug Staimen, Jeff Handel, Kaley Zeitouni, Milana Vayntrub, Pico Cafe, Dr Tsippi Shainhouse, Rabbi Brandon Gaines, Rabbi Hillel Simon, Rabbi Yonah Bookstein, Steve Cohn & Shira Geula Cohn.

Special thanks to The Charles and Lynn Schusterman Family Foundation and ROI for your generous grants and ongoing support. Thank you to Amir Given and the team at Jewcer for your crowdfunding expertise.

CROWDFUNDING SUPPORTERS

I have tremendous gratitude to everyone who supported the crowdfunding. Thank you for your faith in this project and for helping it come to life! The Festive Sutras family are: Aaron Sztarkman, Abigail Coren, Adi & Boaz Hepner, Andrea Hodos, Audrey Jacobs, Babak Kanani, Bal Byron, Barak Raviv, Batsheva & Yossi Frankel, Becca Coren, Benjamin Elterman, Beth R. Steinberg, Brendan Howe, Bronya Gorney, Cantor Lisa Levine, Cantor Rosalie Boxt, Carla Gavzey-Jakobs, Cheryl Rosenstein, Christopher Nicholson & Sara Coppola, Courtney Mellblom, Dahlia & Moshe Bellows, Danny Newman & Zippy Keller, David Chernyavsky, David Pekelney, Desiree Brenner, Dina Saffer-Myers, Eliana & David Weiss, Eric Kingston, Esther Pasternak, Estee & Eric Rosen, Gill & Barry Freed, Gwen Wexler, Jeffrey Van Dyk, Jeremy & Adele Stowe-Lindner, Josh Cohen, Josh Sacks, Julia Soros, Justin Rubin, Keturah Phoebe Attia, Lainie Friedman, Lara Walklet, Leslie Glickman, Liz Feldman, Luca Rubin, Margery Diamond, Mary Connerty, Mary F. Meyerson, Melissa Kurtz, Michal & Brandon Coppel, Michelle Esther Appelbaum, Miriam Levi, Mordechai Fishman, Naomi & Stephen Sacks, Professor Jeremy Kagan, Rabbi Dr Leslie Schotz, Rabbi Louis Rieser, Rebecca Green, Robert & Kelly Messik, Robert Bray, Rya Miller, Sam Talbot, Sandra Razieli, Shira & Jason Rosenbaum, Simon & Emma Kisner, Sonia Cummings, Susie and Eliot Kaye, Tara Mizrachi, William Kingston, Yosef & Jaime Esshaghian.

CONTENTS

The Yogi's Prayer ix
Introduction Xiii
The Hebrew Calendar Xvii
A Note On The Yoga Positions xxiii
THE FESTIVE SUTRAS 1
   Rosh Hashannah 1: From The Depths I Call To You 3
   Rosh Hashannah 2: The Human Shofar 6
   Rosh Hashannah 3: A New Heart 8
   The Fast of Gedaliah: Our Inner Assassin 10
   10 Days of Return: 10 Days of Realignment 11
   Yom Kippur 1: Fasting and Silence 13
   Yom Kippur 2: Living Like Angels 15
   Yom Kippur 3: Five Steps to Enlightenment 17
   Yom Kippur 4: The Physicality of Yom Kippur 19
   Yom Kippur 5: Silence 20
   Succot 1: the Divine body 23
   Succot 2: Ecclesiastes and the Breath of Breaths 27
   Succot 3: Kabbalistic Unity 29
   Succot 4: 7 days, 6 directions 31
   Succot 5: Today I am a Succah 33
   Succot 6: Kabbalah & the Ushpizin 36
   Shabbat Chol HaMoed Succot: 39
   Hoshannah Rabbah: Prayers of Fire 43
   Shemini Atzeret: The Hidden 8 47
   Simchat Torah: The Rabbi Does A Handstand 51
   Rosh Chodesh: Dancing in the Moonlight 53
   MarCheshvan: Feeling Groovy 57
   Chanukah 1: Dark Night of the Soul 59
   Chanukah 2: Warriors of Light 61
   Chanukah 3: Pure Light 64
   Chanukah 4: A New Hope 67
   Chanukah 5: The Hidden Story of Chanukah 68
   Chanukah 6: Dedication 70
   Chanukah 7: Be the light 72
   Chanukah 8: This Is It 74
   Tu B'Shvat: The Human TReE 75
   Purim: It's all about Joy and Gladness 79

    Birkat HaChamah: Here Comes The Sun 83
    Pesach 1: Outstretched Arms 87
    Pesach 2: The Yogi's Hagaddah..90
    Lag B'Omer: Responsibility 103
    Shavuot 1: Equilibrium..107
    Shavuot 2: Desert Freedom 109
    Shavuot 3: The Essence Of Yoga...111
    Fasting: A Yogic Practice 113
    Tisha B'Av 1: Your Body Is A Temple..................................115
    Tisha B'Av 2: Forgiveness Protocol 118
    Tisha B'Av 3: Meditations...120
    Tu B'Av: Valentine's Day For The Soul...............................125
  THE SHABBAT SUTRAS...127
    Tantric Shabbat: Weekly Energy Connections.....................129
    Shabbatasana/Sheva-Sana: Dynamic Relaxation...................141
    Nishmat Kol Chai: Prayer Practice Sequence 143
    Shabbat Meditations..167

Additional Writings
  ETHICS OF THE YOGIS..169
    Introduction...171
    Peace 175
    Truth 179
    Abundance...185
    Power 191
    Non-Attachment 195
    Purity 201
    Contentment 205
    Study 213
    Surrender 217
Appendix 1: Is Yoga Kosher?...221
Appendix 2: Halacha, Shabbat & Exercise...................................223
Bibliography..227
Glossary..231
Book Club Questions..237
Additional Resources 237
Index 239

THE YOGI'S PRAYER

'And I am my prayer to you' Psalm 69:14

Yoga is a form of physical prayer. Through a yoga practice we might have the intention to become aware of our oneness with God. The word yoga means to 'unite' or to 'yoke' and we are consciously unifying our mind with our breath, our heart with our actions, ourselves with the Divine. Traditional yoga classes might precede the *asana* (physical yoga) practice with the traditional *Invocation to Patanjali*. This Sanskrit chant which may leave Jewish practitioners feeling uncomfortable. As such I have written a couple of prayers that you can use as alternatives. Alternatively you may choose to write your own prayer.

Notes on the Yogi Prayers

The Hebrew prayer is inspired by various *yichudim*, Kabbalistic prayers for unity that are said before practices such as putting on the *tallis* (prayer shawl), or shaking the lulav on Succot. There are various borrowings from Psalms and even the opening line of the *Sefer Yetzirah*, an important work of Kabbalah. The English prayer is similarly focused to tune our minds, open our bodies and set a strong intention as we begin a physical practice. Both are also inspired by the medieval devotional writers of *piyyutim* prayers.

You might also use the words of King David *V'ani Tefilati* (Psalm 69:14), which means 'I am my prayer'.

THE YOGI'S PRAYER

May it be Your will Hashem, my God
    and the God of my Ancestors.
Recall how we were freed from the Egypt-mind
    Create new beginnings every day
Unify the letters of your name within our body
    Send us blessings to practice in peace

May abundant blessings flow from high
    And strengthen our vessels to receive Your light
Reveal the Divine spark you placed with us
    Conscious and present, mindful and calm
Uplift our spirit, soul, breath, mind and body
    So all our bones may say *'God, who is like you?'*

"Let every breath praise your name, Hallelujah"

And may it come to pass. Amen v'amen.

MARCUS J FREED   *THE FESTIVE SUTRAS*

תְּפִילַת הַיּוֹגִי

יְהִי רָצוֹן מִלְפָנֶיךָ ה' אֱלֹהֵינוּ וֵאלֹהֵי אֲבוֹתֵינוּ, מֶלֶךְ

רֶמֶז בְּגוּף שֶׁלָנוּ, רֶמֶז הַשֵּׁם

כִּי מֶלֶךְ כָּל־הָאָרֶץ אֱלֹהִים- זַמְּרוּ מַשְׂכִּיל

סוֹמֵךְ נוֹפְלִים, וְהַזוֹקֵף כְּפוּפִים, לְךָ לְבַדְּךָ אֲנַחְנוּ מוֹדִים

מִי כָמֹכָה בָּאֵלִם יְהֹוָה, מִי כָּמֹכָה נֶאְדָּר בַּקֹּדֶשׁ

רוֹמְמוּ ה' אֱלֹהֵינוּ וְהִשְׁתַּחֲווּ לְהַר קָדְשׁוֹ

כֹּל הַנְּשָׁמָה, תְּהַלֵּל יָה וְכֹל הַגּוּף

סַפְּרוּ לָנוּ שֶׁל הַגְּדוּלָה וְהַמוֹפְתִים

מֶלֶךְ הָעוֹלָם

רוֹקַע הָאָרֶץ עַל הַמַּיִם, וּמַתִּיר אֲסוּרִים

כֹּל הַנְּשָׁמָה, תְּהַלֵּל יָה: הַלְלוּיָהּ

סְפָרִים בְּסֵפֶר וּסְפָר וְסִפּוּר, שְׁלוֹשָׁה סְפָרִים הוּא בָּרָא אֶת עוֹלָמוֹ

שָׁלוֹם בְּ'גוּף, שָׁלוֹם בְּ'מוֹכִין, וְשָׁלוֹם בְּעוֹלָם. אָמֵן.

MARCUS J FREED *THE FESTIVE SUTRAS*

INTRODUCTION

INTRODUCTION

Thank you for picking up this book! *The Festive Sutras* is a simple book of essays intended to help you experience God within your body, and connect with the cycle of Shabbat and festivals through with your entire being.

HOW TO USE THIS BOOK

This book is intended as a practice manual that can be used on a number of levels. To begin with you might read a chapter and then do the recommended yoga pose or another posture of your choice. As a student you could read an essay before going to a yoga class or meditation session and use the teaching as the basis for your practice. If you are a teacher, you can create lessons around these essays, and add in postures or sequences as you see fit. Alternatively you might just use the one-line 'Festive Sutra' verse to inspire and motivate yourself. There is also the opportunity to use the book for more traditional chevruta learning, although I would always encourage you to incude some practical movement to integrate the teaching.

MY JOURNEY

I began my body-soul journey in the year 2000 and at the time there was a lack of easily-accessible materials to make the connection between Jewish spiritual ideas and a physical practice. I felt the call to start writing..and writing..and writing. My first book *The Kosher Sutras* explored connections between authentic Torah teachings and the weekly Torah-reading (*parsha*) and my second book *The Kabbalah Sutras* expanded to a physical and emotional exploration of Kabbalistic ideas.

This is Book Three, a collection of essays that I wrote around 2008-2010 on my first visits to California. During the intervening years these essays have been calling out from my bookshelf, as if to say 'our siblings have been published. What about us?'. So here they are. A series of personal musings and reflections around festive times, and a deeper physical dive into the cycle of Shabbat and *Chagim* (festivals). Plus a few more essays thrown in for good measure.

THREE GUIDEBOOKS

Technically this volume is a compendium of three smaller guidebooks to take you through the cycle of festivals, one of the shabbat prayers and a short yogic commentary on Ethics of the Fathers (*Pirkei Avot*), part of the oral tradition (*mishna*) which is traditionally studied on Shabbat afternoons in the summer.

This book is by no means exhaustive. There are lots of ideas that I have not included here, partly due to space and partly because I haven't thought of them yet. As King Solomon wrote 'there is no end to the making of books'[1], although this book is intended as completion to the Sutra Trilogy, and a final wrap-up of my 'Bibli-yoga' journey that began 14 years ago.

---

[1] *Ecclesiastes 12:12.*

INTRODUCTION

There are many other books that can be written in this series. We could have created a complete yogic *Hagaddah* for Passover. Or a series of postures for the morning blessings that mention various parts of the body. Or a sequence for the Friday night *Kabbalat Shabbat* service that would be based on opening and receiving as 'Kabbalat Shabbat' means 'welcoming the Sabbath'. Or a 'unity' sequence for Shabbat afternoon, where the central prayer includes the phrase *Ata Echad* ('you are one'), based on inner unity. There is so much that can be written, and many more teachings to be channeled down. Maybe one day they will be.

There is a brief essay at the end of the book on the *halacha* of exercise and shabbat. Jewish law (*halacha*) holds a fairly stringent position forbidding exercise during Shabbat[2], however yoga falls outside the technical bounds of exercise because technically it can be viewed as prayer of meditation. I would suggest that this is largely a matter of intention, e.g. Whether you are practicing for the purpose purely for your body or as a gateway to Higher connection. Indeed the Yoga Sutras begin by stating that the entire purpose of yoga is to calm our mind, and goes on to discuss how the higher intention of yoga is to connect and unify with God. This can seem a long way from the sweaty and aerobics-like classes that take their place in the mix of modern yoga classes, but as they say, there are many paths to God.

ON ONE FOOT

So what is this book, in a way that can be said whilst balancing on one foot? **The Festive Sutras is a way to tune in your body and soul.** Also, to use the wonderful gifts of the Jewish festivals and Shabbat as a basis for spiritual elevation.

---

[2] *Mishnah Berurah 328:130.*

WHAT THIS BOOK IS, AND WHAT IT IS NOT

These essays are my personal search for answers, to find an embodied Jewish practice where I could feel Shabbat and festivals rather than just pray with my mind. I want kinaesthetic experience, a full-body God experience, and could not (and still cannot) find it in any formal Jewish setting. This book uses the physical language of yoga but is not about the search for a perfect yoga experience. It uses the teachings and framework of Judaism but is not about being Jewish or perfecting a Jewish-ism. Rather it is about using these lenses, my own religious and cultural interests, to experience God and to do my part to reveal more Divine light into the world. *L'Taken [tikkun] Olam b'Malchut Shadai*[3] - 'to rejuvenate/heal the world in the Kingdom of God'

This is intended as a straightforward collection of teachings that I use to motivate myself, for you to enjoy and benefit from as the spirit takes you. Enjoy!

Marcus J Freed
February, 2017
Los Angeles, California

---

[3] This Hebrew phrase is from the *Aleinu* prayer that is said at the end of every Jewish prayer service.

THE HEBREW CALENDAR

THE FESTIVE SUTRAS – A YOGI'S GUIDE TO SHABBAT & FESTIVALS

Holistic living is about being in touch with the rhythm of nature and the world around us. This idea has been taken on by various Green sustainability movements who advocate eating local food that is in season, so that we can support local farmers, reducing our carbon footprint and staying in tune with the land around us. Older yogic and ayurvedic teaching certainly advocated eating locally-grown foods that are in season, and retreat centres are becoming increasingly concerned with having strong organic credentials.

The Biblical cycle of festivals has developed from a largely agricultural basis, although they all fit in with an intensely strong spiritual philosophical system. This book is about finding opportunities for body-soul connections, and the seasonal festivals provide an important gateway for the Bibliyogi.

OVERVIEW

The Hebrew calendar cycle begins with Rosh Hashannah, the new year festival, which usually falls around the end of September. Rosh Hashannah commemorates the creation of the world and the first human, but is not an agricultural festival. It is followed by a week known as the

THE FESTIVE SUTRAS

Aseret Y'mei Teshuvah, or '10 days of return' that culminate in Yom Kippur, the Day of Atonement. The new year celebrations are then concluded, leading into the first of three agricultural pilgrim festivals. Collectively referred to as *Shalosh Regalim*, they are the three 'foot' festivals, so called because farmers in ancient Israel would make the thrice-yearly pilgrimage to Jerusalem by foot. Succot (approximately mid-October) is a harvest festival that marks the ingathering of fruits and remembers when the Children of Israel wandered in the desert living in huts known as succahs (often translated into English as the archaic 'Tabernacles'). Pesach (which falls approximately mid-April) matches the barley harvest and the historical event of the Hebrew slaves escaping from Egypt, whilst Shavuot (May/June) is timed for the wheat harvest, remembering the Torah being given on Mount Sinai. Later non-agricultural festivals also join the fray, such as Chanukah (December) that is a festival of lights and remembers the spiritual survival from Greek oppressors, while Purim (March) is a semi-Bacchanalian celebration commemorating the survival from a potential mass destruction in Ancient Persia.

History is a large part of these festivals but it is history-in-the-present. The Biblical view of time is cyclical rather than linear. The same is true of the 'smaller' events, such as the fast day Tisha B'Av commemorating the destruction of Jerusalem's Temple and the romantic day of Tu B'Av that celebrates rebirth and was a day for marriage proposals (when women would propose to men). Finally, there is the 49-day period of Sefirsat HaOmer between Pesach and Shavuot. It was originally a time for general anxiety about the fate of the crops and the harvest, which was due to be reaped on Shavuot[1]. The crops' abundance - or lack thereof - would have greatly impacted a farmer's quality of life for the coming year. It made sense to pray. Nonetheless, the Sages later revealed hugely kabbalistic dimensions to this 49-day time period (to such an extent than an entire section of this book is dedicated to it with the Omer/Sefirah sequences). If you would like to explore this more deeply with meditations, practices and teachings for each of the 49 days, please take a look at my book *The Kabbalah Sutras: 49 Steps to Enlightenment*.

---

[1] This is explained by the Abudraham, as quoted in *The Book of Our Heritage*, Vol II, p.363, by Eliyahu Kitov.

TIME & MEETING OURSELVES

One of the Hebrew terms for a festival is *mo'ed* which refers to the temporal aspect of the celebration, in the sense that it is an 'appointed time'[2]. There is a very specific rhythm to the way that the festivals fall and we are encouraged to meet each festival with a conscious and mindful appreciation. Although a whole year passes between each celebration, there is a sense that we are visiting a part of ourselves and seeing how we have changed from that time last year. In this way the Kabbalistic calendar is cyclical rather than temporal, as if we are going around in a spiral and visiting the same point each year, recognising where we were the previous year, seeing how we have grown and how we have contributed towards improving the world. Rav Matis Weinberg explains:

> *'This cyclic dimension does not consist of a simple circle, of course, for then we would keep bumping into our past each "time around"! Instead, time is a spiralling cycle in which certain co-ordinates are the same as in the last cycle while others differ. Just as we can repeatedly visit the same space location and not meet our previous selves, so are we annually exposed to equivalent time locations. The differences in our persons and in our history become an actual part of the measurement of time. This combination of recurrence and difference is reflected in the Hebrew word for the year – shana, having the double meaning "repetition/change"'*[3].

We can only measure our own growth and progress when we have some form of measuring stick to place against ourselves. This can happen with our character development when we notice how situations that once provoked us suddenly seem to lose their effect, or we discover on a physical level that we have greater stamina or more flexibility than the last time we approached that posture. By repeatedly visiting these fixed points in time, whether it is celebrating a festival or visiting a posture, we continue on the journey of personal transformation.

---

[2] Other phrases include Chag ('festival') and Zman (literally, 'time'), although they are not directly relevant to this part of the discussion.
[3] *Patterns in Time*, Vol 1: p.54, Rosh Hashannah by Matis Weinberg.

Simon and Garfunkel may have sung that 'after changes upon changes we are more or less the same'[4] but this could not be further from the Kabbalistic viewpoint. *Shana*, the Hebrew word for both 'year' and 'change' is the repetition that leads to the *shana* of change and personal development.

KOSHER SUTRAS: FESTIVALS

The format of these Kosher Sutras continues as in my earlier book *The Kosher Sutras: The Jewish Way in Yoga & Meditation* and *The Kabbalah Sutras: 49 Steps to Enlightenment*. You can use these essays as a motivation for your physical yoga practice, read it to discuss with a group of friends, or use it as a teachers' tool to integrate throughout a class sequence (sometimes there is one idea for a festival and sometimes there will be two or three). Many of these are organic teachings that are continually developing and have often grown out of email correspondence with students. If you would like to receive more ideas and practice sequences on a regular basis, sign up at www.marcusjfreed.com.

HOW DO I USE THE BOOK AND THESE CHAPTERS?

There are three main ways of using this book;

1. To read the chapters on their own
2. To read in preparation for your own personal yoga practice, using the postures and vinyasas described.
3. To read before a general yoga class, so that you can uplift and focus the experience through the ideas.

YOGA PHILOSOPHY AND PRACTICAL PRACTICE.

The focus of a yoga practice is to initially work on technique, concentrating on aspects such as foot placement and alignment of limbs to achieve openness. Good technique will allow energy to flow through your body, enabling you to take the deepest breath possible at any one moment.

---
[4] The Boxer.

THE HEBREW CALENDAR

The next stage is to bring our attention to the breathing. This has several purposes. Firstly, our aim is for smooth, soft and regular inhalation and exhalation, and the idea is that a calm breath will reflect a calm mind. When moving through vinyasa we try to match our movement to the breath so that everything is connected. Our breathing can reveal the internal stillness, or lack of it. Yogis refer to breath work as *pranayama*; more than just breath, *prana* is life-force, and the process of Hatha yoga is to manipulate this life force in a positive way, using breath and movement to cleanse and open our bodies for full spiritual connection.

Posture (*asana*), movement (*vinyasa*) and breath or energy work (*pranayama*) are just three parts of the yoga spectrum; three tools in the hands of a tradesman who is trying to force links between the individual soul and the Great Soul. These links are already there, and the Kabbalah teaches that Divine Light is all around us but hidden by metaphysical curtains. By engaging in prayer, meditation and good deeds we are able to reveal some of this light.

Classical yoga is full of moral instruction, although the phrase seems anachronistic and Victorian in today's world. But each of the ethical principles helps create a world around us that is peaceful, loving and more enjoyable for everyone. The Yoga Sutras describe *yamas* and *niyamas*, ethical/moral ideas that bring healing to society. These include general principles such as *aparigraha*, the instruction to avoid stealing, or *ahimsa*, the idea of non-violence. Some yoga teachers will theme classes around one of these principles.

THE FESTIVE SUTRAS

YOGA POSTURES

A NOTE ON THE YOGA POSITIONS

There are a variety of yoga postures referred to throughout this book and these are all intended to help you physicalise and deepen your internal experience of the teachings. This book is not however intended to teach you the specific postures, but rather to explore the ideas. The best way to learn yoga asana (postures) is with a qualified master teacher, but there are also many other resources including classes and demonstrations on Youtube. I have included comprehensive asana pictures and explanations in my previous books *The Kosher Sutras* and *The Kabbalah Sutras*. These photos are also available for free in the various videos on my Youtube channel (marcusjfreed) that accompany both books.

That being said, here is the most central yoga vinyasa sequence, the Sun Salute ('surya namaskar'). Please remember that yoga is not about whether you can touch your toes, stand on your head or stick your foot behind your ear. It is about whether you can still your mind and join with the presence of God. Now, enjoy!

THE FESTIVE SUTRAS

SUN SALUTATION / SURYA NAMASKAR

The sun salutation is driven by the breath.

1

1. Begin in Mountain Pose with your feet together, shoulders down.

2. & 3. Inhale: Lift your hands up above your head and touch your palms together. Look at your thumbs. Keep your ribs in and your shoulders down.

4. Exhale: Fold your body forwards. Inhale in this position and elongate your spine.

5. Exhale: Jump or float legs backwards.

6. Bend your elbows so that you are in Chatturanga, a low plank.

7. Inhale: Stretch into Upward-Facing Dog.

8. Exhale: Press back and lift your hips into Downward Dog. Hold position for five breaths.

9. Bend your knees on an exhale and jump forwards on an inhale.

10. & 11. Inhale: Lift your hands upwards to a standing position and press your palms together.

12. Return to Mountain Pose (Position 1).

YOGA POSTURES

xxv

THE FESTIVE SUTRAS

6

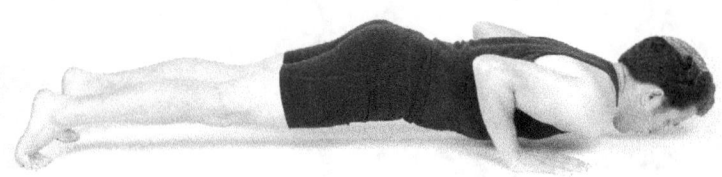

7

8

YOGA POSTURES

xxvii

EASY POSE/SUKHASANA

'This is the day the Lord has made, rejoice and be glad in it'

PSALM 118:24

THE FESTIVE SUTRAS

THE FESTIVE SUTRAS

ROSH HASHANNAH

ROSH HASHANNAH 1: FROM THE DEPTHS I CALL TO YOU

FESTIVE SUTRA: 'From the depths I call to You, God' *Psalm 130:1*

YOGA PRACTICE: *Nadhi Sodhana*, Alternate nostril breathing.

Rosh Hashanah is a New Year festival that can lift you high and take you to profound depths. Rather than being focused on the sort of light-hearted celebrations that characterise a secular new year, it is a time of serious spiritual renewal. The prayers of the day continually mention the theme of *Dsin*, or judgement, reflecting on how this two-day event sets the tone for the coming year. We think about how far we have come from the same time last year, and how we would like to grow in the coming 12 months. We reflect on how we have fared personally, professionally, financially and as a society. We consider who will live and who will die in the coming year. Whilst there is an element of joyousness that is associated with every holiday, this is a time for deepening our spiritual connection. Rosh Hashanah is the beginning of the 10 Days of Return, as we pay full attention to coming closer to The Source.

For the month leading up to Rosh Hashannah we read Psalm 130 which begins with the words, *'From the depths I call to You, God'*. It is about calling to God from a place of depression or despair. Life is challenging, so I look to God for help. I am feeling low, so I raise my eyes to the heavens. And so on. This can be uplifting and healing, and faith can provide us with great hope. We can also take this one stage further when we internalise and physicalise the meditation.

On Rosh Hashanah we remember the creation of mankind, and the first breath that was blown into the first human being, 'the Lord God formed man from the dust of the earth. He blew into his nostrils the breath of life, and man became a living being'[18]. We might say that the ultimate prayer of Rosh Hashannah is *breathed* rather than spoken, as the meditative apex of the day is the sounding of the Shofar, a ram's horn that is blown 100 times. We move beyond words, listening to a primal sound, sounding a war-like rally cry and creating a recital that is somewhere between a cacophony and a symphony. Yet the sound of the shofar has to come from the depths of someone's lungs. As my teacher Rabbi Ebner once shared with me, we might read this as *from the depths [of my body/lungs] I call to you.*

The yogis taught the art of *pranayama* - breathing control and energy manipulation - as something that is far beyond just breathing skills. *Prana* is a life force, an energy that is moved around the body and manipulated in such a way that we can achieve extreme physical feats, such as the extended yogic balances, and create self-healing. Different schools of yoga have been drawn towards the more subtle variations of prana movement, such as the Kundalini energy that is said to rise up the spine like a serpent. Pranayama is therefore much more than just a breathing technique. It can reconnect us with the unused stores of energy in our body, change our mood for the better, move us towards self-healing and restore our mental focus and clarity. Although the breathing itself is processed through our lungs, the oxygen that is absorbed by the alveoli inside our lungs is then transported into our bloodstream for circulation around the body. This goes to all of the body, even to the extremities of our feet, bringing even greater truth to the phrase 'from the depths I call to you'.

---

[18] Genesis 2:7-8.

ROSH HASHANNAH

As we focus on pranayama and the focused movement of breath-energy around our body, we can use it as a tool for renewing our connection with the Source of All Breath and lifting ourselves out of the depths. In this way, we can truly ascend.

ROSH HASHANNAH 2: THE HUMAN SHOFAR

FESTIVE SUTRA: 'My breath shall not abide in a human forever, since s/he is flesh...' *Genesis 6.3*

YOGA PRACTICE: *Bhastrika Pranayama*, Bellows breathing.

Rosh Hashannah remembers the creation of mankind. It is a moment when, according to tradition, all creatures are judged for the coming year. Who will live and who will die - a serious business.

For many years I served as *Baal Tokea*, the official *shofar*-blower at my parents' congregation[19]. The Shofar is a ritual ram's horn and its role is to shake people into a mode of self-reflection, and self-improvement. The day is also called a *'remembrance of the shofar blasts'*[20], or more accurately perhaps, 'a memory of the blowing'.

It was a powerful moment when the first person took their first breath, and the passage in Genesis describes how God blew into Adam's nostrils. This event is worth consideration. How much control do we have over our breathing mechanism? If you try exhaling and hold for as long as you can, you will eventually need to take a new breath. Try it. Whilst we can control our breathing to a large extent, the big inhale is beyond our control as long as we are above ground. We need to breathe and we want to live.

We also cannot consciously stop ourselves from breathing without some external factor. This can be a difficult realisation for some, in that being alive is not our choice but we have to make the most of it. We also do not have much say over when it ends; 'My breath shall not abide in a human forever, since s/he is flesh...'[21]. What are we to do, but reflect on the fragility of this life and of this breath, and make great use of the time we have? One day we will have to return our breath, and it usually is not at a moment of our choosing.

---

[19] Watford & District Synagogue in Hertfordshire, UK.
[20] Leviticus 23:24.
[21] Genesis 6.3

ROSH HASHANNAH

Remembrance is a large part of Rosh Hashanah, thinking about the triumphs and the tragedies that we have experienced during the previous year. What has gone well and where we have suffered, both as individuals and as communities. It is also a time to think about the people who have passed away.

According to the Kabbalah, *nefesh* is the animal part of our soul, the animus force that drives our physical being. But the word is also related to *nashaf*, which means to blow or exhale. As we discover yet another connection between the breath, and the breathing, we can see how the blowing of the shofar is so much more than just a musical prayer; it is a remembrance of the first breath and an appreciation of every subsequent breath. This was stated most profoundly by Rabbi Dov Ber of Mezeritch, an 18th century Kabbalist[22];

> *'You are a shofar. Breath is blown into you and sound emerges. If the shofar-blower walks away, you are silent. So it is that when the Blessed God is absent – God forbid! – it becomes impossible to think or to speak'*[23].

We are the musical instrument, with the breath being blown into us. If the shofar blower walks way, we stop making sound. Today is a chance to appreciate every breath, breathe in deeply and live life to the fullest. 'Let every soul-breath praise You, Hallelujah'[24].

---

[22] Also known as the Maggid of Mezeritch, 1704-1722, who was a disciple of the Baal Shem Tov.
[23] R. Dov Ber of Mezritch, *Maggid Devarav l'Yaakov*, #105, 106.
[24] Psalms 150:4.

ROSH HASHANNAH 3: A NEW HEART

FESTIVE SUTRA: 'Make for yourselves a new heart and a new spirit'
Ezekiel 18:30

YOGA PRACTICE: Heart-opening poses (backbends, Cow Pose arms)

Rosh Hashannah presents an opportunity to begin again and enter the new year with a blank slate. In *The Foundation of Repentance*, the 12th Century teacher Rabbeinu Yonah[18] (1180-1263) quoted the prophet Ezekiel who said:

> *'Cast away from yourselves all transgressions by which you transgressed, and make yourselves a new heart and a new spirit. Why should you die? (Ezekiel 18:30-31)'*[19]

There is a profound beauty in this, to consider how we can make for ourselves a new heart. Some theories hold that our body replaces all of its cells every seven years, and this Biblical teaching speaks directly that that possibility.

Rosh Hashanah has the idea of change hidden within its Hebrew name. Rosh Hashannah literally means 'Head [*rosh*] of the [*Ha*] year [*Shannah*]'. The word *Shaneh* (which is spelled the same way in Hebrew, means 'change'. Rosh Hashannah can thus be translated as 'a change of head' or 'a new head'[20]. We can take this further and think of it as 'a change of perception', or opening up the gates of perception. We can set new intentions in our heart, and broaden our mind to creative new possibilities for the new year.

What does it mean to make a new heart? Perhaps this relates to our intention, as we let go of anger from our hearts and forgive others, or perhaps it relates to a physical element where we keep our body healthy

---

[18] Rabbeinu Yonah's *The Foundation of Repentance*, p7 in *The Complete Artscroll Machzor - Rosh Hashanah* - trans. Sherman, Rabbi Nosson. Mesorah Publications: (New York, 1985).
[19] Ibid.
[20] This teaching is originally from Rabbi Schneur Zalman of Liadi and was shared with me by Rabbi Brandon Gaines.

so that the cells can replenish and nourish themselves. The word *lev* - heart - appears many times throughout the Torah and Bible in general, and can relate to the physical and heart and also the metaphorical levels (e.g. Heart as intention).

The real question is, what must you do to make a new heart for yourself?

THE FAST OF GEDALIAH: OUR INNER ASSASSIN

FESTIVE SUTRA: 'Turn back from your blazing anger' *Exodus 32:12*

YOGA PRACTICE: *Bhakti Yoga* (the yoga of love)

Assassinations happen. Gedaliah Ben Achikam was the Governor of Judea during the time of Nebuchadnezzar II, ruler of the Neo-Babylonian Empire (605-562 BCE). Gedaliah was on a peaceful mission when, along with several colleagues he was murdered by Yishmael Ben Netaniah, a fellow Jew. The Fast of Gedaliah commemorates a Jew-on-Jew assassination and is observed the day after Rosh Hashannah.

What strikes me is the energetic power of this fast day. We can dismiss it as a far-away historical event and not feel the deeper meaning, or we can search for the 'Gedaliah' within ourselves. We might ask ourselves the following questions: Where am I assassinating someone with my thoughts? Am I attacking members of my family in my mind or in my heart? How am I having hateful thoughts or negative intentions towards someone I know?

The path of Bhakti Yoga is one of love. It is considered a spiritual path of love and devotion. From a Torah approach it is closest to *Ahavah*, the love we are commanded to show towards God, or to love other people as we would love ourselves. This yoga practice is internal and external, cultivating love and noticing where we are lacking love towards certain people.

The name Gedaliah literally means 'God has become great'. Perhaps the greatness of Hashem is magnified as we continually remove negative thoughts from our hearts, forgive those who have upset us. Rather than carrying out mental assassinations, today can be an opportunity to increase our love.

10 DAYS OF RETURN: 10 DAYS OF REALIGNMENT

FESTIVE SUTRA: 'Seek God while He may be found, call to him while He is near' *Isaiah 55:6*

YOGA POSE: Twists (e.g. *Marichyasana*)

The ten days from Rosh Hashannah to Yom Kippur are called *Aseret Y'mei Teshuva*, usually translated as the 'Ten Days of Repentance'. The word *teshuva* also means 'return' and we might think of this as returning to our true self, returning to our potential, returning to the best version of ourselves or who we know we can be.

We can also approach teshuva as realignment. In a yoga pose our focus is aligning the limbs in the particular direction of that asana, whether that is standing tall in Mountain Pose, keeping our back straight during Triangle Pose or wrapping our arms behind our back during Marichyasana (a seated twist).

These ten days are considered a time of spiritual sensitivity, and we hear the words of Isaiah who implored people to 'Seek God while He may be found, call to him while He is near'[18]. Whilst God can always be found, these days are considered a more optimum time. There is also a human effect: on the occasions when millions of people are simultaneously praying around the world, there can be a magnified impact.

A focused yoga practice during these days could be to focus on the essence of yoga itself - to unify our breath and spirit, to unify ourselves with God and the oneness of creation, and to unify our thoughts, speech and action.[19] Our realignment, our *teshuva*, can therefore take place within our mind, body and soul.

---

[18] Isaiah 55:6.
[19] This particular unity is mentioned by Rabbi Schneur Zalman of Liadi, the Alter Rebbe, in *Sefer Tanya*.

THE FESTIVE SUTRAS

YOM KIPPUR

YOM KIPPUR 1: FASTING AND SILENCE

FESTIVE SUTRA: 'Is this the fast I desire, A day for men to starve their bodies?' *Isaiah 58:5*

YOGA PRACTICE: Total fasting for 25 hours.

Fasting can be transformative. There are both yogic and Jewish practices for fasting but the common theme is whether our fast is going transform how we interact with the world, or whether it is purely refraining from eating. Every Yom Kippur the morning Torah reading is followed by a passage from Isaiah which asks:

> *'Is this the fast I desire, A day for men to starve their bodies? Is it bowing the head like a bulrush and lying in sackcloth and ashes? Do you call that fast, a day when the Lord is favourable? No, this is the fast I desire: to unlock fetters of wickedness, and untie the cords of the yoke, to let the oppressed go free; to break off every yoke. It is to share your bread with the hungry, and to take the wretched poor into your home: when you see the naked, to clothe him, And not to ignore your own kin. Then shall your light burst through like the dawn and your healing spring up quickly..'*[1].

---

[1] Isaiah 58: 5-8. JPS translation.

Rabbi Mendel Furtefas (1906-1995) is said to have taught that if someone does not play close attention to the way that they fast, they can actually increase their ego. While the intention of our fast is for inner transformation, there is always the possibility of achieving the opposite result[2].

Mahatma Ghandi considered fasting as a time for reflecting on how we are controlling our impulses. He taught that 'fasting can help curb animal passion [but] only if it is undertaken with a view to self-restraint...if physical fasting is not accompanied by mental fasting, it is bound to end in hypocrisy and disaster'[3]. The yogic concept of an *upavasa* fast is based around self-purification and cleansing the body with a view to cleansing the mind and soul.

My very first yoga students were a group of teenage anorexic patients who were regularly fasting in a bid to lose weight and change their bodies[4]. They were suffering on many levels and this kind of fast is not what we are aiming for in a Yom Kippur practice. Ghandi's concept of 'mental fasting' stresses the internal aspect of the fast; and we can meditate on how we will be different at the end of Yom Kippur and how the fast will change us.

Isaiah follows his criticism of a shallow fast with a powerful promise of revitalisation. If your fast raises social consciousness and community awareness and if your fast brings about real and measurable change to the lives of the poor, 'then shall your light burst forth like the dawn'[5]. We might view this is as a restoration of *prana*, *chi* or life-force, or as a metaphorical spiritual awakening, but the message is clear that the intention of every fast is to bring change into the world.

---

[2] I was taught this by my friend Rabbi Hillel Simon.
[3] *Gandhi's Life in His Own Words (My Life is My Message)*, p406, Ghandi as.
[4] I was teaching at Rhodes Farm, a unit for teenagers with eating disorders in Mill Hill, North London.
[5] Isaiah 58:8.

YOM KIPPUR 2: LIVING LIKE ANGELS

FESTIVE SUTRA: 'Who may ascend the mountain of God, and who may stand in the place of His sanctity? One with clean hands and a pure heart...' *Psalms 24:3-4*

YOGA PRACTICE: *Tadasana,* Mountain Pose.

Yom Kippur is a day of spiritual cleansing when we reflect on the year that has passed, meticulously questioning our behaviour during the previous 12 months. The Bible explains how the day itself brings atonement for our various actions[6] and there is a physical rhythm for tuning into the energy of Yom Kippur.

Five prohibitions come into being for the 25-hour period and they all relate to the body. They are; eating, drinking, bathing, anointing oneself with oil (ie perfume, make up and hair products), and sexual relations. This is a day when we focus entirely on the spiritual aspect of ourselves, praying, meditating and of course breathing. We dress in white and are compared to angels, who are beings of pure spirit[7]. On a slightly more rational note we understand the idea of angels as esoteric forces that carry out the will of God, rather than human-like forms with halos on.

One aspect of fasting is that it forces us to overcome our most basic physical desires of eating and drinking. An early explanation I heard was comparing the body-soul relationship to that of a horse and rider. If the body is essentially a creature of want, continually trying to satisfy a variety of desires – almost like an untamed horse, then on Yom Kippur we

---

[6] Leviticus 16:30.
[7] The Maharal of Prague wrote that: *"All of the mitzvot that God commanded us on [Yom Kippur] are designed to remove, as much as possible, a person's relationship to physicality, until he is completely like an angel"*, as translated by Rabbi Shraga Simmons. Originally from *Drashot Maharal - Drush L'Shabbat Teshuva, s.v. "U'B'Perek Get Pashut."*.
During the *Shema* prayer we also say the second line out loud, *Baruch Shem Kavod Malchuto L'Olam Va'ed* (Blessed is the Holy name of His Kingdom for all eternity); on every other day this 'angelic chorus' is recited in silence. The Midrash in *Devarim Rabbah 2:36* explains how we are compared to angels on Yom Kippur, which is why we say it out loud.

assume a position of responsibility to 'tame' the horse.[8] We are stepping above the desires of our ego and using the body as a direct gateway.

One of the earliest recorded fasts is when the Hebrews stood by the side of Mount Sinai and fasted for three days prior to receiving the Torah. They cleansed themselves inside and out, reducing their physical involvement in the world whilst preparing for the ultimate elevation as the Torah was revealed. Later we read of prophets who took on extensive fasts, such as Elijah who also goes to the mountain of God on the strength of one meal. Moses also fasted each time he ascended Mount Sinai.

The climax of Yom Kippur is the *Neilah* service which takes place as the sun is setting. Communities will traditionally stand up throughout the hour-long service. The yogi may relate to this through *tadasana*, Mountain Pose. A position which is both grounding and uplifting, Mountain Pose is simple and effective. The posture is accessible by everyone and can even be practiced in a modified form of sitting with a straight back. It encourages strength and stillness, rooting into the feet and lengthening up through the spine.

Yom Kippur is an opportunity to focus on our souls and temporarily step out of the restrictions of physicality. As we simplify our physical life for 25 hours, minimising our bodily functions by reducing digestion or any major physical activity, we can face the spiritual 'mountain' and focus on how we would like to elevate our thoughts and intentions in the coming year.

---

[8] I originally heard this in July 1994 from Rabbi Noach Weinberg z"l.

YOM KIPPUR 3: FIVE STEPS TO ENLIGHTENMENT

FESTIVE SUTRA: Hear O Israel, Hashem is our God, Hashem the One and Only

שְׁמַע יִשְׂרָאֵל ה׳ אֱלֹקֵינוּ ה׳ אֶחָד

YOGA PRACTICE: *Pranayama*/ Breath meditation

Yom Kippur is a five-step process that consists of five services[9] during the 25 hour period, corresponding to the five services in the Temple. The Kabbalah refers to five parts of the soul and the yogis refer to five energy sheaths around the body, which are known as *koshas*.

We might use Yom Kippur to lift us from the focus of our own life. It can be an opportunity to meditate on the expansive nature of our spiritual self and how we are all connected at the highest level of our soul.

According to Kabbalistic teachings, the five parts of the soul are: *Nefesh* (Spirit), *Ruach* (Breath), *Neshama* (Soul), *Chaya* (Life-force) and *Yechidah* (Oneness). The first three, *nefesh, ruach* and *neshama* reside within our body, the *chaya* is more of an energy field around us, and *yechidah* is the highest level on a Godly level - this is where we are all connected. Yechidah has the same root as *Echad* which means 'one'. Another way to consider these different aspects of our soul is as vibrations, with each level vibrating at a higher frequency. These are sometimes translated as follows:

1. *Nefesh* - 'Spirit' – Biological Life.
2. *Ruach* – 'Breath' – Emotional Life.
3. *Neshamah* – 'Soul' – Intellectual Life.
4. *Chayah* – 'Life' – Transcendental Life.
5. *Yechidah* – 'Oneness' – Essence.

---

[9] There are five services through Yom Kippur, which are *Kol Nidrei/Maariv* (Evening service), *Shacharit* (morning service), *Musaf* (additional service), *Mincha* (afternoon services) and *Neilah* (closing service). Whereas a usual day includes three services and Shabbat has four services, it is only Yom Kippur that features five.

The yogis teach of five energetic sheaths that surround our body: 'The five 'sheaths' or 'casings' are: (1) the sheath composed of food (*an-na-maya-kasha*), or physical body, (2) the sheath composed of vital energy (*prnaa-maya-kosha*), (3) the sheath composed of the lower mind (*mano-maya-kosha*), (4) the sheath composed of understanding (*vi-jnana-maya-kosha*), and (5) the sheath composed of bliss *(ananda-naya-kosha)*[10]. B.K.S. Iyengar taught that we might integrate these five aspects of energy during every yoga asana, so that the pose is both a contemplation and a deeper meditation[11].

Another translation of these five levels of energy can also form the basis of a Yom Kippur meditation. Elsewhere Mr Iyengar translated them as physical body (*annamaya kosha*), physiological body (*pranamaya kosha*), psychological body (*manomaya kosha*), intellectual body (*vijnananamaya kosha*) and the body of joy (*anandamaya kosha*). A meditation could take our awareness through these different aspects of our being and into a space of blissfulness as we find God within[12].

Should you choose to approach this from a purely Kabbalistic meditation, you might meditate through five *sefirot* (Divine spheres), counting *hod* (humility), *netzach* (endurance) *tiferet* (compassion), *gevurah* (strength) and *chesed* (love).

Yom Kippur can be contemplative, meditative and raise our consciousness through the five levels of our soul.

---

[10] Georg Feuerstein, *The Deeper Dimension of Yoga*, p 234. He references B.K.S. Iyengar, *The Tree of Yoga* (Boston: Shambhala, 1989), p.48.
[11] Ibid.
[12] Mr Iyengar described these levels in *Light on the Yoga Sutras of Patanjali*, p141. He mentions a further two sheaths there, the *Cittamaya Kosha* - the body of consciousness and the *Atmamaya Kosha* - the body of the Self.

YOM KIPPUR 4: THE PHYSICALITY OF YOM KIPPUR - TEMPLE, JONAH & NEILAH

FESTIVE SUTRA: 'God is One' *Deuteronomy 6:4*

YOGA PRACTICE: *Balasana*/Child's Pose, *Matsayanasa*/Fish Pose and *Tadasana*/Mountain Pose

The culmination of Yom Kippur is a proclamation of the unity of God and creation, *Hashem Echad*. This is the goal of all yoga, as an awareness of unity. There are several opportunities to engage our bodies throughout Yom Kippur and we can borrow from yoga *asana* (postures) to engage more deeply with the prayers.

Three physical opportunities offer themselves during *Mussaf* (the additional service), the afternoon reading of the story of Jonah (during *Mincha*) and the concluding service of *Neilah* (which means 'closing').

There is a moment during Mussaf in the *aleinu* prayer when the congregation gets to its knees and bows forwards, during the words 'we bend our knees and bow and acknowledge our thanks before the King who reigns over kings, the Holy One, Blessed is He'[13]. At this point we can remain vigilant of our breathing and posture, as if performing Child's Pose (*balasana*).

The afternoon reading of The Book of Jonah may be an opportunity to explore Fish Pose or to do a series of flowing sun salutes with a focus on the element of water. Finally there is the concluding *Neilah* service, during which it is customary to stand for the entire 45-60 minutes of the prayers. We can once again engage our legs, torso, focus and breath to use Mountain Pose (*tadasana*) during these prayers.

Yom Kippur yoga does not need to look like a usual yoga practice complete with rubber mat and stretch clothing, but it is more important to get the essence of the principle. That may look like standing straight, stretching as you are able or purely focusing on the breath and internal processes.

---

[13] *The Complete Artscroll Machzor - Yom Kippur*, p550.

YOM KIPPUR 5: SILENCE

FESTIVE SUTRA: 'All my days I have been raised among the Sages, and I have found nothing better for the body than silence' *Ethics of the Fathers, 1:17*

YOGA PRACTICE: Any seated posture, held in silence for 50 breaths. Silently count down from 50 to 0.

Yom Kippur can be viewed as a day of silence or at least a substantial quieting.

The 1st Century sage Rabbi Shimon Ben Gamliel said: 'All my days I have been raised among the Sages, and I have found nothing better for the body than silence'[14]. We might consider how silence can bring us physical and emotional healing and lead us towards spiritual growth. When I am silent, I am able to listen to you. When I am silent, I can make space for you. When I am silent, I can allow the surface noise to gradually fade and begin to connect with the world on a much deeper level as I really hear what is going on.

Speaking too quickly can cause problems. Whether it is making promises that we are unable to keep or spreading a story that makes someone else upset. Using language to attack people is equally hazardous – if we reprimand someone with unnecessarily unkind words then it can eventually rebound on us and create problems in the long term. Silence can be good for us in many ways.

Temporary withdrawal from food creates another kind of silence for the body. The body is an instrument for a variety of natural digestive sounds. When we fast it gives our bodies a chance to purify and self-cleanse, to slow down the flow of the digestive juices and give the bowels some time to rest. The 12th century Rabbi Moses Maimonides claimed that many diseases are due to the foods that we consume[15]. Fasting is a form of silence that can heal.

---

[14] *Ethics of the Fathers (Pirkei Avot), 1:17.*
[15] *Hilchot Deot* Chapter 4.

YOM KIPPUR

But Rabbi Shimon ben Gamliel must have known that there is no true silence with our bodies; no absolute quiet. How can there be? There are always going to be the minute noises, whether it is a lung inhaling or a muscle stretching. While we are alive, there is the dynamic silence of our breath. Breath is the soul food of Yom Kippur – a day to remember that we are a soul in the body. A day to shut out the white noise of life, the incessant flow of emails and the thousands of advertisements that assault our senses on a daily basis.

Yom Kippur ends with a universal declaration of oneness: 'God is One'. And we are all part of that oneness, whatever our race or religion. This is a simple, powerful and refreshing message, but one that can only get through if we really quieten ourselves to hear it.

THE FESTIVE SUTRAS

SUCCOT

SUCCOT 1: THE DIVINE BODY

FESTIVE SUTRA: 'Rabbi Manni began his discourse with the following [verse]: 'All of my bones shall declare: Who is like you, God?' *Psalms 35:10*.

YOGA PRACTICE:
1. Lying Supine Twist or Marichyasana sequence (Spine/Lulav)
2. Sun Salutations (Heart/Etrog)
3. Forward Bend (Eyes/Myrtle)
4. Headstand (Eyes/Myrtle)
5. Lion Pose (Mouth/Willow)
6. Wheel Pose (Spine/Lulav)

Succot is a very physical festival. There are many ways to deepen our spiritual experience and explore the festival's themes through a vigorous yoga practice.

On Succot we celebrate by living outdoors in huts for the entire week and mark each day by taking four species, binding them together and shaking them in every direction. After the angel-like spiritual asceticism of Yom Kippur where we abstain from physical pleasures, Succot takes us deeply into the natural world, grounding us back down to the species of the earth. This harvest festival is a powerful opportunity to connect with spirituality from inside our body.

An early Midrash (rabbinic commentary) compared the four species of Succot to different parts of the human body. These four species, the *arba minim*, are bound together and held as part of the prayers. They are; the *lulav* (date palm), *etrog* (a kind of citrus fruit), *hadas* (myrtle branch) and *aravah* (willow). The 5-7th century Midrash wrote that:

> 'Rabbi Manni began his discourse with the following [verse]: "All of my bones shall declare: who is like you, God?"(Psalms 35:10). This verse refers to the lulav. The spine of the lulav resembles the spine of the human being, the hadas [myrtle leaf] resembles the eye, the aravah [willow] is like a mouth, and the etrog is shaped like a heart. King David said: "These [four] are the greatest of the body's organs, for they are as important as the whole body." This is the meaning of the verse "All of my bones shall declare..."for taking the lulav signifies the dedication of one's whole being to God]'[1].

This text encourages a body-consciousness that is often missed in contemporary practice but can be genuinely enriching during this time of year. We will later explore the "All my bones" verse as a key component of the *Nishmat Kol Chai* ("Soul-breath of all living things") prayer on Shabbat, Rabbi Manni offers an entirely new perspective on the phrase in the light of the four species.

Each of the four species has a close physical counterpart. The date palm is straight like a spine, the etrog is heart-shaped, the myrtle leaf has the oval silhouette of an eye and the willow leaf resembles a thin pair of lips. Just as four species are brought together as one and waved in different directions to unify the four corners of the earth, we are to fulfil the challenge set by King David and bring all of our bones together as one. This unity might also be translated as 'yoga'.

---

[1] *Vayikra Rabbah* Chp. 30 – from the *Midrash Aggadah* to the book of Leviticus, which was compiled in the 5th-7th Century in Israel. Translation courtesy of David Harbater, FMAMS *Teacher's Guide for 'Rhythms of Jewish Living'*, p271 (Jerusalem: 2002).

SUCCOT

Try practicing a yoga sequence with the intention of uniting your body and mind with God. Are your eyes totally focused whilst you are moving your spine? Is your mouth fully relaxed as you happen to notice something with your eyes? Is your heart beating a steady pace whilst you are moving your spine?

Rabbi Manni's challenge is to invoke a stillness and unity within our body during Succot, taking inspiration from these four species that sit together as one. We might begin with postures that activate each of these body parts, as follows;

Spinal twists for the lulav (Date palm), which move the back in a lateral motion – marichyasana A, a spinal twist pose, is excellent for this. Backbends are very good strengtheners for the shoulder muscles and encourage flexibility with the spine, so a strong dhanurasana/Wheel pose would be ideal to close the sequence.

Heart-opening poses would suit the etrog/citrus. These are achieved in two of the 'lulav' postures, both in the backbend and in the marichyasana-twists, but we can also focus on opening our heart as we move through a high arch into the sun salutes. It is important to keep the heart space open throughout all stages of a sun salute, including downward-facing dog and the cobra, because by opening the thoracic chest cavity we are able to take a more powerful breath. Deeper breathing also results in more oxygenated blood, which also invokes the heart.

Inverted postures are excellent for the eyes. The eyes correspond to the hadas/myrtle. By practicing a headstand, or some variation of it, we cause an increased blood flow to the head which, in moderation, can refresh our eyes. On the other hand there is also the yogic practice of *pratyahara*, which involves closing the eyes during a yoga practice. By temporarily shutting off the faculty of vision we 'see' with our other senses, and use all of the receptors in our skin as 'eyes', moving carefully and thoughtfully into postures as our eyes are closed.

Lion pose is one of the few asanas that directly involves the mouth, which is a perfect tribute for the arava/willow. The pleasingly-named

Simhasana (well, pleasing for 'Lion King' fans at least) involves kneeling and sitting on one's feet with a straight back, hands on knees, mouth open and tongue out, and eyes crossed. There's also a double-hit as we get our eyes working in a different manner.

It may be easy to hold four species together in one bundle, but it is more challenging to focus the entire body as one. This is one opportunity presented by Succot, to unify our body, mind and soul.

SUCCOT 2: ECCLESIASTES AND THE BREATH OF BREATHS

FESTIVE SUTRA: 'Vapour of vapours! Said Kohelet. All is Vapour! What real profit is there for a person in all the gains he makes beneath the sun?' *Ecclesiastes 1:1.*

YOGA PRACTICE: *Pranayama,* breathing practice.

King Solomon's book of Ecclesiastes, *kohelet*, begins with the words *Hevel Hevelim* which are usually translated as 'Vanity of vanities!', 'Futility of futilities' 'Vapour of vapours'. The phrase could also be interpreted as 'nothingness of nothingness' or 'breath of breaths', as it is an exclamation of the transient nature of life. Breath work, *pranayama*, is a key tenet in the eightfold path of yoga.

Our breath connects us to the world, and there are many allusions between the breath and the soul: the three aspects of the soul that are within the body all correspond to words for breath. *Neshama* (soul) has the same letters as breath (*neshima*), *Ruach* (spirit) is another kind of belly-breath. *Nefesh*, another part of the soul, has the same letters as *Nashaf* which means 'exhale'.

On Succot we contemplate the temporality of life and during that Shabbat that falls in the festival, we read Kohelet, the Book of Ecclesiastes, written by King solomon. He ruminates on the frustrations of life, and the apparent futility of everything, reflecting that 'what has been is what will be, and what has been done is what will be done' and exclaiming 'Is there nothing new under the sun?'[2].

A traditional answer is that there is nothing new beneath the sun, but we can set our spiritual sights above the sun, to the realm of the spirit and of God. Humans may create great societies, build structures and then go to war and destroy them. There are huge advancements in human inventions, but however successful or innovative we are, everyone still ends up the same as their ancestors: dead. Life passes quickly. The

---

[2] *Ecclesiastes 1:9.*

opposite side of Kohelet's words is that although there might be nothing new under the sun, and human behaviour may be destined to repeat itself interminably, the true source of newness comes from that which is above the sun. God is not bound by the rules of nature or the narrow-minded view of human beings here on earth.

> *The original festival of Succot saw extreme festivities in ancient Jerusalem. The Talmud relates how all of the courtyards were lit up with burning candles through the festive nights, and that the levels of the fun were unrivalled: 'The flute-playing would sometimes go on for five days and sometimes six days. This was the flute-playing at the Libation Water-Well which didn't take place on a Sabbath or Festival. They said that anyone who had not witnessed the rejoicing at the Libation Water Well (Simchat Beit HaShoevah) had never seen rejoicing in his life'[3].*

We can interpret 'futility of futilities' as the words of a bitter old man who is disillusioned with life, as an angry young man who sees everything as a waste of time, as someone who is being positive about spiritual possibilities and looking to accomplish things beyond the physical realm, or just as a neutral statement, as if to say 'life is short. Everyone dies. Physicality is passing, like a breath, but what will last is how we elevate our consciousness and how we unify with the Divine'. In other words, the mission of the yogis which was to unite with the Oneness.

Succot has the unique mitzvah (commandment) telling us to be happy and celebrate - 'you shall rejoice on the festival'[4] and underscoring the command with 'for seven days..you shall be joyful'[5]. Hebrew prayers refer to Succoth as Zman Simchateinu, 'the time of our rejoicing'. All of this is accomplished through very physical means. We simultaneously live in the realm of our bodies and the realm of our soul, and continually strive to find the unity between the two, as if to say 'All is One'.

---

[3] Mishnah Succot 5.1.
[4] Deuteronomy 16:14.
[5] Deuteronomy 16:15 .

SUCCOT 3: KABBALISTIC UNITY

FESTIVE SUTRA: 'My intention is to unify the Name of the Holy One... in perfect unity...'[6] *Vayikra Rabbah, Chp. 30*

YOGA PRACTICE: 5 rounds of Sun Salutations.

The *kabbalistic yichudim* were meditations for Divine unity that were spoken at various times to help people refocus on the ultimate goal of their actions. These are in essence mini internal yoga exercises, to bring us back in tune with our intention. Here is the meditation that was designed to be said before the waving of the four species on succot;

> *'May it be Your will...that through the fruit of the etrog tree, date-palm branches, twigs of the myrtle tree, and brook willows, the letters of your Unified name may become close to one another, that they may become united in my hand...and when I wave them, may an abundant outpouring of blessings flow from the wisdom of the Most High...For my intention is to unify the Name of the Holy One...in perfect unity...'*[7]

When we bring our hands into prayer position, with palms pressed together and thumbs pointed into our sternum, our aim is to connect our breath and feel the sense of unity in our bodies. Elsewhere the rabbis describe how each of the four species comes to represent a different type of person – some who are spiritual seekers with wisdom, some who have wisdom but behave badly, some who behave well but are ignorant and some who don't have spiritual knowledge or good deeds to their credit. Rather than placing one kind of person as more important than another, the waving of the four species is about reminding us of the importance of everyone in society, and finding connections with all of our community[8].

---

[6] Meditation before the ceremony of waving the The Four Species, as found in *The Complete Artscroll Siddur*, p631.
[7] Ibid.
[8] 'Just as the etrog has a taste and fragrance, so are there individuals [among Israel] who have spiritual knowledge and good deeds... just as the date possesses a taste but no smell, so are there individuals [among Israel] who have spiritual knowledge but no good deeds... just as the hadas/myrtle has a fragrance but no taste, so are there individuals [among Israel] who have good deeds but no spiritual knowledge... [and] just as the willow has no taste and no fragrance, so are there individuals [among Israel] who possess neither knowledge of Torah nor good deeds. What does God do? To destroy them is not possible. Rather, he says: 'Let them all be bound up and taken as one, so that they will atone for one another,' *Vayikra Rabbah* Chp. 30.

THE FESTIVE SUTRAS

We can feel most alive and be most effective when all of our energy is focused in one direction. The distractions of modern living can make it harder to feel internal stillness and to operate at the best of our ability; the continual buzzing of mobile phones and reminders of emails are designed to help our life but often make it hard to carry out one task at a time. The four species on Succot may be seen as another reminder to find peace and stillness within, as we bring together disparate elements that would not normally be combined.

Our yoga will only be successful when all of our being is focused in one direction and it is not enough for our body to be in a perfect asana/posture if our mind is wandering away. Just as the entire community is represented in the four species – and the blessing cannot be made unless all four species are there - our entire person is needed to achieve a state of yoga.

SUCCOT 4: 7 DAYS, 6 DIRECTIONS

FESTIVE SUTRA: 'You shall dwell in booths for a seven-day period'
Leviticus 23:42

YOGA PRACTICE: *Surya Namaskar*/6 Sun Salutations (any style). As you practice, keep an awareness of the six directions of space that you are moving through (forwards, backwards, up, down and diagonals).

During the festival of Succot we remember the temporary nature of life, as we spend the entire week eating and even sleeping in a hut which can be blown away at any time. Life is fragile and we are poignantly reminded of this during a festival of temporality.

In building a Succah there are various laws that ensure it is a temporary structure that contains reminders of its impermanence. The roof has to be made of a harvested material that was once living, such as palm branches or bamboo, and these are laid on thinly enough so that it is possible to see the stars through them at night or the sun at day. The covering is thick enough to provide some shelter but not so dense that it would protect us from the driving rain (which is more of an issue when celebrating in harsher climes such as England). The four walls cannot be permanent round walls that are up all of the year and the ideal is to have a succah that is constructed especially for the festival and taken down shortly afterwards. From a historical perspective this reminds us of when the Hebrews were wandering through the desert and constructing temporary shelters, and from the agricultural aspect it ties in with the time of the final harvests, as it says 'you shall keep the festival of Succot for seven days after you have gathered in from your threshing floor and from your wine harvest'[9]. One theory is that farmers would put up these huts in the fields as short-term storehouses to gather and guard their crops during the harvest; it would have been essential to keep a close watch on all of the gleanings because the wheat they had just harvested represented their wealth for the coming year[10].

---
[9] *Deuteronomy 16:13.*
[10] Thanks to Dr Raphael Zarum for teaching me this idea.

THE FESTIVE SUTRAS

The Kabbalah underscores the significance of the succah, explaining a spiritual aspect to the six sides of the hut. The Torah describes six constant remembrances which relate to historical identity[11]. The Kabbalah describes a cube as the ultimate meditational space because its 8 vertices (corner points), 12 lines and 6 faces (areas) add up to 26 which is the numerical equivalent of one of God's key names in Hebrew, *Havayah*[12]. Although there is no need to build a succah in a perfect cube, it does have to be a square structure so perfectly fits with this idea of being a form of permanent kabbalistic meditation that we access with our entire body. By entering this six-sided, 26-numbered matrix we place ourselves within a continual reminder of the presence of God, and using this as a meditation whilst eating, drinking and in some examples sleeping, during the seven days of the festival.

Your Succot yoga practice might pay close attention to the space you are in, bringing your awareness to the walls, ceiling and floor of the room in which you are practicing (unless you are lucky enough to be in a country where it is warm enough to do yoga outside during October). Our time on earth is limited but whilst here we can mindfully connect with our physical space rather than passing through it unconsciously. We bring attention to the fact that we are not our bodies, as they are vessels that will eventually be 'gathered in' to the earth whilst our souls are returned to the Creator. As we move through our sun salutes, we can reach a level of appreciation and gratitude that is a source of sheer joy. Life may be temporary but through these moving meditations, we can connect with the higher source and elevate the spirit in the process.

---

[11] These six remembrances are: the Exodus from Egypt (*Deuteronomy 16:3*), receiving the Torah at Mount Sinai (*Deut. 4:9-10*), Amalek's attach (*Deut. 25:17-19*), Golden Calf (*Deut. 9:7*), Miriam's punishment (*Deut. 24:9*) and the Sabbath (*Exodus 20:8*). See Artscroll Siddur, p.177.

[12] *Likutei HaGra* at the end of *Sefer Yetzira* (2:25b), as referenced by Rabbi Yitzhak Ginsburg in *Living in Divine Space: Kabbalah and Meditation*, p.129.

SUCCOT 5: TODAY I AM A SUCCAH

FESTIVE SUTRA: 'You have clothed me with skin and flesh, and knit me together with bones and sinews' *Job 10:11*

YOGA PRACTICE:
1. Jumping and Shakeout (stir up the energy).
2. Triangle and Reverse Triangle.
3. Wheel or Bridge.

Succot is described as *zman simchateinu*, 'the time of our rejoicing', and it is a poignant coincidence that the Sanskrit word for joy is *sukhah*. This yogic concept for deep happiness can literally translates as a 'good space', composed of *su* (good) and *khah* (space)[13]. Ideally the succah (i.e. our temporary hut rather than the yogic concept of joy) is going to be an excellent space where we can celebrate the joy of being alive. We celebrate the festival for seven days with our friends, family and community, spending as much time as possible dwelling within the succah.

One irony about the 'time of our rejoicing' is that Succot is also a continual reminder of the fragility of life and the fact that everything can be overturned in a moment. However secure our lives appear, the temporary hut is a poignant symbol that we might die at any moment and we are susceptible to the winds of fate as the walls of the succah are to nature's winds. Especially when celebrating Succot in England on a windy night. No human beings are immune from a sudden change in their life circumstance and our security can be 'blown away' at any moment, as we see during financial crises, personal tragedies or natural catastrophes.

The Succah's roof contains a continual reminder of death and the temporary nature of life. The temporary covering, or *skach*, is made of materials that have been harvested and are therefore no longer alive. The Bible continually refers to Succot as *Hag Ha-Asif*, 'the festival of ingathering', and this ingathering may be understood as a metaphor for death. The Bible uses this phraseology when referring to the deaths of Abraham,

---

[13] See Feuerstein p.162, quoting the *Yoga-Bhashya 1:31*, and comparing suffering (duhkha) with its counterpoint of joy (sukha).

Isaac, Jacob, Moses and Aaron. They all have one thing in common in that they are described as being 'gathered unto [their] people'[14].

This powerful symbolism sits quietly within the subtle ceremony of the *Ushpizin*, a series of readings where we metaphorically welcome a Biblical figure into our succah for each of the seven nights. The first five are those mentioned above, the 'ingathered', whilst the last two are Joseph and King David, who are both associated with future redemption.

We have a choice on Succot whether to use the opportunity for a pessimistic or an optimistic outlook about the fragility of our lives. At the turn of the 17th Century there were British playwrights who looked towards this dark side of life and the fact that our lives are continually decaying and we are dying from the moment we are born. John Webster, a contemporary of Shakespeare, wrote in *The Duchess of Malfi*;

> *'Thou art a box of worm seed, at best, but a salvatory of green mummy:*[15] *what's this flesh? A little cruded milk, fantastical puff-paste: our bodies are weaker than those paper prisons boys use to keep flies in: more contemptible; since ours is to preserve earth-worms: didst thou ever see a lark in a cage? Such is the soul in the body: this world is like her little turf of grass, and the heaven o'er our heads, like her looking-glass, only gives us a miserable knowledge of the small compass of our prison'*[16].

On Succot we do remember that our bodies are fragile shells that will one day be gathered in the same way as our ancestors, and that the soul only dwells in our body for a relatively short time. Rather than allowing these thoughts to lead us towards despair, this is a time for unadulterated optimism. The Book of Job describes how our bodies are

---

[14] The following figures are referred to as being 'gathered to his people'; Abraham (*Genesis* 25:8), Ishmael (*Genesis* 25:17), Isaac (*Genesis* 35:29), Jacob (*Genesis* 49:33), Aaron (*Numbers* 20:24, 26) and Moses (*Deuteronomy* 32:50). Succot is referred to as Chag HaAsif (Festival of Ingathering) in the following places: *Exodus* 23:16 and *Exodus* 34:22, and there are references to 'ingathering' in *Leviticus* 23:39 and *Deuteronomy* 16:13). Thanks are due to Dr Raphael Zarum for developing and teaching this idea.

[15] This refers to mummia, a medicinal preparation made from Egyptian mummies.

[16] *The Duchess of Malfi* Act 4, Scene 2

'clothed together with skin and flesh and knit together with bones and sinews'[17]. The Hebrew phrase for 'knit together' is *T'sacheini*, which has the same root as the word *skach*, the decaying matter that forms the roof of a succah. In other words, our bodies are a succah!

From this perspective we can see the entire week as a metaphor, and the seven days we spend in the succah are akin to the time that the soul spends within the body, as seven is the number that the Bible connects with life cycles such as weddings (*sheva brachot*), funeral weeks (*shiva*), creation (seven days of creation) and more[18]. During the seven days of being in the succah we are re-enacting the time that our souls spend within the temporary physical confines of our body[19]. We leave the succah in time for the eighth day, which is symbolic as the number eight is traditionally associated with metaphysical experience and God[20]. As if to underscore this, the Torah reading for the eighth day mentions the fact that although lots of sacrifices were brought in the Temple during the week of Succot, on the eighth day the number was reduced to one. Our seven days of being 'alive' during Succot are followed by a day of closeness with the creator, which the Kabbalah refers to as *Yechidah*.

Today's yoga practice is focused around a subtle appreciation of the fragility of our bodies. The appreciation of our soul-breath is more important than ever, as the *neshama* (soul) or *neshima* (breath) is the only thing that will ultimately last. When we take our final breath our soul will be returned to the Creator, but our task right now is to appreciate every breath, and bring this powerful spiritual infusion into our bones, sinews, muscles and flesh.

---

[17] Job 10:11.
[18] The theme of sevens also continues with the sets of seven circuits, or hakafot, that are performed in the synagogue on the mornings of the festival.
[19] The body-succah connection continues in the liturgy as the rabbis instated a farewell to the succah that refers to a future time when the world will be united in peace under a succah of skin: "May it be your will, Hashem, our God and God of our forefathers, that just as I have fulfilled [the mitzvah] and dwelled in this succah, so may I merit in the coming year to dwell in the succah of the skin of the Leviathan. Next year in Jerusalem".
[20] The Brit Milah circumcision ceremony is performed on the eighth day after a child has been born, partially in reference to the fact that it is a sign of a covenant between human beings and the non-human, or metaphysical element, ie God.

SUCCOT 6: KABBALAH & THE USHPIZIN

FESTIVE SUTRA: 'I invite to my meal the exalted guests: Abraham, Isaac, Jacob, Joseph, Moses, Aaron and David'[21] - *Ushpizin Prayer*

YOGA PRACTICE: Kabbalistic Yoga Practices

The Aramaic word *Ushpizin* means 'guests'[22] and there is a custom throughout the seven nights of Succot to welcome in other-worldly guests. We are taught that 'the Succah generates such intense spiritual energy' that the Divine presence manifests within this space[23]. According to the Kabbalah, the souls of these 'seven shepherds' descend to join the festivities[24], and the festival has a consciousness of both life and death, as we celebrate life but do it in a temporary structure that is covered with *scach*, cut-off branches or leaves that are no longer connected to a living tree. There is a sense of slow decay above us, thin Succah walls are around us, but we celebrate nonetheless. Succot is the closest that Jewish culture has to Halloween or Dia de Muertos (Day of the Dead), and the seven *Ushpizin*-guests we welcome in are Abraham, Isaac, Jacob, Joseph, Moses, Aaron and King David.

There is an additional Lubavitch tradition to welcome in a different Rebbe each night (in order: The Baal Shem Tov, the Maggid of Mezeritch, the Alter Rebbe, the Miteller Rebbe, the Tzemach Tzedek, the Rebbe Maharash and the Rebbe Rashab).

THE DANCE OF SEVENS

The number seven occurs throughout Succot, whether it is the sets of seven *hakafot* circuits we dance in synagogue, the seven nights of the festival, the seven mystical Ushpizin guests. As we dance the seven circles we might think of the seven planets which are circling the sun, the seven times that men wrap a *tefillin* strap around the left hand, and of course

---

[21] Ushpizin prayer, *The Complete Artscroll Siddur* p722.
[22] This occurs in the Tosefta, Ma'aser Sheni 1:13.
[23] According to the Zohar as quoted in https://www.geni.com/projects/The-Holy-Shepherds-Ushpizin/8193.
[24] *Zohar, Emor* 103a.

the seven days of creation. There is a tradition that each day of Succot also represents a thousand years in the life of the planet, based on the psalm that says 'a thousand years in Your eyes are like a single day'[25]. For our practical purposes, to experience this energy in our body, we might consider the Kabbalistic connections for each of the Ushpizin.

YOUR BODY & KABBALAH

As I explored in *The Kabbalah Sutras*, each of the seven Biblical figures correspond to a different *sefira* a cosmic light or Divine energy. Each of these *sefirot* are also represented in the body, and each have a corresponding characteristic (e.g. Lovingkindness, Discipline, Compassion, Endurance, Humility, Bonding and Nobility):

1. Day One - Abraham - *Chesed* - Lovingkindness - Right Arm
2. Day Two - Isaac - *Gevurah* - Strength or Discipline - Left Arm
3. Day Three - Jacob - *Tiferet* - Compassion or Balance - Body
4. Day Four - Moses - *Netzach* - Endurance, Ambition or Victory - Left Leg
5. Day Five - Aaron - *Hod* - Humility or Gratitude - Right Leg
6. Day Six - Joseph - *Yesod* - Bonding, Foundation or Grounding - *Brit Milah*
7. Day Seven - David - *Malchut* - Nobility, Kingship, Divine Feminine - Mouth, Feet, Hands

KABBALISTIC YOGA PRACTICE

There is a tremendous variety of postures that can be associated with each of the sefirot - and each of these Ushpizin. At a basic level you might choose a different pose for each day or choose the *same* pose, but focus on the specific characteristic of the day and the specific part of the body. On the first day you might focus on your right arm, reflect on

---

[25] Psalm 90:4.

Chesed, the quality of Lovingkindness and so forth. Take a look at *The Kabbalah Sutras* for an extensive Kabbalistic yoga practice with detailed pictures and explanations.

The most important principle here is to consider each day as the epitome of a different character trait, and to use your physical practice as a way to deepen that spiritual growth within your body.

We learn about the physical placement of the *Sefirot* directly from the Tikkunei Zohar 17b:

> *"Elijah began and said: Master of the Worlds! ...You are He that has produced ten constructs (tiquninn) - and we call them 'the ten sephirot' – with which to direct hidden worlds that are not revealed, and worlds that are revealed... And they are called in this order: chesed is the right arm, gevurah is the left arm, tipheret is the body, netzach and hod are the two thighs; and yesod is the completion (siyuma) of the body – the sign of the holy covenant. Malkhut is the 'mouth'– we call it the Oral Torah"*[26]

---

[26] Tiqqunei haZohar 11b, Qustha 1740: An English Translation. (from private manuscript, currently awaiting publication. Translation by Professor David Solomon, reprinted with gratitude).

SHABBAT CHOL HAMOED SUCCOT

SHABBAT CHOL HAMOED SUCCOT:

FESTIVE SUTRA: 'Vanity of vanities, all is vanity...' *Pesach Hagaddah*

YOGA PRACTICE: *Pranayama*/Breathing practice

How can we enjoy life with grace, peace and joy? The Biblical wisdom traditionally offers an approach that is both profound and easy-to-apply.

The Sabbath that falls in the middle of the week-long festivities of Succot is called Shabbat Chol HaMoed Succot[1]. This double layer of celebration, being both a Shabbat and a festival, includes the special custom of reading the book of Ecclesiastes, *Kohelet*, written by King Solomon.

Ecclesiastes opens with the following words: '*Vanity of vanity, all is vanity*'. I spent many years touring as an actor performing a one-man play about King Solomon, and early in my research I discovered two approaches to this verse. It might be the words of a man who is old, cynical and angry, or a young man who is open and optimistic[2].

'*We are all buried in the end, the wise man along with the fool*', it continues, and this may be read as the words of someone on the verge of despair.

---

[1] Roughly translated as 'the sabbath of the festival days of Succot'.
[2] Thank you to Clive Lawton for this dual interpretation.

There is, however, an opposite approach. Rabbi Rami Shapiro's translation of Ecclesiastes[3] translates it as 'vapour of vapours', as the Hebrew word *hevel* represents a kind of mistiness, an exhale, a nothingness, an intangibility. We could extend this to 'nothingness of nothingness' or 'breath of breaths'.

Rather than a cynical, nihilistic, world-coming-to-an-end despair, we can use these words to enter a zen-like state. On one level King Solomon might be writing 'breath of breaths, everything is breath'. We take this as both a yogic instruction and an awareness, bring attention to our breath, to be aware that our breath is with us throughout our life, and at the end of our days we will take a final exhale. Instead of judging life or death to be good or bad, we can focus on our breath, meditate on it and become completely mindful. In that moment we enter the present with full mindfulness, and this very act of awakening consciousness will liberate us from any pain, sorrow or grief.

In other words, breathe.

Shabbat Chol HaMoed Succot: Time

FESTIVE SUTRA: 'There is a time for everything beneath the heavens' *Ecclesiastes 3:1*

YOGA PRACTICE: *Shavasana*/Corpse Pose

Years ago I was invited to do a storytelling piece on the theme of time. A phrase drifted through my head, that 'there is a time for everything beneath the heavens', and I wondered if those could be the final words of a play, so the audience sees everything that leads up to that speech. That was the birth of my play *Solomon: King, Poet & Lover - A Tale of One Man & 700 Wives*, and 16 years later I still love performing it, always discovering something new from the incredible wisdom of King Solomon.

---

[3] *The Way of Solomon: Finding Joy and Contentment in the Wisdom of Ecclesiastes*, by Rami M. Shapiro.

He teaches that *'There is a time for everything beneath the heavens, a time to be born and a time to die'*[4].

I love the words of King Solomon.

"For everything there is a season
A time for everything beneath the heavens
A time to give birth, and a time to die
A time to plant and a time to uproot..."

As one teacher taught that true wisdom is knowing which time it is.

Anthony Robbins teaches this is a practical version, explaining that there are different seasons in life, whether it is in regard to relationships, finances, or physical. If you are experiencing a winter, whether it is a bad economy or a bad relationship, do not get upset that things are not 'blossoming'. See the winter for what it is. Similarly, when you are in a 'summer' season, and things are at full bloom, be aware that may be a good time to fill your storehouses (e.g. if it is a financial summer and money is flowing, that is a good time to save). Or if it is a financial winter - and there are no extra 'crops' to put aside as your savings, do not get upset.[5]

I was recently comforting a friend who had experienced the sudden death of a loved one and we were working through various aspects of her mourning process. She asked me what she should do when overcome with a wave of grief? My response was 'cry'. Sometimes that is all there is to do. To feel the emotion and to allow the tears to flow. As Ecclesiastes says, 'there is a time to weep and a time to laugh'[6]. At that moment it was a time to cry.

A yoga practice will typically end with Corpse pose, and this is an opportune moment for reflection that early life does not last forever and one day there will be a time to die.

However, if you are reading this, right now it is most definitely a time to live. *L'Chayim!*

---

[4] Ecclesiastes 3:1-2.
[5] The specific examples are my own.
[6] Ecclesiastes 3:4.

THE FESTIVE SUTRAS

HOSHANNAH RABBAH

HOSHANNAH RABBAH: PRAYERS OF FIRE

FESTIVE SUTRA: '[Please save us] for the sake of the courageous one [Abraham] who was hurled into a flame of fire' *Hoshanna Rabbah prayers*[1]

YOGA PRACTICE: *Tapas*/an intense and fiery yoga practice

Hosannah Rabbah, the day of 'great salvation' is the last day of Succot, and considered chol or 'weekday' without the restrictions of Shabbat and festivals. From a spiritual perspective it is believed to be the day when our New Year prayers ascend to heaven. If the prayers are signed on Rosh Hashanah, sealed on Yom Kippur, they are 'delivered' on Hoshannah Rabbah.

I would like to share a series of ideas that interplay on Hoshannah Rabbah, around our thoughts, our energy and our fiery potential.

1. THE THOUGHTS WE HOLD

    The day has Spiritual Potency. I would extend this further, suggesting that we practice during the day as if everything counts: the thoughts we hold, the intentions in our heart and the love we emanate. Who do we want to be for the coming year? What

---
[1] Artscroll siddur p730-731

vibration do we want to hold? Can we cultivate ourselves towards an optimum of being loving, optimistic and faith-filled? Today is the day to raise our consciousness and elevate our game.

There are a series of prayers said during the morning service known as '*Hoshannahs*'. Hoshannah is translated as 'please save [us]', as if they are a final set of prayers to close out the intense festive season of the new year.

2. ENERGETICS

There is also the practice of beating willow branches on the ground. One idea which occurred to me is a kind of grounding that takes place during this ceremony. Throughout Yom Kippur we beat our chests, as if to clear blocked energy and bring healing for the year ahead, and on Hoshannah Rabbah we continue the beating, although this time it is willow branches to the ground. I have not seen any sources that connect these two actions, but if earth represents the Divine sphere of Malchut (Kingship, Nobility or the Divine feminine), it feels as if we are taking any final sparks of negativity and allowing them to be absorbed directly into the ground. The earth has the ability to absorb energetic negativity and transform it into the positive, as we see with the case of farmers who spread manure - waste material - over the earth and this becomes the fertile ground for new crops[2].

We might play some more with the idea of releasing blocked energy. For the last 30 years, Dr Roger Callaghan developed what is sometimes known as EFT (Emotional Freedom Technique), TFT (Thought Field Therapy)[3]. It shares some similarity with acupressure and other chi-related techniques, with the focus being on tapping energetic meridian points in the body to bring emotional healing.

---

[2] There is however a limit to the amount of negative energy we can place into the earth.
[3] See more at www.tfttapping.com.

3. FIRE

Some of the Hoshannah Prayers are focused on fire:

> *For the sake of the son [Isaac] who was bound upon the wood near the fire, for the sake of the strong one [Jacob] who wrestled with a prince of fire. For the sake of him [Moses who was raised to the heavens and became as exalted as the angels of fire"*[4].

This stands as a contrast to many of the Succot festivities which are connected with water, such as the *Simchat Beit HaShoevah*, the water-drawing ceremonies that took place in the Temple during Succot. One idea might be that whereas water falls to earth, fire burns upwards towards heaven, and on this day we are focused on our prayers ascending to the heavenly realm.

Eastern teachings considered fire to be yang energy, male and potent, compared with the *yin*, or feminine of water. We need a balance of both fire and water, and Hoshannah Rabbah is a day for this male energy. The site of many men parading in synagogue holding lulavs looks similar to a tribal procession with swords, so the case could be made that we are fighting with our prayers. If we connect this with the *Tikkunei HaZohar* (Kabbalistic) teaching that prayer is considered to be a form of battle, fighting with our negative thoughts and fighting through negative shells (*klipot*), then it is certainly time to hold our fiery swords aloft!

A yogic practice can be used to generate heat, or tapas. One reason that Ashtanga Yoga practitioners do not drink water during a yoga practice is because it can quench the subtle fires within, and there is healing to be experienced when we channel this heat.

The following day, on Shemini Atzeret, we say *Tefillat Geshem*, the prayer for rain. There is a dance of water/fire/water that goes on through these festivities, a subtle interplay of energetics, the Divine Feminine dancing with the Divine Masculine. The prayer

---
[4] Artscroll siddur, p732.

for rain has its basis in fertility, as we ask for the all-important rains to come to the land so that we have a fertile year ahead.

There is probably much more to be said about the overall flow of fertility in these prayers and the ongoing interplay between masculine and feminine…but at the time of writing, that is all that has been revealed to me!

We can be aware of these subtle energies within our body, whether it is the delicate or refined cooling emotional flow of water, or the strong, masculine heat of fire. We have both of these energies within our body, both masculine and feminine. Today, Hoshannah Rabbah, appears to be a day of fire, the day we are focused on sending our prayers to heaven. Fire is the messenger. And so it is.

SHEMINI ATZERET

SHEMINI ATZERET: THE HIDDEN 8

FESTIVE SUTRA: 'The eighth day shall be a solemn rest' *Lev. 23:39*

YOGA PRACTICE: *Vrksasana*/Tree Pose (or other postures that involve balance)

There is a hidden secret on Shemini Atzeret. The technicalities of the day can be confusing[1] but we can build on the previous essay (Hoshannah Rabbah) to see how there is an invitation for deeper healing.

Before we go any further, does *Shemini* not sound like *Shaman*? Shemini means 'eight', *Atzeret* means 'stop', and it is a kind of stopping day to end the festival. The number eight also represents the Divine or the supernatural, and the symbol 8 has deeper meanings across various Eastern spiritual practices.

Here then is a path to healing and energetic retuning on Shemini Atzeret.

---

[1] Shemini Atzeret occurs at the end of Succot, an adjunct which is also a festival in its own right, can be somewhat confusing. Many people still eat their meals in the Succah but do not say a blessing (because it is not technically Succot) and others have the custom not to eat in the Succah at all. In Israel there are two-festivals-in-one as *Simchat Torah* is celebrated on the same day, but in the rest of the world, these days run contiguously.

THE FESTIVE SUTRAS

THE HEALING OF WATER, FIRE, YIN & YANG

As we began to explore in the Hoshannah Rabbah essay, Succot is strongly connected to water. There are the water-drawing ceremonies of the *Simchat Beit HaShoevah*. The last day of Succot, *Hoshannah Rabbah*, is a day of prayers that invoke fire. Water represents feminine yin energy, the idea of intuition or going with the flow. Fire is considered masculine, the heat of the warrior, the anger that can rise upwards in someone's body to make their face go red.

The day after, the day following the water and fire interplay, is called 'the final eight' or *Shemini Atzeret*.

The book of Genesis teaches that we are created 'male and female', as if to say we have both fire and water, or masculine and feminine energies in our body. The majority of the body is water (feminine energy) although we do radiate heat (masculine energy) throughout our body. Infants are made of 75-78% water while the average human adult consists of 57-60% water.

We see this balance of feminine and masculine, or yin and yang, throughout nature. 71% of the planet Earth is covered with water (feminine), but we still require the other 29% which is our dry land.

When children are growing up, the majority of their time might be spent with their mother - which is perfectly healthy - but if their father is never present, there can be irreparable damage which may last a lifetime.

In other words, we need the balance of masculine and feminine. The feminine waters of Succot, the masculine fires of Hoshannah Rabbah and the energetic balance of Shemini Atzeret. Or we could just say: get in balance.

This takes place on a more subtle level, deep within the body. We can only touch on it here in a couple of paragraphs, although the Taoist teacher Mantak Chia has written at least *three books* on this topic if you would like to study further.

Chia describes the Microcosmic Orbit, an energy circle which runs from our genitals, under the body and up the back of the spine, over the head, down through the tongue-lock (when the tongue is pushed to the top palate), down through the centre of the body and back to where it started. This circle of energy can recycle sexual energy within the body, leading to greater longevity and potency. This is basically a one-paragraph summary of his book *Sexual Kung-Fu*, and I would recommend reading the entire book.

When a man and woman make love and practice the Microcosmic Orbit, a form of inner sexual meditation, or 'sexual Kung Fu' as Mantak Chia puts it, they form two circles. When you place these circles together, you get the shape of a number eight, the centre of the '8' being where the man and woman are physically connected.

Is it any surprise then, that *Simchat Torah*, the festival of rejoicing of the Torah (which is celebrated simultaneously in Israel or on the next day in the diaspora), is all about marriage?

On both of these days there are customs to dance around the synagogue in a circle, and to complete seven circuits. These seven circuits are similar to the seven times a bride walks around her bridegroom under the *Chuppah* (marriage canopy).

THE BIG REVEAL

With full respect to my teachers, here is what I believe is occurring: we are re-enacting getting married to God but we are also re-enacting a lovemaking process.

Mantak Chia describes this from the perspective of Taoist Yoga, explaining: *"You simply make love internally, between the yin and yang poles within your body, imaging you are pulling the ching chi up to make love to your highest centre, the crown"*[2]. He is talking in the context of internal healing and inner balancing, but it is all related.

---

[2] *Taoist Secrets of Love*, p135.

As if to compound this further, Simchat Torah also includes *Tefillat Geshem*, the prayer for rain. Ancient cultures would combine fertility rituals with prayers for rain, and many of these elements are present in the mix of these festivals and prayers, albeit on a very subtle level.

These subtle energetics and the practices of Taoist Yoga are really a subject for another book. There are more clues throughout the Torah and the Zohar is more explicit, although in a coded form.

For now we can focus on getting a healthy balance within our bodies and harmonising areas of our life where there may be a lack of equilibrium.

Symbolism flows throughout this festive season as Succot represents water and Hoshannah Rabbah represents fire. Shemini Atzeret represents the number 8, a stopping point, where fire and water intermingle, where yin and yang balance and where harmony is achieved for the coming year.

SIMCHAT TORAH

SIMCHAT TORAH: THE RABBI DOES A HANDSTAND

FESTIVE SUTRA: 'We learnt about Rabban Shimon Ben Gamliel that when he was rejoicing/partying at the Simchat Bet HaShoevah, he would take eight flaming torches, throw one up in the air and catch another [i.e. juggle them] and none of them would touch. And when he prostrated himself, he would stick his two thumbs into the earth, bow, kiss the ground, and stand upright. Nobody else was able to do it like him. And this is called 'Kiddah'. Levi tried to do Kiddah like the Rabbi, and crippled himself [or made himself crooked]'. *Babylonian Talmud, Succah 53a*

YOGA PRACTICE: Handstands and arm balances.

Shaolin Monks are known for their ability to do a handstand whilst resting only on one finger, a move which is likely to cause us a hand fracture if we were to try it. The monks use their balances and acrobatic displays in the context of meditative martial arts, but there is no evidence of a rabbinic equivalent, with the sole exception of Rabbi Shimon Ben Gamliel. The Talmud describes this somewhat mysterious meditative acrobatic movement, explaining that the practitioner '*should not lie down so that his body touches the ground*'. In the time of Reb Shimon, 'nobody knew how to do [the kiddah handstand] but him'[1].

The Rabbi Shimon anecdote took place at the festival of water drawing, the *Simchat Beit HaShoevah*. This event is no longer officially celebrated but is mostly thought of in the context of both Succot and the festival of rejoicing for the Torah, *Simchat Torah*, which takes place at the end of Succot. A time of intense joy, the Talmud relates how Rabbi Shimon would juggle eight flaming torches before performing a complicated balance that outshone his colleagues. Whereas the juggling is presented purely as a form of entertainment, the kiddah-handstand appears to be some form of prayer posture, which would fit our yogic understanding of the handstand as another type of meditation posture.

Simchat Torah, literally 'Joy of the Torah', is the only festival with the word joy in the title, and there is an element of behaviourism going on – the idea that we can affect our internal emotions through our external actions. This theory is the essence of Neuro-linguistic Programming (NLP) and there are many examples where dancing or moving will kick-start a state of euphoria. Modern science backs this up as we have discovered how endorphins are released through exercise.

How can we get into the spirit of deep happiness if we are not in the mood? By getting physically involved. Rabbi Shimon was the *Nasi*, the leader of the generation, and he would prostrate himself, 'stick his two thumbs into the earth, bow, kiss the ground, and stand upright'. It is not entirely clear how he linked these positions, from the prostration to the bow, to kissing the ground and then standing erect, but there seems to be some kind of flowing dynamic between the different stages. Either way we can approximate the action and the effect through a hand balance. We can induce feelings of joy, of *simcha*, through physical play and lift ourselves up both physically and metaphorically. Just take care in the balance rather than following the example of Levi who had a bad technique and injured himself…

---

[1] BT Talmud 34b.

ROSH CHODESH

ROSH CHODESH: DANCING IN THE MOONLIGHT

FESTIVE SUTRA: I have created you and I have appointed you a covenant people, a light unto the nations, opening eyes deprived of light, rescuing prisoners from confinement, from the dungeon those who sit in darkness' *Isaiah 42:6-7*

YOGA PRACTICE:
1. Restorative postures.
2. *Ardha Chandrasana*/Half-moon pose.

The Hebrew calendar is known as lunisolar, based on both the sun and the moon. Although each new month is based around the appearance of the moon, and the *nolad*, or rebirth of the moon is announced in synagogues prior to the mini-celebration, there is also a solar element underpinning the calendar. Due to the 11-day difference between the lunar and the solar calendar, an entirely moon-based system would mean that festivals move throughout the year which would play havoc with seasonally-based celebrations – this is why Muslims who follow an entirely lunar calendar can find themselves observing the Ramadan fast during the short days of winter or the hard long days of summer. The Hebrew calendar therefore runs on a 19-year cycle with leap years that add an extra month once every seven years.

THE FESTIVE SUTRAS

Hatha Yoga literally means sun-moon yoga, as it pays tribute to the balance between these two lights in the sky, and the physical postures can help us to unlock and connect with the new month.

The celebration for a new month, *Rosh Chodesh*, lasts for one or two days and is a kind of mini-festival[1]. We first learn about this in the Book of Exodus, where the very first commandment that is given out is that of marking the new month; 'And the Lord spoke to Moses and Aaron in the land of Egypt, saying: "This month shall mark for you the beginning of the months; it shall be the first of the months of the year for you"'[2]. The name Rosh Chodesh literally means Head of the Month, but Chodesh, or month, is a play on words that also means 'newness'. Hence the word *Chadashot* in modern Hebrew, which is the daily news. Whilst there is nothing new about the moon in the sky, it does remind us of new potential and our capacity for refreshment, as the white orb appears to grow larger in the night sky.

One irony is that the new month is celebrated when the moon is almost at its least visible point. Surely it makes sense to have the celebration when the night sky is full of light? The full moon appears in the middle of a solar month. At the point of Rosh Chodesh, the moon appears darkest because it is directly between the sun and the earth, and is not able to reflect any of the sun's light[3].

Kabbalists have long taught that the darkest moments in our life are the points when the greatest good is about to happen, and that light is about to be revealed. The spiritual master Rav Nahman of Breslov explained this with reference to the positioning of the moon at the new month celebration, when the moon is seemingly absent in the night sky but actually in close proximity to the sun. Rosh Chodesh is the exact

---

[1] There are some halachic (legal) differences for the day, such as extra prayers (e.g. Hallel, Mussaf, insertions into the Amidah), additional Torah readings and extra blessings. Some people have customs to dress more smartly and it is also treated as a 'Women's Festival' by many communities. Ask a competent halachic authority if you have any further questions, or visit Chabad.com for great educational resources.
[2] *Exodus 12:1-2.*
[3] The full moon happens when the moon is on the opposite side of the earth to the sun, and able to fully reflect the solar rays.

moment when the moon is about to start revealing itself in preparation for the full moon at the middle of the month.

In the Ashtanga Yoga system, the dawning of a new moon is marked as a day to refrain from a heavy yoga practice, as the Ashtangis believe that the moon's cycle corresponds the breath and energy cycles[4]. A full moon energy is high, whereas the new moon – where we can hardly see anything in the sky – corresponds to low energy. This makes sense on a basic human level, as we tend to feel more inspired by a brightly-lit sky than when it is overcast. We can consciously do a lighter yoga practice and in doing so raise our awareness of nature's rhythmic cycle. Jewish sages teach that Rosh Chodesh should be a special holiday for women, whose bodies undergo a menstrual cycle that is not dissimilar to the waxing and waning of the moon.

The rebirth of the moon also reminds us of our potential to become great and the possibility of renewing lost hope. In some ways the moon serves as a screen onto which we can project our positive hopes, just as it receives the healing light of the sun.

When travellers are lost in the countryside on a dark night, the moon can help guide the way. Similarly, if you have ever been in a state of depression, it is incredibly comforting when a friend steps in to help you feel better. When we are perplexed with a difficult problem, it is refreshing to 'spread some light on the matter'.

---

[4] The concept of a 'Moon Day' is eloquently put by well-known Ashtanga Yoga teacher Tim Millier: *'Like all things of a watery nature (human beings are about 70% water), we are affected by the phases of the moon. The phases of the moon are determined by the moon's relative position to the sun. Full moons occur when they are in opposition and new moons when they are in conjunction. Both sun and moon exert a gravitational pull on the earth. Their relative positions create different energetic experiences that can be compared to the breath cycle. The full moon energy corresponds to the end of inhalation when the force of prana is greatest. This is an expansive, upward moving force that makes us feel energetic and emotional, but not well grounded. The Upanishads state that the main prana lives in the head. During the full moon we tend to be more headstrong. The new moon energy corresponds to the end of exhalation when the force of apana is greatest. Apana is a contracting, downward moving force that makes us feel calm and grounded, but dense and disinclined towards physical exertion'*- http://ashtangayogacenter.com/moon-days/

Rosh Chodesh is a time for refreshment and renewal. This takes place on a physical and spiritual level, as we choose postures that are gentle towards our bodies. It allows us the chance to be still, quiet, and to take a moment to prepare us for the weeks ahead. It is also called a *Zman Capparah*, a time for return and renewal, as we start afresh for the new month.

We can be like the moon, reflecting spiritual energy and bringing light into the lives of others. Whether it is guiding a traveller, helping a friend or cheering people up, we can play an important role in the lives of others, but first we must take a moment to recharge our batteries.

MARCHESHVAN

MARCHESHVAN: FEELING GROOVY

FESTIVE SUTRA: 'This too is for the best' *BT Taanit 21a*

YOGA POSTURE: *Pincha Mayurasana*/Scorpion

To cope with the stresses of modern life where we are overwhelmed with news and data, it has been suggested that we go on an information diet, limiting the amount of media we consume on a daily basis[1]. This advice proves particularly sage when the media is peddling doom and gloom about the economy or life in general. We frequently hear of recessions and redundancies but perhaps it is time for some rejoicing.

Marcheshvan is the name of the Hebrew month following the festive month of Tishrei (when we celebrate Rosh Hashanah, Yom Kippur and Succot). The proper name of the month was originally Cheshvan but it gained the prefix *mar*, which means bitter, because it does not contain any festivals and some people consider it to be an energetic low point. One challenge is to redeem these days and find reasons to rejoice in life, regardless of what is being presented to us.

The Talmud teaches that everything is ultimately good and that the entire universe is a part of Divine Light. As a result we need to be

---

[1] Suggested by Tim Ferris in his blogs and first book *The Four Hour Work Week*.

positive about apparently negative occurrences[2]. Even when things seem to go wrong, there is the rabbinic custom of saying *Gam Zu L'Tovah*, or 'this too is for the good'[3]. All well and dandy, but what about the times when life does not smell of roses? What can you do when you face a rotten turn of events?

The mystics taught that there are two types of light; revealed light and hidden light[4]. Revealed is the goodness we can see, the boons of joyful living, happy relationships and abundant wealth. Hidden light is the things we find painful, be it loss of a loved one or career misfortunes, and for much of the time we just cannot discover any positive aspects about it, hence the light being considered hidden.

Sometimes there is too much light, and things can actually seem dark. A healthy dose of sunlight will brighten the world around us, but if we stare directly into the sun and get an overdose of intense, pure light, then we may burn our retina and plunge into darkness. Hidden light may be seen in a similar manner: it is not that the light is not there, only that we cannot see it. Another analogy would be at night when we cannot see the sun. The sun still exists, but it is our perspective that is obscured. Similarly we consider that God's light always exists and part of our work is to continually reveal it.

Yoga is about the movement of energy around our bodies, and light is another form of energetic vibration. Well-practiced yoga gives us more energy – or light - and can actually en-lighten us as a result. You remember that feeling of glowing after a great yoga session? Or the fact that some yogis seem to have more positive, radiant skin? Let's leap into a powerful yoga postures, release more energy into our bodies and get ready to radiate more light into the world.

---

[2] *Mishna Brachot, 9:5.*
[3] *Based on the Talmudic story of Nachum Ish Gamzu, Babylonian Talmud 21a.*
[4] *Tanya, Likutei Amarim, Chp 26.*

CHANUKAH

CHANUKAH 1: DARK NIGHT OF THE SOUL

FESTIVE SUTRA: 'The life-breath of a human is the lamp of God' *Proverbs 20:27*

YOGA PRACTICE: *Virabhadrasana 1/*Warrior 1

The Chanukah story is inspiring. It tells of how the Greco-Syrian Empire had taken over Jerusalem and expelled the Jews, placing idols of foreign gods in the sanctuary of the Temple. The Hasmonean fighters staged a civil war and reclaimed the capital city. On re-entering the holy Temple, their very first action was to relight the eternal flame that was intended to burn continuously. Legend tells that there was only enough kosher oil to last for one day before supplies would run out, but a miracle occurred and the flame burned for eight full days, by which time all of the stocks had been replenished[1]. This is celebrated today by lighting the menorah throughout the eight nights of Chanukah, remembering the spiritual victory, and taking this as our cue to spread light into the world.

One way of understanding the story is to reflect on how a group of people fought for what they believed in – a system of living that is based around the idea that we are all connected and that we are all One – rather

---

[1] *Babylonian Talmud, Shabbat 21b.*

than accepting the idolatrous gods of the Greco-Syrian. The Hebrew Bible is a system centred around social justice and the unity of Hashem, creating communities that look after the oppressed and impoverished and seeing the Godliness in one another. Lighting the candles was a reminder of these values which are supposed to last for an eternity. But the fires will only burn if we light them.

Correctly practiced yoga leads to increased light within the body, as our skin becomes healthier and more translucent, giving us that super-healthy yogic glow (rather like the glowing kid from the Ready Brek adverts for those who grew up in Britain during the 80's…although in retrospect perhaps he just lived too close to a nuclear power reactor…). You know the feeling – you have just worked out or had some kind of amazing physical experience and you are feeling that glow. It is also a lot more fun when other people are glowing as they are often a lot more pleasant to be around.

The Book of Proverbs calls our soul the 'lamp of God' or 'flame of the Lord'[2] and it is our challenge to see how we can allow the light to shine forth. This comes through removing physical blockages by way of a powerful yoga practice that will heal our body and reconnect our soul, before taking that light into the world. The first Lubavitcher Rebbe taught that 'the body of a person is a wick and the Light is kindled above it'[3], and he explained that we draw this Light down through our good deeds and positive actions.

As we invigorate our bodies with a fit and healthy physique, we will be well placed to bring light into the world by helping other people through their dark nights.

---

[2] Proverbs 20:27.
[3] Tanya, Likutei Amarim, Chp.35.

CHANUKAH 2: WARRIORS OF LIGHT

FESTIVE SUTRA: 'The Lord goes forth like a warrior, like a fighter he whips up his rage...I will turn darkness before them into light' *Isaiah 42:13-16*

YOGA PRACTICE: *Virabhadrasana 2*/Warrior 2

The Greco-Syrians presented a unique threat to Jewish tradition because of their novel approach to spiritual warfare. Rather than staging mass executions as with the Romans or later anti-Semites like the Nazis, the Alexandrian Empire sought to crush the Hebrew religion and replace it with their own. They had a completely different set of values which did not believe in the oneness of God, and was all about body-soul separation. These so-called Hellenisers represented the opposite of a Jewish spiritual practice. Rather than everyone combining a sense of Godliness within their body, the Greek approach was to separate between athletes who focused on the body, philosophers who focused on the mind and priests who focused on spiritual matters. This disunity is the opposite of the unity of God (*Hashem Echad*) that is mentioned twice a day in the *Shema* prayer.

The Hasmonean family was a Jewish priestly family who became warriors and fought the path back to Jerusalem. Chanukah means 're-dedication' and with the help of these fighters, the Temple was re-established for the body, mind and spirit.

Yet the whole message nearly got lost due to politics. When the Talmud was being written down a couple of hundred years after the event, the Hasmonean family had gone out of favour because they had married out of the faith and had begun bringing idols into the Temple. This was the exact opposite of what their ancestors intended. In addition, the land of Israel was now called Judea, under Roman rule, and it was not a good idea for Jews to send out a message of religiously-inspired military uprisings against the ruling power.

The Talmud describes the Chanukah story from a completely different perspective, choosing to focus on the miracle of light and almost ignoring the whole military victory:

> *'What is Chanukah? Our Rabbis taught: On the 25th of Kislev begins the eight days of Chanukah, which are eight days on which mourning and fasting are prohibited. For when the Greeks entered the Temple, they defiled all the oil in it, and when the Hasmonean dynasty defeated them, they searched and found only one container of oil with the seal of the High Priest, enough for only one day of lighting the lamp. But a miracle happened and the oil lasted for eight days'*[4]

The lights of Chanukah, can be seen as a metaphor for the Light of God in the world, and by physically lighting the candles we are reminded of the ways that we can bring light into the world, brightening the lives of other people through our actions. The 19th Century Rabbi Yehuda Leib Alter, known as the *Sfat Emet*, said that as we stare into the candles, '[our] *"inner light" suddenly realises its own true essence, and its ultimate mission – to draw light into the world. These are the inner lights*[5]. He explains that the Hebrew words for lights, wick and oil – the three components of the menorah on Chanukah – are an acronym for the human soul (ie *N*er = Light, *F(p)tilah* = Wicks and *Sh*emen = Oil. *NeFeSh* = soul). This idea was written about elsewhere, viewing human beings as channels of Divine Light. In other words, as we light the lights and bathe in the luminescence, we are reminded of our goal to bring light into the world.

Similarly the Alter Rebbe wrote in Tanya:

> *'For the body of a person is a wick, and the Light is kindled above it. And King Solomon cried, saying "Let there be no lack of oil above your head". For the Light on a person's head must have oil, meaning good deeds…the Light of the Shechinah [the feminine presence of God] is compared to the flame of a lamp which produces no light nor clings to the wick without oil, and likewise a person's body, which is likened to a wick, except through good deeds alone, and it is not sufficient that*

---

[4] *Babylonian Talmud, Shabbat* 21b.
[5] Paraphrased from Sfat Emet, in *Days of Joy*, p113.

his soul (Neshama), which is a part of Godliness from Above, should act for him as oil to the wick…'[6].

Similarly the prophet Isaiah, whose school was exceptionally concerned with social justice, uses the metaphor of light to explicitly describe how God can transform negative situations, saying that *'The Lord goes forth like a warrior, like a fighter he whips up his rage…I will turn darkness before them into light'*[7].

Bringing Light into the world can require hard work. It can take training to raise our consciousness, which is more akin to an internal battle for light. Chanukah is about spreading light and it begins through an inner practice of unity and reintegrating our separated parts. The Greek culture divided the body, mind and soul but every *mitzvah* and every yoga pose is a practice of unity, bringing together our thoughts, words and actions. Chanukah reminds us that when we are living in a state of Oneness, and aligned with God in all of our deeds, we have the power to bring light into the darkness of other people's lives, although this may sometimes need the persistence of a warrior.

---

[6] *Likutei Amarim* Chapter 35, p44.
[7] *Isaiah* 42:13-16.

CHANUKAH 3: PURE LIGHT

FESTIVE SUTRA: 'There was only enough [pure] oil for one day's lighting. But a miracle happened, and with that oil [a lamp] was lit for eight days' - *Babylonian Talmud, Shabbat 21b*

YOGA PRACTICE: *Virabhadrasana*/Reverse Warrior (i.e. one hand in air at front, other hand placed on back thigh)

The festival of Chanukah celebrates a key moment in the history of Judaism. It remembers the moment when a group of dedicated Jewish priests regained control of the Temple in Jerusalem, relit the holy menorah (candelabra) and secured the future of the religion. Chanukah is a family festival that is associated with fun activities and hot food to warm up the winter nights, but it also has inherent symbolism for the Jewish yogi.

The Talmud[8] states how the Hasmonean fighters entered the sanctuary following their exile by the ruling Greek powers, and found that there was only one remaining jar of oil with the seal of the Kohen Gadol (High Priest). This was expected to supply enough fuel to light the menorah for one day, but ended up surpassing expectations and miraculously stayed alight for eight days.

Patanjali's *Yoga Sutras* describe the principle of 'sauca' as part of the second limb (*Niyama*) of the Ashtanga system. Sauca translates as 'purity' but can be interpreted as relating to the purity of our choices. The sutras state that 'when the body is cleansed, the mind purified and the senses controlled, joyful awareness, needed to realise the inner self, also comes'. We can use our yoga practice to bring an awareness to the motivations of our everyday actions; how pure are our intentions? A simple application of this begins on the yoga mat when we reach an asana (posture) that appears to be beyond our reach. If we are pushing towards the posture in order to satisfy our ego then there will usually be a sense of annoying frustration, but if we face the challenge with a detached acceptance, then our motivation is presumably more pure.

---
[8] *Babylonian Talmud, Shabbat 21b.*

CHANUKAH

The Hebrew word for purity is *tahor* and just as the priests were only allowed to use pure oil to light the Temple's candelabra, we too might only attempt our yoga – and our daily actions – with this ego-less aim.

There are two final yogic clues in the name of the festival. Chanukah means 'dedication' and this is a key part of yoga, with regards to the need for regular practice. We are able to accomplish a phenomenal amount when we dedicate ourselves to a cause – whatever the cause may be – and perhaps we can use the burning lights of the menorah to remind us of this principle.

Chanukah is sometimes dismissed as being a festival for children, and it is from the word Chanukah that we get the word *Chinuch*, meaning 'education' – usually the type that is geared towards the young. Another one of Patanjali's niyamas is *Svadhyaya*, referring to 'education of the self' or 'self study'. Perhaps Chanukah is reminding us to connect with our inner child, to educate ourselves through our daily practice as if we are in the prime of our youth. It has been repeatedly proven that yoga practice can slow down the effects of ageing, so let's put it to the test.

Happy Chanukah.

TREE POSE/VRKSASANA

'Is a human a tree of the field?'

DEUTERONOMY 20:19

CHANUKAH 4: A NEW HOPE

FESTIVE SUTRA: 'Greeks entered the Sanctuary..the Hasmonean monarchy overcame them and became victorious' *BT Shabbat 21b*

YOGA PRACTICE: *Drishti*/Focus

Chanukah can be an internal practice. The traditional Chanukah story is based around how the Greek-Syrian forces entered the Temple in Jerusalem and the Hasmonean forces, a group of Jewish rebel fighters also known as the Maccabees ('hammers'), reclaimed the Temple. They found one day's portion of priestly-anointed oil to light the Menorah and it miraculously lasted for eight days until more supplies could be found.

From an internal, yogic perspective, we might consider our body or mind as the sanctuary, and the 'Greeks' as foreign thoughts. If we choose to make our yoga practice about love, then foreign thoughts would be anything other than loving thoughts. Similarly we could think about the oil as our positive deeds or *mitzvot*.

The seventh chapter of Ecclesiastes opens with the Hebrew poeticism *'Tov Shem Mi Shemen Tov'* which means 'a good name is better than oil [9]. The Hebrew word for oil is *SheMeN* which contains the word *Shem*, name, and *Men*, which has the same spelling as the word for Manna. The word for oil could be loosely translated as 'a name of heavenly sustenance'.

An important part of any yoga posture is the *drishti*, or focus. Like the Hasmoneans driving the Greeks out of the Temple, we can drive out unwanted thoughts. Typically there is a physical focus point for every posture, so in Warrior Two you might choose the end of your index finger as the *drishti*, or a point on the wall ahead of you.

When your focus is tight you can then imagine yourself glowing, radiating out heat and warmth through your posture. Try this for eight days in a row and see if any miracles happen.

---

[9] *Ecclesiastes 7:1.*

CHANUKAH 5: THE HIDDEN STORY OF CHANUKAH

FESTIVE SUTRA: 'The Chanukah lamp is to be lit in the same manner as the sacrifices of the feast', *BT Shabbat 21b*

YOGA PRACTICE: *Sukha*/Joy

I love the hidden story of Chanukah. I first learned about it in a beautiful booklet *The Great Sukkot Cover-Up* or *The True Story of Hanukkah*[10]. The alternative narrative simmers just below the surface and is hinted at in the Talmudic discussion between the schools of Hillel and Shammai. Hillel argues that we should light one candle on the first night and add each night until we have eight candles on the last evening, because we 'increase in holiness'. Shammai says that we should like eight candles on the first night and remove one each night until there is one candle burning on the last night because this would correspond with the sacrifices on Succot[11].

What has Succot got to do with it?

The Books of Maccabees, which were Jewish primary texts that never made it into the Bible but instead became classified as apocrypha and ended up as Christian holy books, tell a different version of the Chanukah story. Instead of the miracle of oil, they explain that Chanukah is celebrated over eight days because the Jews were belatedly celebrating the festival of Succot, as they had been exiled from the Temple and were unable to observe the Succot festivities at their proper time:

> '*Maccabeus and his company led by the Lord, recovered the Temple and the city of Jerusalem. He demolished the altars put up by the heathens in the public square and their sacred precincts as well. When they had purified the sanctuary, they constructed another altar: then*

---

[10] This was written by my friend and teacher Joel Lurie Grishaever and is available at *http://www.torahaura.com/item_True_Story_of_Hanukkah.aspx*

[11] The discussion takes place on *Babylonian Talmud, Shabbat 21b*, with Shammai referencing the order of sacrifices on Succot from Numbers 29:12-31.

striking fire from flints, they offered a sacrifice for the first time for two whole years, and restored the incense, the lights, and the Shew Bread...the sanctuary was purified on the twenty fifth of Kislev... This joyful celebration lasted for eight days; **it was like Succot, for they recalled how only a short time before they had kept that festival while living like animals in the mountains, and so they carried lulavim and etrogim,** *and they chanted hymns (Hallel) to God who had so triumphantly led them to the purification of His Temple. A measure was passed by the public assembly that the entire Jewish people should observe these days every year*"[12].

As mentioned in an earlier Chanukah essay, the Hasmonean dynasty eventually gained a poor reputation amongst the Jewish people and this was one contributing factor as to why their stories were edited out of the Biblical canon. The family's eventual fall from grace was compounded in 134 BCE when Simon Maccabee, the last remaining son of Matisyahu, was murdered by his son-in-law Ptolemy.

Additionally, when the Talmud was being compiled, the land of Israel was under the foreign rule as a client kingdom of Rome. For this reason, it was not helpful to recount tales of Jewish militants because it may have been seen as a call to insurgency. Nonetheless, the stories are here and we can now make use of them for our inspiration and motivation.

Here is a simple yogic practice for Chanukah: to be joyful. We can take any warrior-like energy and direct that passion towards the pursuit of happiness. As the Book of Maccabees says, 'this joyful celebration lasted for eight days; it was like Succot'[13], so why not practice joy? Sukha is the sanskrit word for joy, as explored earlier, in the Succot essays, so this seems a perfect opportunity for eight days of happy practicing.

Happy Holidays.

---

[12] This is from 2 *Maccabees 10:1-6*, which was written in Greek c.120 BCE for the Egyptian Jewish community).
[13] Ibid.

CHANUKAH 6: DEDICATION

FESTIVE SUTRA: 'A psalm. A song. For the dedication of the temple', *Psalm 30:1*

YOGA PRACTICE: Acknowledge our teachers

What are you dedicated to? Or, Where are you lacking dedication and what would you *like* to be dedicated to? Or, can you be more committed to your goal than you are to your fear of pursuing or achieving it?

Chanukah means 'dedication' and one way we can use the week is to meditate on how we are pursuing our most important goals. Another word that comes out of Chanukah is *Chinuch*, meaning education. The Hebrew word *MeChanech* means 'teacher' or guide'. As we teach we are 'dedicating' our students and future generations.

I want to take this moment, in the middle of Chanukah, to acknowledge one of my teachers who has helped along this journey. My first and primary yoga teacher for many years was Edward Clark. I met Edward at drama school, Webber Douglas Academy of Art in South Kensington, London, where he was the Head of Movement and Dance for over two decades. Edward would begin every class with a short yoga sequence that taught us how to breathe and focus our minds in a way that would enhance physical awareness, vastly improve our acting technique and a host of other physical and artistic benefits.

After graduating from drama school I hassled Ed until he would allow me to come along to his company class, the regular yoga practice at his home that would take place before rehearsals for his innovative Yoga Dance Theatre company, Tripsichore Yoga[14]. Fast forward several years and I did a yoga teacher training programme with Edward[15].

---

[14] www.tripsichoreyoga.com
[15] Also taught by the late Elizabeth Connolly, may she rest in peace.

CHANUKAH

One of the best ways to learn is also to teach, as the interaction with students forces us to clarify and articulate our practice. Chanukah can be an opportunity both to renew our dedication and also to be a teacher.

Like the candles on a menorah, we shine out with our own brightness, and use our light to ignite the flames in others.

CHANUKAH 7: BE THE LIGHT

FESTIVE SUTRA: 'Make for yourself a teacher', *Ethics of the Fathers 1:6*

YOGA PRACTICE: Listen to your body

One of my teachers helped me out of a funk. At the time I was spending a lot of energy trying to teach other people. Meanwhile, I was suffering myself. 'Be the light you are seeking' he said, quoting a great teaching. 'Stop focusing on helping other people. Help yourself first'.

In *Ethics of the Fathers*, Rabbi Yehoshua ben Perachiah instructed, *Oseh Lecha Rav*, *'Make yourself a teacher'*[16]. One thing this means to me is to listen very closely to the advice I want to give out to other people, and immediately start following it myself.

I also allow my body to teach me during yoga practices. For years I might ignore physical twinges whilst doing hip-openers and I would then cause myself an injury that lasted weeks, months or years. These days I try to be mindful and conscious of what my body is seeking, aiming to strike the balance between not giving up too easily but also not over-pushing myself to the point of pain. The body is different every day as it ages, as the weather heats or cools, as other external factors come in to play, but such is the nature of lessons: they are not always easy.

Our bodies are miraculous organisms, made up of billions of micro-organisms and performing thousands or millions of biological processes every single day. Our body also possess innate wisdom. Who are we not to listen to our body?

There is great merit in having deep understanding and being able to teach information, but the returns can be infinitely increased when we apply our own wisdom.

---

[16] *Ethics of the Fathers* 1:6.

CHANUKAH

For many years I would look for wisdom outside of myself, even though I had a very clear idea of what I was seeking. Around 2001 I was very keen to find a book that connected Jewish wisdom with yoga, taking us through a cycle of Torah readings and Jewish festivals. A long time went by during which I kept looking, and finally realised that I had to write that book, or at least my version of it. This principle has repeated itself many times in my creative process. We do of course need external teachers from time to time, but there comes a point when we have to apply the teachings or otherwise they will remain 'just' theories.

Be the light you seek.

CHANUKAH 8: THIS IS IT

FESTIVE SUTRA: 'This is Chanukah', *Numbers 7:88*

YOGA PRACTICE: *Tapas*/A heat-generating practice

The final day of Chanukah, day eight, is referred to as *Zot Chanukah* or 'This is Chanukah'. The name comes from the list of sacrifices and offerings that were brought by all of the tribal princes upon the dedication of the sanctuary, which concludes with the phrase *'This was the dedication-offering of the altar, after that it was anointed'*[17]. The Hebrew word for dedication is *Chanukah*.

Chassidic teaching views this final day as the epitome of the festival, as if to say that what happens on this day will summarise your entire Chanukah and be the final push of Chanukah spiritual energy for your coming year. The Sfat Emet comments that on the eighth day of Chanukah it is considered as if we are the candle, and based on this we might meditate on all of the ways that we can share light into the world.

There are also Kabbalistic teachings that suggest a certain kind of spiritual light is only available during Chanukah and how we act during these eight days will affect our coming year.

An intense yoga practice can generate a lot of heat within our body, what the yogis referred to as tapas. This idea can be expressed in a number of ways: you are the candle of Chanukah, the verse from Proverbs that 'the soul of man is the flame of God'[18], or the science-based biological perspective that our body literally radiates light-energy, as is seen when heat-seeking devices are used to detect survivors under collapsed buildings.

Generate heat, burn brightly and have a meaningful last day of Chanukah.

---

[17] Numbers 7:88.
[18] Proverbs 20:27.

TU B'SHVAT

TU B'SHVAT: THE HUMAN TREE

FESTIVE SUTRA: 'Is a human a tree of the field?' *Deuteronomy 20:19*

YOGA PRACTICE: *Vrksasana*/Tree posture

The 15th Day of the Month of *Shvat* is the New Year for Trees, In ancient Israel, *Tu B'Shvat* marked the beginning of the agricultural tax year and the date from when tithing began for crops.

The festival is an opportunity to stop and reflect on the lessons that trees might have to offer us. They can remind us of the interconnectedness of everything, as trees absorb the carbon dioxide that we emit and replace it with life-giving oxygen. They have roots that burrow deep into the ground, unseen to passers-by but essential for giving them stability and groundedness, helping to withstand against passing winds. Trees can provide shelter for entire families of animals, food for humans, shelter to travellers, and complete ecosystems. Or we can simply cut them down and pulp them into a newspaper which will end up in the recycling bin within 24 hours.

The Bible commands absolute respect for trees, especially fruit-giving ones, demanding that we avoid unnecessary destruction even when attacking the owners of the tree: *'When you besiege a city for a long time and make war against it, do not destroy the trees by wielding an axe against them, because you can eat from them. You must not cut them down – are trees of the field human to withdraw before you into the besieged city?'*[1].

If only this environmentally-sensitive advice had been heeded by the US Forces who set up a 370-acre military base on top of the Hanging Gardens of Babylon when they invaded Iraq in 2003, building a heliport and trenches for draining fuel. The environmental disaster is akin to the military blunders that happened in the film *Team America: World Police* where the army task force destroyed everything in sight. Life imitates art.

Are trees of the field human? The commentator Rashi switches the emphasis of the words to ask a different question on this verse. He initially suggests that there is no reason to discriminate against trees because they are not the ones that you are fighting against. Besides, you might need to eat from them. Rashi then retranslates the phrase to mean '*Perhaps* a human is a tree of the field'. This makes even more sense in light of the Garden of Eden where *'God planted a garden and placed the human, and caused to grow from the ground every tree that was pleasing to the sight and good for food'*[2]. The book of Genesis is virtually suggesting that the first human was planted rather than born.

The Talmud later suggests that we should be 'flexible like a reed rather than firm like a cedar'[3], and the Psalm 92 takes the human-tree analogy even further:

'The righteous bloom like a date-palm;

they thrive like a cedar in Lebanon;

planted in the house of the Lord,

they flourish in the courts of our God.

In old age they still produce fruit;

---
[1] Deuteronomy 20:19.
[2] Genesis 2:8-9.
[3] BT Taanit 20b.

TU B'SHVAT

They are full of sap and freshness

Attesting that the Lord is upright

My rock, in whom there is no wrong[4]

However we look at it, we are intricately connected with trees. We breathe the oxygen that trees produce and we eat their fruit. If we are buried next to a tree then we will fertilise its growth. Like trees, we are stronger when we have firm roots, be it family, cultural or spiritual, and we have the ability to provide shelter and protection for one another just like an oak with broad branches. Trees do a lot for us and we can learn from them.

Tree posture, *Vrksasana*, requires balance and alignment, firmly planting our foot onto the ground and drawing our energy upwards towards the sky. As we hold the pose it shows us how rooted we are and where we can improve our balance (e.g. if we fall over). This is a helpful metaphor for the rest of our life, as we can find success and happiness through remaining connected to our passions, ideals and heritage. Whether your personal roots include a strong faith or deeply grounded confidence, they may leave you standing strong throughout the storms of life.

---

[4] Psalm 92: 13 – 14.

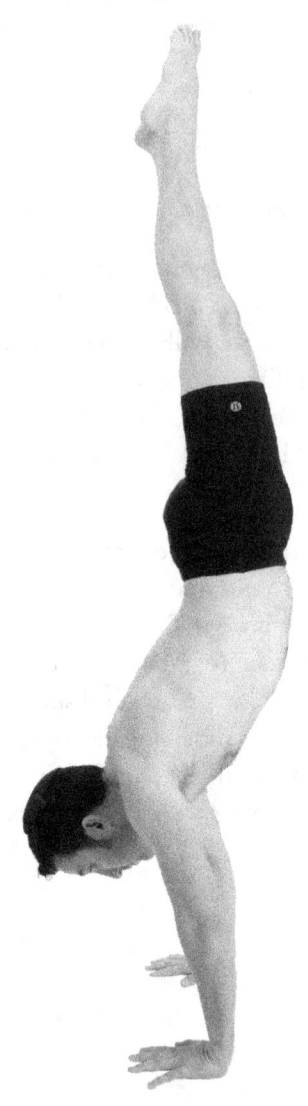

HANDSTAND/ADHO MUKHA VRKSASANA

'there was light and gladness, happiness and honour'

ESTHER 8:13

PURIM

PURIM: IT'S ALL ABOUT JOY AND GLADNESS

FESTIVE SUTRA: 'They gathered themselves together [as one]' *Book of Esther 9:2*

YOGA PRACTICE: *Karma Yoga*, e.g. Sharing gifts with others.

Purim celebrates oneness and unity. Unifying our thoughts, speech and actions is the goal of much Chassidic philosophy[1], and unity is the essence of any yoga practice. The story of Purim revolves around a tale of persecution when evil forces were bent on the destruction of the Jews, but events changed direction and the people survived. The initial attack began when the Persian Prime Minister Haman argued that 'they are one people who are dispersed abroad and scattered'[2]. From one perspective, he saw that there was an internal problem with the Jewish people as they were not unified in one place, but spread across a large geographical area.

Yoga is primarily concerned with internal unity and focusing our energy. The Sanskrit word yoga means oneness, combining or yoking, as we bring together our breath, thoughts and physical being. There is no separation between yoga and meditation as every posture (asana), breathing

---
[1] As taught by Rabbi Shneur Zalman of Liadi in *Tanya*.
[2] *Esther 3:8*.

exercise (prayanama) or flowing movement (vinyasa) is intended to unify our mind, body and soul.

We might explore the Festive Sutra from the perspective of our own bodies, *'They gathered themselves together [as one]'*[3]. How is our body not currently 'gathered together'? How scattered are our thoughts? Where are our intentions different from our actions, and where do we say one thing and do another? Our hands may put food into our mouth while our brain feels guilty. Our mouth might speak words that our heart does not mean to express, or we may refrain from saying things that we want to say, and hold on to resentments. Our feet can take us into situations that we would really rather avoid. True unity, where we are conscious and mindful at all times, involves unifying our thought, speech and action.

The yoga of Purim runs even deeper. The Sfat Emet, a 19th Century commentator, said that the miracle of Purim was that people recognised God's actions within the world even though God was hidden. The Purim narrative tells how a massive pogrom was avoided through a series of events, and these could be attributed to either sheer coincidence, or the hidden hand of God. We go for the latter explanation. Our Festive Sutra describes how the people 'gathered themselves together' because they recognised that everything is connected. The Divine is working around us, all of the time, every day. When I stand on the yoga mat taking a powerful breath and connecting my entire body and mental focus with that breath, I tune into this oneness and reconnect with the Creator. This is why yoga is so much more than a sport, gymnastic or a weight-loss technique; it is about nothing less than achieving total unity and complete inner power.

The Sfat Emet taught how when the people gathered themselves together on Purim, it contrasted with the receiving of the Torah at Mount

---

[3] Book of Esther 9:2.

PURIM

Sinai when the people where gathered together by Moses[4]. Mount Sinai was a passive experience where they were brought together by an outside leader, but on Purim they gathered themselves as one, and the healing leadership came from within[5].

Purim presents an opportunity for gathering ourselves together: getting our thoughts together, getting our actions into alignment and getting our act together. We begin on the yoga mat, bringing into alignment our thoughts, body, breath and spirit. This overwhelming oneness can be intense and uplifting, as we reconnect with God in the world. We then take this oneness out into the world, gathering with friends, family and loved ones. The customs of Purim include giving gifts to the poor and gifts of food to our friends. These are all techniques to connect with other people, all methods that lead us towards a greater unity. There is even a rabbinic opinion that our 'gifts' include sharing our own form of spiritual wisdom and talents with one another[6]. These are all forms of yoga, as we take that which is scattered and bring it together. The yoga of Purim can be about sharing with other people, strengthening our communities through giving to those around us and empowering others, and strengthening our own lives as a result.

---

[4] *Deuteronomy 9:2.* There is a further Talmudic teaching on this which explains how the spiritual principles that were given on Mount Sinai at a time of obvious revelation were finally established at Purim when God's presence was most concealed (this is taught with specific reference to the Hebrew phrase "Kimu v'Kiblu", i.e. established and received, and the Talmud explains Kimu man v'kiblu far - that which was earlier received (on Mount Sinai) was finally established on Purim).

[5] *Days of Joy: Insights of the Sfas Emes*, trans./commentary Rabbi Yosef Sterne, p255.

[6] *Talmud Bavli, Megillah 7b*, which relates how one scholar sent his friend a pungent food and in return he received something sweet. This is seen as an allusion to everyone sharing their own unique talents, and their own brands of learning.

BIRKAT HACHAMAH

BIRKAT HACHAMAH: HERE COMES THE SUN

FESTIVE SUTRA: 'What real profit has a human in all the work he does beneath the sun? a generation comes and a generation goes, and the world stands forever. And the sun rises and the sun sets, and it returns back to its place' *Ecclesiastes 1:3-6*

YOGA PRACTICE: *Surya Namaskar*/ 28 Sun salutations

Birkat HaChamah, the Blessing of the Sun, is a once-in-every-28-years-event. Tradition holds that the sun begins a new cycle on this day, when it is sitting at the exact same point in the sky as it did when it was created on Day 4 of the Genesis narrative[1].

'What real profit has a human in all the work he does beneath the sun?'[2]. The words of King Solomon resonate: human life is short but the world lasts for a long time. Tradition teaches that King Solomon wrote Ecclesiastes as an old man, reflecting on how he had misspent much of his time on earth. It took him many years to find meaning and fulfilment, and that only came in his final years. What are we to do when all of our efforts

---

[1] *'Our Sages taught: The one who sees the sun starting on its new cycle, the moon in its power, the planets in their orbits, and the signs of the zodiac in their orderly progress should say [the blessing] 'Blessed be He who wrought the work of creation'.* Babylonian Talmud, Brachot 59b.
[2] Ecclesiastes 1:3-6.

will eventually fade to nothing? What is the point of everything we do on earth? What is the point of working hard to innovate and be creative when there is nothing new under the sun?

The pivotal phrase in our Kosher Sutra is 'beneath the sun'. If our life is purely focused on material pursuits, pleasures of the flesh and material possessions, then things can appear meaningless because we know that everything will eventually be lost. But if the question is rephrased, to read; 'What real profit has a human in all the work s/he does above the sun', then we have a new perspective. What is above the sun? The realm of the spirit. The realm of God.

If we read further between the lines, we can understand that although our possessions do not travel with us when we die, we can take our consciousness. The work we do to refine our spirit does travel with us, and these spiritual merits carry forward from one lifetime to the next[3].

In 2009, Birkat HaChamah fell on the eve of Passover. The festival of Pesach is a celebration of liberation. The exodus from Egypt is a reminder that we are not slaves to our physical body. We are free people. We look towards a metaphorical Mount Sinai and remember there is something beyond our human material existence, and we can strive towards continual awareness of God. We have free will to choose to believe or not, and that choice is entirely ours. Nonetheless, in recognising there is something beyond our mere physical existence we begin to free ourselves from earthly limitations.

The cornerstone of Hatha yoga is the sun salutation; a choreography that is traditionally done at sunrise whilst facing the sun. There are many variations on *Surya Namaskar* and there is no 'right' version as different styles suit different needs. As we face the sun we might recognise what is beyond it and lift our hearts and intentions beyond the sun, towards our Creator. The sun is a source of energy to our planet but on a spiritual level it is merely representative of the greater source of energy behind it; the Source who made the sun on Day 4 of creation.

---

[3] This may apply both to reincarnation on the planet Earth and also as we move between different spiritual realms, i.e. what is commonly referred to as *Olam Haba*, the next world.

BIRKAT HACHAMAH

The Kabbalah connects the sun with Moses[4], and explains how the phrase 'the sun rises' (from Ecclesiastes, above) refers to when Moses led the people out of Egypt, which began a new dawn. The Zohar, the Kabbalistic 'Book of Splendour' (again, another play on spreading Light), also teaches that 'the sun is the body'[5].

Birkat HaChamah, the Blessing of the Sun, is a chance to celebrate in one of the most glorious aspects of creation, and to remember what is truly beyond it, namely the glory of the Creator. Enjoy your sun salutes and be nourished by the Eternal Light.

---

[4] 'And Moses was the chariot to Zeir Anpin, referred to as "Sun". We see here that the right arm was broken and the body, which is the sun, became darkened' (Zohar, Parshat Chukkat, 37-38).

[5] 'Since that generation was receiving from the moon, which is Malchut, and the sun was gathered, because they did not receive from Zeir Anpin, referred to as "Sun". During the time of Moses, the moon was gathered, so that they did not receive from Malchut, and the sun was dominant, as they were receiving from Zeir Anpin, referred to as "Sun". Zohar, Parshat Chukkat, 37-38

TRIANGLE /TRIKONASANA

'The Lord freed us from Egypt with a strong hand, an outstretched arm and awesome power, and by signs and portents'

DEUTERONOMY 26:8

PESACH

PESACH 1: OUTSTRETCHED ARMS & HEALTHY HEARTS

FESTIVE SUTRA: 'I will harden Pharoah's heart...and the Egyptians shall know that I am the Lord when I stretch out my hand over Egypt... say to Aaron: "stretch out your arm"' *Exodus 7:3, 5 & 8:1*

YOGA PRACTICE: *Ustrasana*/Camel Pose

The story of Passover is a symphony that tells of slavery and freedom, as an oppressed people are redeemed from their captors. So powerful is the imagery that the emancipation of Hebrew slaves has become a leitmotif for other peoples throughout history, such as the African-American slaves who reached the ultimate freedom with the success of the American Civil Rights movement.

The Bible uses body-centred language when introducing the ten plagues. God says that He will 'harden the heart of Pharoah'[1]. This phrase is repeated at least eight times during the next few chapters, and there are two different verbs applied to Pharoah's heart – both hardening (*Eksheh*) and strengthening or stiffening (*Yehezak*)[2].

---
[1] Exodus 7:1.
[2] Exodus 7:22.

When somebody's heart gets hardened or stiffened, this is a threat to cardiac health. I experienced this up close when my father underwent emergency heart surgery, having a double bypass to enable clearer blood flow around a blocked artery. Thank God the operation was a success. We learned that clear blood flow is everything.

Pharaoh's heart was hardened, stiffened, strengthened, and these actions effectively blocked the channel of freedom, arresting the movement of the Hebrew slaves towards their eventual freedom. Moses responded with the first of the ten plagues, which took place by the Nile, the biggest artery in the whole of Egypt. The river flowed with blood.

One of the first things I did following my father's heart operation was to ask an experienced yoga teacher what sort of remedial postures could be prescribed to help him on the road to healing. The answer was not that different from the exercises that had already been set by the hospital's physiotherapists, namely heart-openers. A recovering heart patient should begin with gentle movements that get the blood moving and open the thoracic cavity, by moving their arms to either side and creating as much space as possible in the upper chest. Those early days were very difficult for my father as every stretch, however simple, brought a painful reminder that his ribcage had just been sewn back together following several hours in the operating theatre. Nonetheless he continued, persevered and healed. If we look at the Biblical text, there is an important stage that takes place between hearing about Pharaoh's closed heart and the river of blood flowing through the Nile;

> *'And the Egyptians will know I am the Lord when I stretch forth my hand...And the Lord said to Moses: "Say to Aaron: Take your rod, and stretch out your hand over the waters of Egypt..."'*[3]

God's prescription for healing the situation is to do this heart-opening posture of stretching out the hands! Shoulder rotations are an essential part of many postures, ranging from sun salutations to triangles to warriors, and every one of these variations will help create space around the heart. Several of the plagues are introduced with this physical action,

---

[3] Exodus 7:5 and 19.

as is the splitting of the Red Sea, and it is performed by Moses and Aaron following God's instruction.

> *'And Aaron stretched out his hand over the waters of Egypt; and the frogs came up…'*[4]

> *'And Moses stretched forth his rod over the land of Egypt, and the LORD brought an east wind'*[5]

> *'And lift up your rod, and stretch out your hand over the sea, and divide it'*

The Rabbis warned about viewing God as a human being and made it clear that any anthropomorphic descriptions of the Creator are only supposed to be metaphorical. God's 'outstretched arm' is a metaphor for the force with which He acts in certain situations. The repetitive mentions of his fingers, hand and arm in the Passover Haggadah is reinforcing this sense of His involvement within the world.

We might use this festival to open our hearts to other people who are oppressed, and even to open our hearts to love ourselves if we are oppressing ourselves with our thoughts. Healing can arrive when we keep our hearts open and healthy, and we may get to see some miracles of our own.

Chag Sameach.

---

[4] Exodus 8:2.
[5] Exodus 10:13.

PESACH 2: THE YOGI'S HAGADDAH

FESTIVE SUTRA #1: 'And the more one expands the story of the coming out of Egypt, the more admirable it is', *Pesach Hagaddah*

YOGA PRACTICE: Yoga opportunities throughout Seder Night

For several years I have been dreaming of *The Yogi's Hagaddah*, a hands-on guide to the first two nights of Passover. In lieu of a full book, here are some outline ideas for a creative experience during the festival.

Seder Night, the annual retelling of the Passover story, presents the opportunity for a creative feast. *Leyl HaSeder*, literally translated means 'evening of the order' and goes through the order of events on the path to freedom. We remember the Children of Israel's slavery in Egypt, subsequent miracles and eventual liberation. Our guide is the *Hagaddah*, a book which means 'the storytelling' or 'the retelling' and shares an important principle: 'the more one expands the story of leaving Egypt, the more one is praised', or 'the more admirable it is'[6]. In other words, get creative!

There are many creative ways to enjoy Seder Night and get deeper into the story. Here are some ideas to get started with, and if you generate some more yogic approaches to Pesach, please let me know via my website. Let *The Yogi's Hagaddah* begin.

FESTIVE SUTRA #2: 'With a Strong Hand and an Outstretched Arm'

YOGA PRACTICE: Stretch your arm and hand.

This is the yoga equivalent of a drinking game. It is also a great warm-up exercise which the whole family can do, from young children through to the elderly. At the beginning of the Seder night, tell people that every time you hear the phrase how God

---

[6] I like 'the more admirable' translation which is by Emeritus Chief Rabbi Lord Jonathan Sacks in *The Jonathan Sacks Haggada* (Maggid Books, Koren Publishers: Jerusalem, 2013), p30.

liberated the Hebrews 'with a strong hand and an outstretched arm'... you reach your arm with strength and vigour. The arms are similar to a *Trikonasana* (Triangle) or *Virabadhrasana* (Warrior) pose, with the anatomical effect that reaching out your arm can create more space around your heart. Either way, it is also a fun group exercise.

FESTIVE SUTRA #3: 'Go and learn what Laban the Aramean did to Jacob'

YOGA PRACTICE: Balance poses (e.g. *Vrksasana*/Tree Pose)

The first mention of Jacob is an opportunity to introduce some Kabbalistic yoga. Jacob represents the *sefirah* (Divine sphere) of *Tiferet* which is compassion or internal balance, and you might play with this idea through a one-legged balance such as tree pose. For a very extensive exploration of the Kabbalistic connections to yoga and the sefirot, take a look in my previous book *The Kabbalah Sutras - 49 Steps to Enlightenment*.

FESTIVE SUTRA #4: 'Pharaoh condemned only the boys to death...'

YOGA PRACTICE: Neck rolls or *Jalandhara Bandha*, the Chin Lock.

The word *Pharaoh* has three letters in Hebrew - *Peh, Resh, Fey* - and if you rearrange these letters you get *Oref* which means the back of the neck. The Jews are called a 'stiff-necked people'[7] - *Am K'shei Oref*, and this stubborn quality can be used for good or evil. Pharaoh was stubborn, making life difficult for his slaves, and we can meditate on where we too are making life difficult for ourselves and others. Similarly, having a 'stiff neck' can also be a healthy quality when it comes to being focused and persevering in the pursuit of a vision. There are various ways you can play with this idea: one is to breath as you do some neck rolls, carefully and slowly moving your head around in circles. Another idea is to bring your chin down to your clavicle, the 'v' shape at the top of your chest, and breathe deeply in that position. This is a yogic 'chin lock' called *Jalandhara Bandha* which is said to have various healing qualities including regulating our metabolism.

---

[7] Exodus 32:9.

FESTIVE SUTRA #5: 'The Egyptians dealt cruelly with us, and oppressed us, and imposed hard labour on us'

YOGA PRACTICE: *Trikonasana*/Triangle Pose or *Parsvottanasana*/Pyramid Pose

The Hagaddah does not explicitly mention Pyramids or the landmarks of Ancient Egypt, but we can still use Pyramid or Triangle-related postures as a meditation on freedom and liberation.

FESTIVE SUTRA #6: 'And the Lord heard our voice...and remembered the covenant with Abraham, Isaac and Jacob'

YOGA PRACTICE: Standing balance poses

There are ways to physicalise each of these phrases, depending upon how deeply we want to internalise the experience. 'The Lord hearing our voice' could be any moment when we pause and consider when God has listened to our prayers, when those prayers have been answered and *how* they have been answered (and sometimes God says 'no').

Any mentions of Abraham, Isaac and Jacob can be practiced through the kind of Kabbalistic yoga that we explore in greater detail in my book *The Kabbalah Sutras*. The first three chapters explore how these three patriarchs each correspond to a different *sefirah* or Divine Sphere, namely, different Godly energies that are present within our body. Abraham represents *Chesed*, the attribute of lovingkindness which is associated with the right arm. Isaac corresponds with *Gevurah* or discipline, which is the left arm. Jacob is associated with *Tiferet*, compassion or balance, the middle path that is embodied in our body. We might re-read the phrase that God 'remembered the covenant with Abraham, Isaac and Jacob', stretch and move the upper parts of our body, and think about how the Divine energy 'remembers' us at every moment as the life-force flows throughout our body and thousands of tiny biological processes take place as every second passes.

FESTIVE SUTRA #7: '"With signs" - this refers to the staff, as it is said, "Take this staff in your hand and with it you shall perform the signs"'
YOGA PRACTICE: *Dandasana*/Staff Pose

We can do a modified Staff Pose in our chair, which would look like placing your feet firmly on the ground, hands by your side pressing into the base of the chair on either side of your hips, and keeping your back straight.

FESTIVE SUTRA #8: '"And with wonders" - this refers to the blood, as it is said: "I shall make wonders in the sky and on the earth"'
YOGA PRACTICE: Meditations from head to toe

The next phase of the work, which I may explore in a future book, is to consider how the entire Torah is happening in our bodies right now. A simple reading of this sutra phrase would be to consider the wonders within our body, from the 'sky' of our head to the 'earth' of our feet. We might meditate on how our blood is the great connector, and breathe whilst visualising the connections from our feet through to the crown of our head.

There are various internal energy exercises and visualisations that might be connected here. *The Bahir*, for example, mentions how the 10 sefirot (Divine Spheres) are represented by the fingers and toes, and we can see the fingers as the 10 sefirot in the upper world(s) and the toes as the 10 sefirot in our 'lower' world[8].

FESTIVE SUTRA #9: 'Blood, and Fire, and Pillars of Smoke'
YOGA PRACTICE: Fire Breath

There are different versions of a fire breath, and one is to inhale, hold your breath, make tight fists, close your eyes and shake your fists vigorously for five seconds before exhaling with your mouth open and tongue pushed out to your chin. The breath-hold and shaking have the effect of heating your breath and building up some pressure before a fiery exhale[9]. A meditation on this may be to reflect upon the fire aspects within our body, as we build heat.

---

[8] *The Bahir*, p125.
[9] I learned this version from the yoga teacher & practitioner David Sye.

THE TEN PLAGUES

We can use the Ten Plagues as an opportunity for cultivation and a mindful practice. There is a Kabbalistic idea that each of the Ten Plagues is trying to liberate a different power of the soul. Examples of this are how the plague of blood, a warm liquid, was trying to heat up the cold spiritual void of Egypt, and we could use this to meditate on how we need to 'heat up our spirituality'. Similarly, the second plague, a swarm of frogs, leapt into the ovens of Egypt and the coolness of the frogs was intended to cool down the Egyptians' hot passion for negativity[10].

FESTIVE SUTRA 10.1: The Plague of Blood
YOGA PRACTICE: Inverted poses, e.g. *Salabama Sirsasana*/Headstand.

There are times when we do not feel 'spiritual' and may experience a distance from God. From one perspective reading about the first plague can be the basis for a practice where we take our areas of spiritual coolness and warm them up towards God. On a physical energetic level we might think about the *chi* or *prana* flowing through our veins, literally warming up the 'rivers' of blood within our body.

The first plague can be seen to represent a kind of warming. Egypt had an indifference to spirituality and transforming the blood to water represented the way that the country was being 'warmed up' to accept the Oneness of God. A commentary in the name of the Lubavitcher Rebbe explains: *'Water is cold, whereas blood is warm. There are two types of coldness and two types of warmth: a person whose primary orientation*

---

[10] These ideas are explored more fully in both the *Likutei Torah* of Rabbi Yitzhak Luria (the Ari) and Kabbalistic prayer books (siddurim). Each of the plagues also correspond to a different sefirah, as if to break down the shells or energy blockages surrounding them: Blood = *Malchut*, Frogs = *Yesod*, Lice = *Hod*, Wild Beasts = *Tiferet*, Boils = *Gevurah*, Hail = *Chesed*, Locusts = *Binah*, Darkness = *Chochmah*, Death of the Firstborn = *Keter*. More detailed explanation in 'Ten Ways to Destroy Your Life' by Rabbi Yosef Y. Jacobson on www.chabad.org and in *Sefer Tanya* chapters 3 and 6.

in life is material will be cold to spiritual concerns and warm to material concerns; a person whose primary orientation is spiritual will be cold to material concerns and warm to spiritual concerns...Allegorically [the plague of blood] signifies the transformation of cold indifference to Divinity into warm enthusiasm for it[11].

FESTIVE SUTRA 10.2: The Plague of Frogs
YOGA PRACTICE: *Mandukasana*/Frog Pose

Once we have warmed our body towards the spiritual presence within, and increased our prana flow or life-force, we can practice thought control and choosing positive thoughts.

There is a ying-yang reading of the first two plagues, according to the Lubavitcher Rebbe's teachings. Whereas the plague of blood 'signified how Egypt's cold indifference toward God must be replaced with warm enthusiasm', the heat of the Egyptian's evil inclination then had to be cooled down with frogs, which represent a cold energy: *'First the evil (the cold Nile river) was turned into good (the hot blood), and only then was the evil (the hot Egyptian ovens) neutralised (by the cold frogs)'*.[12]

Just as the cold frogs leapt into the metaphorical evil of the Egyptian ovens, we can 'cool' negative thoughts within our head. There are areas where we blame, judge or complain about life, or project negativity towards others. The higher levels of yoga practice are concerned with raising our vibration and and controlling or directing our thoughts.

Another meditation is based on this teaching: *'A frog's natural habitat is water, for a frog to jump into a piping-hot oven is an act of self-sacrifice'*[13]. A question to ask, in the name of spiritual growth, might be: Where can we sacrifice our ego or fears or negative beliefs?

---

[11] *Chumash Shemot: The Book of Exodus* - With an Interpolated English Translation and Commentary Based on the Works of the Lubavitcher Rebbe, Rabbi Menachem M. Schneerson, p47.
[12] Ibid, p.48.
[13] Ibid.

FESTIVE SUTRA 10.3: The Plague of Lice

YOGA PRACTICE: Mountain Pose and be aware of the sensations on your skin.

If the second plague is a reminder to raise our consciousness through holding positive, loving thoughts, then the third plague can prompt us to keep our thoughts at a higher vibration.

> *'The louse is a parasite; it lives off animals and people without contributing anything beneficial to their lives…it is therefore seen as a metaphor for evil, inasmuch as evil thrives by sucking the life force out of holiness rather than on its own merits. Just as a louse can attach itself to a person only if its hygiene is lax, evil can only suck vitality out of holiness when we allow our Divine consciousness to lapse'*[14].

One way to drop our consciousness is to take more than we give, or allow other people to drain our energy. This is a larger discussion - how we attract 'energy vampires' who will suck our energy, how we can behave like this towards other people, and how to protect ourselves and others - but a solid starting point is to focus on having healthy boundaries within relationships and making sure that we give as well as take. Similarly, if someone in our life is taking more than giving in a way that is unhealthy, we must be careful to establish a positive balance in the relationship.

FESTIVE SUTRA 10.4: The Plague of Wild Beasts

YOGA PRACTICE: *Pinchamayurasana*/Locust Pose

When I discuss meditation with people who do not have a regular practice, one of the most frequent responses is 'I can't control my thoughts'. This, of course, one of the best reasons why we practice meditation. Personally, I prefer meditation techniques that get you to think of something specific rather than the sometimes unhelpful 'empty your mind'.

---

[14] Ibid, p.50.

The plague of wild beasts might be interpreted as the 'wild beasts' of our thoughts that can run through our mind when we are in a limited state. Egypt, or *Mitzrayim* represents a limited consciousness because the Hebrew word mitzrayim literally translates as 'from narrow straits' or 'from a limited place'. That limited place can be our mind. The Book of Exodus records the words that Moses was told to speak to Pharaoh, *'If you do not send out My people behold, I shall incite against you, your servants, your people, and your houses, the mixture of wild beasts; and the houses of Egypt shall be filled with the mixture of wild beasts'*[15].

Our challenge is thus to send out liberating thoughts, to raise our consciousness from the patterns that constrict and constrain us, the 'Egypt' consciousness. If we allow the wild beasts of negative thoughts to run free in our mind, then we too experience a plague of these beastly thoughts. As our thoughts are integrally connected to our bodies, this can manifest as stress, pain or disease. The Yoga Sutras begins with the mantra that yogic oneness is achieved when the mind becomes still and there is an end to the wild fluctuations of our thoughts[16], so we can achieve deep inner peace.

FESTIVE SUTRA 10.5: The Plague of Diseased Livestock
YOGA PRACTICE: *Gormukhasana*/Cow-face Pose

The Torah describes how Moses was commanded to tell Pharaoh that 'the hand of God will be directed against your livestock in the field - against the horses, the donkeys, the camels, the cattle and the flocks'.[17]

On a straightforward level we can think about the battle between our Divine soul (*Nefesh Elokit*) and our Animal Soul (*Nefesh Behamit*)[18]. Our animal, physical desires are those that keep us energetically tied to the physical world, whereas our higher soul is focused on the

---

[15] Exodus 8:17.
[16] Yoga Sutras 1:2.
[17] Exodus 9:3.
[18] This concept is explained in *Sefer Tanya*.

vibrations and thoughts that raise us to an awareness of God's emanation. For example, I can think about how to get some food and quench the hunger in my stomach, or I can think about how I would like to eat to nourish my body so that it can fulfil the mission of my soul.

As a spiritual practice we can view every physical desire as something that can be harnessed for a higher spiritual goal. The drive for sex, power, strength, food or anything can all be connected with a goal that will serve others and serve God.

FESTIVE SUTRA 10.6: Boils
YOGA PRACTICE: *Tadasana*/Mountain Pose

There are times when we are so fed up with our behaviours that we do not want to do them anymore. Our tricks no longer work, whether it is subtle lies, manipulations or just ways of being that we have grown out of.

The plague of boils specifically affected the Egyptians' bodies, rather than the River Nile, their homes (as with the plague of frogs), the fields or the animals. We are told that Egypt's necromancers, the black magic sorcerers who had been able to replicate several of the earlier plagues on a smaller scale, 'could not stand before Moses because of the boils, because the boils were on the necromancers and on all of Egypt'[19]. The Ramban explains that 'they were embarrassed and covered their heads [in shame] because they were full of boils and could not save themselves [from the plague]'[20].

There can be something empowering about this image of the magicians no longer being able to stand up because their skin was in such a boil-ridden condition. We can think about behaviours we want to let go of, those aspects of our personality that no longer stand up to the image of who we want to be and who we want to become. Each of these plagues is an opportunity for us to step into our full potential, liberated from the shackles of narrow thinking and small-minded behaviours.

---

[19] Exodus 9:11.
[20] Ramban on Exodus 9:11, Artscroll translation.

PESACH

FESTIVE SUTRA 10.7: The Plague of Hail
YOGA PRACTICE: Hand on heart

The Zohar teaches that the plague of hail represented selfish love. Normal hail consists of water, which represents *Chesed*, the Divine light (*sefirah*) of lovingkindness. This plague, however, combined the naturally-frozen hail with flaming fire. Fire represents *Gevurah* - discipline or restriction - and in the realm of relationships this represents a kind of frozen love.

Rabbi Yosef Y Jacobson explains that *'In Kabbalah, the flow of love is compared to a flow of water, irrigating and nourishing a human soul with its refreshing vibrancy. Yet a person who finds himself in "Egyptian" bondage knows only an icy love—a love that is based entirely on self-seeking motives and self-centred considerations. This person's rain-like flow of love becomes cold and frozen like hail, harming his loved ones instead of nurturing them'*.[21]

One meditation is to place one hand on our hearts and consider where we are freezing our love towards ourselves, one another, or God. The intention is thaw our love, and balance it so that our hearts are open and connected. This openness is a further counter-balance to the restrictions of Egypt-consciousness.

FESTIVE SUTRA 10.8: The Plague of Locusts
YOGA PRACTICE: *Salabhasana*/Locust Pose

The plague of locusts was highly destructive. So many of them descended upon the land that it looked dark, and they devastated all of the remaining crops:

> "Moses raised his staff over Egypt...the locusts came up over the whole land of Egypt and descended over all the territory of Egypt, very severely; never before had there been such a

---

[21] As written in his commentary 'Ten Ways to Destroy Your Life' at Chabad.org.

plague of locusts, and never again will there be anything like it. They covered the surface of the land so that the land became dark. They ate all the grass of the land and all the fruit of the trees that the hail had left over; no greenery was left on the trees or among the grass of the field, throughout all Egypt"[22].

Where are we being destructive with our thoughts or actions? Where do our minds flood out all light or goodness, because we are so locked into a particular way of thinking?

The inner Kabbalistic aspect of this plague is Binah, which represents understanding or intelligence. A deeper understanding of a higher intelligence will keep us safe from the negative, low-vibrating thoughts that tear us up in the way that locusts ate up the crops.[23]

FESTIVE SUTRA #10.9: The Plague of Darkness
YOGA SUTRA: Meditate with eyes closed (*Pratyahara*)

Rashid taught that four-fifths of the Hebrew people died during the three-day plague of darkness. This Rashi comment is part of an amazing word-play on Exodus 13:18. The Hebrew says that the Children of Israel were armed when they went up from Egypt, but the Hebrew word for armed, *Chamushim*, also means 'one-fifth'. The hidden teaching is that only a fifth of the people survived.

Where are we dying through darkness, or through not telling ourselves the truth? Where would we rather defend our negative behaviours or refuse to cultivate, refine and enlighten our thoughts so that we can be liberated? The choice is not to evolve ourselves or continue with the status quo, but rather to raise our consciousness or to die.

---

[22] Exodus 10: 14-15, Kehot translation p6.
[23] Rabbi Yosef Y. Jacobson's Article, *'Ten Ways to Destroy Your Life'* at Chabad.org.

PESACH

FESTIVE SUTRA #10.10: Death of the Firstborn
YOGA PRACTICE: *Savasana*/Corpse Pose

There are times when we need to let things die. Our bodies replace dead blood cells, expels waste material and exhales carbon dioxide. *Savasana* or Corpse Pose is more than a relaxing lie-down on the ground. It is not only to come face to face with our own death, to realise that life leads towards death, but also to recognise that our souls never die and that there is an immortal part of ourselves that is part of God and lives on after we have exited our physical body.

The Death of the Firstborn can lead us to question the parts of our ego that we might let die, such as inflated self-images, unhealthy beliefs, mental misconceptions or negative behaviours that are holding us back.

FESTIVE SUTRA #10.11: 'Against all the Children of Israel, a dog will not sharpen its tongue, against man or animal..' *Exodus 11:7*
YOGA PRACTICE: *Adho Mukha Svanasana*/Downward-facing dog

The Torah teaches that when during the tenth plague, the death of the firstborn, the dogs in Egypt would not be barking amongst the Israelites. Dogs are considered to have their special place as a result. Indeed the Hebrew word for dog, *Kelev* means 'like [our] heart' - *k (like) lev (heart)*. One practice for this would be to do a downward facing dog position and focus on opening your heart. You may also do a modified version of this against the wall, standing a couple of feet away from the wall and pushing your hands into the wall, rather than on the floor.

***

הוד
Hod-Humility

EXTENDED CHILD'S POSE/BALASANA

'If I am only for myself, what am I?'

ETHICS OF THE FATHERS 1:14

LAG B'OMER

LAG B'OMER: RESPONSIBILITY

FESTIVE SUTRA: 'All of Israel are responsible for one another' *BT Shavuot 39a*

YOGA PRACTICE: *Natarajasana*/Supported Dancer Pose, practiced with a partner (e.g. face one another and rest palms together so you are slightly leaning towards one another).

Yoga practice can be easier when you are doing it with a friend. There is something special about the energy of having someone else in the room. My morning yoga practice is generally a solo affair and it is easy for my mind to wander, lose focus and suddenly find myself staring into space. Whenever I am going through yoga sequences with a friend there is a subtle energy shift that takes place – like having a running partner, it can be easier to get motivated and stay motivated when there are two of you.

Lag B'Omer has become the Jewish mystical bonfire night, a time when we pause in our metaphorical journey up the mountain of spiritual development. The journey from the festival of Pesach to Shavuot is a movement from freedom to liberation and there are exactly 49 days, seven complete weeks in between. Leviticus describes this 49 day period as counting the 'Omer' as it corresponded with seven weeks of marking the barley harvest[1]. The Kabbalists later introduced the mystical attributes to the 49-day count (see my book *The Kabbalah Sutras - 49 Steps to Enlightenment* for a more in-depth study).

Lag B'Omer, which literally means the 33rd day of the Omer count, is a day of celebration because of a major historical incident that occurred. During the Roman occupation of Israel, there was a plague that affected the students of Rabbi Akiva. All of his 24,000 disciples died. The Talmud records that this happened because they did not respect one another and they were punished as a result of their jealousy and disagreements. As scholars they were supposed to be peaceful and loving, but allowed negativity and ego to take over their daily existence[2]. Rabbi Akiva showed the ultimate resilience after this tragedy and reconstructed his school with just five students. One of the new students was Rabbi Shimon Bar Yochai who became the most noted teacher of Kabbalah and is attributed with revealing the Zohar, or Book of Splendour. Rabbi Shimon Bar Yochai, the *Rashbi*, was responsible for bringing great light into the world through his teaching of Kabbalah and he also died on the 33rd day of the Omer. Thousands of people gather every year on this night at his gravesite in Northern Israel and Jews all over the world light bonfires on Lag B'Omer. The fires represent the immense light that the Rashbi brought into the world with his revelation of the Divine teachings.

There are various energies we can connect with on this day as we explore the theme through a physical practice. The ancient yogis taught how the physical practice of yoga helps light inner fires as we generate heat through our body, so we might focus on an 'inner bonfire'. Holding postures and breathing deeply through our vinyasa all helps power-up our energy and stokes these inner fires. We have all experienced getting hot through exercise, but the yogic heat is slightly different because it is

---

[1] 'You shall count for yourselves – from the morrow of the rest day, from the day when you bring the Omer of the waving – seven weeks, they shall be complete'. Leviticus 23:15.
[2] Babylonian Talmud, Yevamot 62b.

not about sweating for the sake of it, but creating a warmth that will be both healing and energising.

One focus for Lag B'Omer is on friendship and having respect for our companions. The Biblical tradition of spiritual learning is to sit with a friend and discuss texts rather than to be silent in a library. A learning partner is known as a *chevruta*, or friend. The 2nd-century Rabbi Yehoshua ben Perchyah advised that we 'acquire for ourselves a friend'[3] on this spiritual journey. The Hebrew word he used for acquire was *koneh* which is usually associated with purchasing something. Building a friendship is an investment and it may cost us time and energy, but this is essential to create strong relationships. Whereas we are still connected to family members regardless of what we do, even when communications break down, friends are only there if we give them a reason to be so and it is a connection that does require some effort.

We might take this teaching on an internal level, seeing how we can be a friend to ourselves. Where are your thoughts self-critical, or where do you not act as a friend towards yourself? How can you invest some time and energy into choosing positive thoughts that are self-loving?

The Kabbalistic quality of this day, the *Sefirah* or Divine sphere, is *Hod She b'Hod* which translates as ultimate humility, or grateful gratitude. These qualities are essential to developing friendships. How can I be a friend to someone, to really be there for them, if I cannot listen to what they really need? How can I be humble towards another person? How can I make a space and be grateful for our relationship? In *The Kabbalah Sutras* book we look at how the Sefirah energies correspond with the body. The Kabbalists noted how the Divine energy of Hod is represented by the left leg. Hence the one-legged balance!

Wishing you a powerful Lag B'Omer, full of inner fire, deep gratitude and ever-improving friendships.

---

[3] *Ethics of the Fathers* 1:6.

THE FESTIVE SUTRAS

YOGA PRACTICE GUIDELINES

Supported Dancer Posture (with a friend):

1. Stand on your left leg, raise your right ankle to the buttock, drop your right hand to the side and turn it outwards (i.e. thumb pointing behind you and palm open) and take hold of your right ankle.
2. Now, kick backwards with your right foot (on an inhale) and lift the foot as high as you can.
3. Lean forwards and reaching out with your left hand (exhale). Hold for 5 breaths.

SHAVUOT

SHAVUOT 1: EQUILIBRIUM

FESTIVE SUTRA: 'Rise up to the mountain and wait there' *Exodus 24:12*

YOGA PRACTICE: *Tadasana*/Mountain Posture

Shavuot commemorates receiving the Torah, a moment of revelation where the 10 commandments were brought into the world along with the rest of the tradition. These moments forever changed the course of human history as can be seen by the commandments' centrality in Western law and constitutions, but how can we experience this through our body?

There are a number of yogic access points to Shavuot which we will explore through these Shavuot meditations. Firstly, the command to 'rise up to the mountain'. We can literally take mountain posture, *Tadasana*, and refine our practice of that one pose throughout Shavuot.

Mountain pose is the basis of all standing yoga postures and it requires stability, balance and strength. The pose asks us to aim for perfect symmetry throughout the body, finding equilibrium between the height of our shoulders and hips - and to adjust where necessary, to straighten right and left parts of our back, and to consider where else our body needs balancing. We begin aiming for physical symmetry with the intention that we also reach for balance in our mind and soul. *In Anatomy of Hatha Yoga*, David Coulter wrote:

> *'For perfect symmetry, every right-left member of every pair of bones, skeletal muscles, joints, and ligaments must be identical on both sides of the body – right and left knee joints, hip joints, femurs, and clavicles; and right and left erector spinae muscles, quadriceps femori, hamstrings, adductors, and gluteals'*[1]

Mountain pose is an opportunity for rebalancing and it occurs at the beginning of all sun salutations. This may be a reminder for us to come back to base, to re-find ourselves and to stay grounded. As we root down to the ground with stability and equilibrium, we create a strong base to reach for the spiritual heights that are offered by Shavuot.

---

[1] *Anatomy of Hatha Yoga*, p227

SHAVUOT 2: DESERT FREEDOM

FESTIVE SUTRA: 'Why was the Torah given in the desert?' *Mechilta HaHodesh, 1*

YOGA PRACTICE: Seated meditation (*Padmasana*/Lotus pose optional)

Mount Sinai is something of a mystery we still do not know its exact location to this day. Perhaps that is part of the point: the *where* is less important than the *what*: rather than having a mountain to pray at (or to), we have the essence of what was revealed - a series of commandments which are spiritual connection points to uncover the Divine at every moment we are on earth. Nevertheless we can still meditate on the essence of the mountain. The Midrash (a rabbinic story-commentary) suggests why a nondescript mountain was selected as the place of spiritual revelation:

> *'And why was the Torah given in the desert? To teach you that unless one makes himself "hefker" (open, free, ownerless) as the desert, s/he will not merit the words of Torah'[2].*
>
> *'And they camped in the desert' (Exodus 19:2). 'The Torah was given in an open ownerless [desert]. Because had the Torah been given in the land of Israel, they [The Jewish People] would have said to the Nations of the World "You have no portion in the Torah". Therefore it was given in the open ownerless (desert); whoever wants (enlightenment) can come and take it[3].*
>
> *Just as the desert has no end so too the words of Torah have no end, as it says; [the wisdom of the Torah] "is longer than the measure of the earth and wider than the sea" (Job:11). Just as it has no end so too its reward has no end as it says "how great is the reward that you have hidden for those who fear you"(Psalm 31:7)[4].*

---

[2] Pesikta R. Kahana Chapter 12.
[3] Mechilta HaHodesh Section 1.
[4] Yalkut Shimoni, Yitro 272.

Yoga is designed as a liberation practice, to continually remind us that we have a spiritual essence that is part of God. The yogis identified a form of living liberation, calling it *jivan-mukti*[5]. An earlier yogic dialogue from the *Yoga-Vasishtha* states that:

> 'He is a *jivan-mukti* for whom, even though he is busy with ordinary life, all this ceases to exist and [only] the space of ultimate Consciousness remains.
>
> He is a *jivan-mukta* whose face neither flushes nor pales in pleasure or pain and who subsists on whatever comes his way...
>
> He is a *jivan-mukta* who, though responsive to feelings such as detachment, hatred, fear and other feelings, stands wholly pure within, like space.
>
> He is a true *jivan-mukta* whose real nature is not influenced by egotism and whose mind is not subjected to attachment, whether he remains active or is inactive'[6].

And so it continues. Shavuot can remind us of the boundless nature of the desert and the freedom to be found there. We are in a physical space which can be one of emotional, mental and spiritual liberation. Part of us is of the world, in the world but not bound by the world. We are free.

---

[5] *The Deeper Dimension of Yoga - Theory and Practice* by Georg Feuerstein, p374.
[6] Ibid, pp375-6.

SHAVUOT 3: THE ESSENCE OF YOGA

FESTIVE SUTRA: 'I am Hashem, Your God' *Exodus 20:2*

YOGA PRACTICE: Twist poses (e.g. *marichyasana*) with a focus on freedom

The Ten Commandments, part of the Torah reading for Shavuot, provide extensive opportunities for a physical yoga practice. Part of this is explored in the later part of this book *Ethics of the Yogis*. Here are two ideas to begin with.

Prior to the receiving of the Torah, Moses warned the people to prepare for three days, saying 'Be ready for a three-day period. Do not approach a woman'[7]. The prohibition against marital relations was a physical and energetic cleansing, and this might be understood through the yogic principles of *brahmacharya* (non-lusting) or *sauca* (cleansing)[8]. On a practical level we can look at our preparation prior to morning prayer, which includes saying a blessing on washing our hands as part of a physical cleanse. On a deeper level we may consider the thoughts and intentions we are bringing to the prayer process, or to the yoga mat, as our innermost thoughts directly affect our prayers[9].

The Ten Commandments begin with *'I am Hashem, your God, Who took you out of the land of Egypt, from the house of slaves. There shall not be unto you the gods of others before me'*[10]. There are a number of ways we can directly apply this through yoga:

'I am Hashem (the Lord), your God' - consider the essence of yoga which means unity. At this point we can focus on the unity of all creation, the Oneness that is everywhere and seeing beyond the duality of the world we live in, the illusory world which looks as if we are separated from our source.

---

[7] Exodus 19:1.
[8] See the later dedicated chapters in *Ethics of the Yogis* to explore these topics more extensively.
[9] See *Alter Rebbe, Tanya* Chapter 39.
[10] Exodus 20: 2-3.

'Who took you out of the land of Egypt' - the Hebrew word for Egypt, *Mitzrayim*, translates as 'from narrow spaces' or 'from restrictions' and we can physicalise this through freeing our body of tightness, seeing where we are restricted, exploring where our mind is restricted and seeing where we can be more free.

'from the house of slaves' - we can use this is an inner yogic practice, to question where are we enslaved? Where are our thoughts subservient to a power other than God? How can we reclaim our freedom? (See the previous essay which discusses *jivan-mukti*).

'You shall have no other gods before me' - if the concept of One God is the essence of Yoga, that is, being unified with all of creation, then we can ask: where are we not in the state of yoga, or where are we not unified? Every place where we are stressed about paying our bills and forgetting God, or out of touch with our creator is an opportunity to reconnect.

We live in a world of duality where it looks as if we are totally independent from God. We walk, breathe, work and feed ourselves. Yet we cannot survive without the oxygen and air that connects us all (albeit invisible), we cannot survive without gravity that keeps us connected to the earth (albeit invisible) and we could not survive unless nature kept our trees growing, our earth revolving around the sun and if our bodies did not perform a million functions (also invisible to the naked eye).

Shavuot asks us to remember that there is one God, one Creator, one central force. This is a lifelong practice. Wishing you a meaningful, enlightening and liberating Shavuot!

FASTING

FASTING: A YOGIC PRACTICE

FESTIVE SUTRA: *'Moses anger was hot…Aaron said "Let not God's anger be hot"' Exodus 32: 19-22*

YOGA PRACTICE: *Upavista*/Fasting

The purpose of fast days is to focus on our behaviour and 'awaken hearts towards repentance through recalling our forefather's misdeeds[1]. We consider how we have behaved, how we can modify our behaviour, and undergo some physical discomfort with the purpose of self-transformation.

The Fast of 17th Tammuz commemorates five events that happened on the same day in history: Moses broke the first tablets on Mount Sinai when he saw the golden calf, the Daily Sacrificial stopped being offered in the First Temple, the walls of Jerusalem were breached during the Second Temple, Apostomos burned the Torah and an idol was placed in the Sanctuary. This day marks the beginning of the 'three weeks', a time to focus on the loss of the Temple and the exile of the presence of God and it culminates in Tisha B'Av, the ninth day in the month of Av when the Temple was destroyed.

---

[1] *The Book of Our Heritage*, Vol III p193.

The Zohar and other Kabbalistic writings compare the Temple to our own body, and we might focus on how we exile God from our hearts. We can push away the presence of Godliness through angry impulses and continual negative thinking, even if we do not voice them out loud.

There is a special morning and afternoon Torah reading on the fast day, which talks of how 'Moses' anger burned hot'[2], how his brother Aaron said 'let not God's anger be hot'[3] and talks of God as being 'slow to anger'[4].

There is a yogic approach to fasting, explained Georg Feuerstein:

*'Two important yogic means of self-purification are fasting (*upavasa*) and dieting (*ahara*). Fasting has long been known as a highly efficient way of inducing an altered state of consciousness. Abstinence from food changes the chemical composition of the blood, which inevitably has an effect on the mind. But fasting has to be undertaken from the right inner disposition to bear spiritual fruit'*[5].

This fast day, the 17th Tammuz, can be an opportunity for considering where we are holding inner anger. Who are we holding anger towards, even in the depths of our heart? Some people are angry at God but do not want to admit it. Others are angry at their parents but cannot say so. Most of us are angry at ourselves. We are taught that the Temple was destroyed through baseless hatred[6], and perhaps we are damaging and even destroying our own lives for the same reason.

Just as baseless hatred drove the presence of God from the Temple, perhaps we can bring back the presence of God by meditating on our hidden angers, forgive who we need to forgive, and make our bodies a temple for love. This, however, may take some serious practice: the Fast of Tammuz is an excellent place to start.

---

[2] Exodus 32:19.
[3] Exodus 32:19.
[4] Exodus 34:6.
[5] The Art of Purification in *The Deeper Dimension of Yoga*, p149.
[6] Babylonian Talmud Yoma 9b.

TISHA B'AV

TISHA B'AV 1: YOUR BODY IS A TEMPLE

FESTIVE SUTRA: 'The curtains (of the Tabernacle) are the inner garments; corresponding to the skin upon the flesh'. *Zohar, Shemot, Section 2, Page 76a.*

YOGA PRACTICE: *Pranayama/* Inner breath and energy practice

The first nine days in the summer month of Av are an energetic low point in the Hebrew calendar. During this time people refrain from physical pleasures, culminating in a total 25-hour fast on the ninth of Av, Tisha B'Av, which commemorates the tragic destruction of the Temple in Jerusalem. That was the end of a globally centralised Jewish practice which revolved around the Temple, and the beginning of Rabbinic Judaism which encouraged the *Mikdash Me'at*, the 'small Temple' that people would carry around in their hearts and replicate at their Shabbat tables[6].

THE PAINFUL ABSENCE

Tisha B'Av is a challenge as people are encouraged to mourn the Temple even though we have never seen it in our lifetime. We can take

---
[6] Elements of the sabbath table replicate the temple in Jerusalem, most notably the two *challah* loaves of bread, representing the showbreads in the Temple.

an embodied spiritual approach, based on the Kabbalah's teachings that objects in the Temple correspond to parts of our own bodies:

> *The beams were fixed into the sockets, and in the body the ribs are fixed into the vertebrae…the beams were covered with gold and the ribs are covered with flesh…the veil divided between the Holy place and the Holy of Holies, and in the body the diaphragm divides the heart from the stomach*[7].

We are taught that the temple was destroyed on account of 'baseless hatred'[8] so we might look to see where we are holding hatred, anger or blame within us. To spend Tisha B'Av getting upset at the Romans seems a little futile, but we could engage in a deep practice of introspection, to examine where we have impulses towards anger or blame. A first step would be to recognise where we are holding angry thoughts, before forgiving and releasing them, and then replacing them with loving intentions.

YOGA AND TISHA B'AV

There are yogic practices for fasting and one approach is to complete the full 25 hour fast of Tisha B'Av with total awareness. Mat-based yoga practices can include a focus on different body parts as they correspond to the Temple, for example doing heart-opening postures as the heart corresponded to the *Kadosh Kadoshim*, the Holy of Holies in the sanctuary's epicentre. The key however is to free oneself of upsets and anger, and to pursue pathways of peace. The first of the Yoga Sutras' ethical principles, *ahimsa*, preaches non-violence on all levels[9].

This essay may be short but there is enough here practice to last a lifetime. Although the Temple was destroyed with baseless hatred, and many relationships are destroyed through the same negativity, we can

---

[7] Midrash in *Genesis Rabbah*, as quoted by Raphael Patai in 'Man and Temple' (New York: Ktav 1967).

[8] 'The first Temple was destroyed because of the sins of idolatry, harlotry, and murder. The second [Temple] – in spite of Torah studies, Mitzvot, and deeds of love executed during its existence – fell because of sinat chinam (baseless hatred)' BT Talmud, Yoma 9b.

[9] *Yoga Sutras* 2:30.

rebuild with baseless love. Tisha B'Av was the beginning of the Jewish exile which has lasted for 2000 years, and is seen as the exile of the presence of God. As one of my teachers says, the true exile is from ourselves, not seeing God within, and being disconnected from our own hearts. May Tisha B'Av be an opportunity to rebuild through love, and may that love start from within.

TISHA B'AV 2: FORGIVENESS PROTOCOL

FESTIVE SUTRA: 'Why was the Second Temple destroyed? Because of baseless hatred' *Talmud, Yoma 9b*

YOGA PRACTICE: Forgiveness Protocol (details below).

The path of Karma Yoga is a practice of good deeds, of *chesed* (lovingkindness) and healing through giving. This can be difficult when we find it hard to clear upsets and have not forgiven people. Many people live with perpetually unresolved anger, whether it is anger at their parents and siblings, anger at God or anger at themselves for what they did or did not do. There are old people who are angry with their families for things that happened 60 years ago, and there are many people who die angry (and possibly have to reincarnate because their consciousness is still angry). One solution is forgiveness).

The Talmud asks *'Why was the First Temple destroyed? Because of three evils in it: idolatry, immorality, and bloodshed. But why was the Second Temple destroyed, seeing that during the time it stood people occupied themselves with Torah, with observance of precepts, and with the practice of charity? Because during the time it stood, hatred without rightful cause [baseless hatred] prevailed. This is to teach you that hatred without rightful cause is deemed as grave as all the three sins of idolatry, immorality and bloodshed, together'*[10].

WHY FORGIVE?

Forgiveness is an essential path to healing.

We do not forgive to be kind to the other person (just in case you are still angry), but we forgive so that we can relieve ourselves of the burden of the anger. Forgiveness is a process and can take some time. If you are clearing 20 years of anger or more, it will mostly likely take more than just a few minutes to release.

---

[10] *Babylonian Talmud, Yoma 9b.* Translation from *The Book of Legends, Sefer Ha-Aggadah,* p193

FORGIVENESS PROTOCOL

Here is a Forgiveness Protocol that I learned from a teacher and it has changed my life. I use it whenever needed. There are four steps to it.

1. Write an Anger Letter to the person you are angry with. It could be your Mum, Dad, boss, anyone. They will never see the letter: this is for you. Get out all your feelings. Swear if necessary. Curse. Say everything. Be real. Really real.
2. Re-read the letter to yourself. Witness what you have written.
3. Burn the letter. This is very important. Burn it and get rid of the energy that is in your letter. If there is nowhere to burn (e.g. if you are on an aeroplane), then rip up the letter and put the pieces in a plastic bag and seal it.
4. Write the person a Forgiveness Letter.

That is it. You might begin by first making a long list of everyone you have become upset with in your entire life. I wrote headers for all the decades I have been alive and then a list of everyone I was upset with from all those decades. It was a long list and it took me many months. Then I had to do another 6 months of anger and forgiveness letters towards myself.

It has been said that 'not forgiving someone is like drinking poison expecting the other person to suffer'. Forgiveness is the next stage to releasing anger and replacing it with love. Even if you have a fantastic backbend on the yoga mat, God sees what is in your heart.

Wishing you a meaningful Tisha B'Av and an easy fast.

TISHA B'AV 3: MEDITATIONS

FESTIVE SUTRA: "The Temple corresponds to the whole world, and to the creation of man who is a small world"[6] *Midrash Tanchuma*

YOGA PRACTICE: Sequences described below.

There are secrets upon secrets within *Tisha B'Av*. The Temple in Jerusalem, the *Beit HaMikdash*, is a spiritual energy centre that lies at the apex of several world religions. Deep within the walls of the Old City of Jerusalem, its remaining Western Wall is the global focus of Jewish prayer, while the site of the Holy of Holies (*Kadosh Kadoshim*) is deep beneath the Dome of the Rock and the Al-Aqsa Mosque.

There is something of a disconnect on Tisha B'Av, as we mourn the destruction of the Temple, because the majority of people have a difficult time mourning for something we have never seen in our lifetimes. That is another discussion, but what I would like to focus on is some of the deeper symbolism of the Temple.

As mentioned in the earlier essay, the different parts of the Temple correspond to our body, and for many years I desired to take this meditation even deeper. With the help of some key midrashim compiled in Raphael Patai's *Man and Temple*, we can dare to find even more relevance and more emotional connection to the Temple if we venture deep within ourselves. This path is not for everyone, but it is an alternative, legitimate and heartfelt route about which I feel passionately and want to share with you.

---

[6] Midrash Tanchuma, Pequde, 3. Quoted in *Man and Temple* p116.

FESTIVE SUTRA #1: *'In the hour when the Holy One blessed be He said to Moses, Make me a temple, Moses said, How shall I know how to make it? The Holy One blessed be He said, Do not get frightened; just as I created the world and your body, even so will you make the Tabernacle. How [do we know] that this was so? You will find in the Tabernacle that the beams were fixed into the sockets, and in the body the ribs were fixed into the vertebra, and so in the world the mountains are fixed into the fundaments of the earth'*[7].

YOGA PRACTICE: Pranayama breathing, and focus on the expansion of your ribs

A Tisha B'Av yoga/meditation practice can begin with broadening and deepening our breath. Our heart is compared to the Holy of Holies, the *Kadosh Kedoshim*, and in this passage our ribs are compared to the beams in the Tabernacle. The Tabernacle, or *Mishkan*, was the portable sanctuary carried through the desert. Its ark carried the two tablets that Moses received on Mount Sinai, and we might consider these as the equivalent of our heart. To begin the practice we can focus on our breath, expanding and contracting our ribs and be aware of them as Divine creations[8].

FESTIVE SUTRA #2: *'In the Tabernacle the beams were covered with gold, and in the body the ribs are covered with flesh, and in the world the mountains are covered and coated with earth'*[9].

YOGA PRACTICE: Mountain Pose

We now bring our attention to flesh, to skin and to the earth element. The creation story describes how Adam, the first person was taken from the earth - hence his name *Adam* which is a part of *Adamah* (earth). As you practice Moun-

---
[7] *Man and Temple,* p114. Footnote on p135, quoting Bereshith Rabbati, ed. Albeck, p.32; cf. ib. additional sources.
[8] You might also meditate on the role of the rib in the creation story.
[9] Ibid.

tain Pose, be aware of earthing your energy, feeling the ground beneath you and connecting with this. In Taoist thought, Earth corresponds to *yin* or feminine energy.

FESTIVE SUTRA #3: *'In the Tabernacle there were bolts in the beams to keep them upright, and in the body limbs and sinews are drawn to keep man upright, and in the world trees and grasses are drawn in the earth'*[10].

YOGA POSE: Extended Mountain Pose

Raise your hands above your head in extended mountain pose and adduct (draw together) your limbs within the posture. Bring your shoulder blades towards one another and squeeze your legs together whilst keeping aligned and upright. Focus on your ligaments and tendons, and to the best of your ability, imagine you are strengthening them from within.

FESTIVE SUTRA #4: *'In the Tabernacle there were hangings to cover its top and both its sides, and in the body the skin of man covers his limbs, and his ribs on both his sides, and in the world the heavens cover the earth on both its sides'*[11].

YOGA PRACTICE: Awareness of skin

Practice 'listening' with your skin. Notice what sensation you feel on your face, your stomach, your back, your arms, your legs and your feet. Be aware of the textures of your clothes from the inside, and bring awareness to your skin as external covering for your bones and muscles.

---

[10] Ibid.
[11] Ibid.

FESTIVE SUTRA #5: *'In the Tabernacle the veil divided between the Holy Place and the Holy of Holies, and in the body the diaphragm divides the heart from the stomach, and in the world it is the firmament which divides between the upper waters and the lower waters'*[12].

YOGA PRACTICE: Pranayama breathing, focusing on diaphragm

One helpful breathing exercise is to lie on your back in semi-supine position (knees bent), breathe into your upper chest (clavicular breathing), ribs (thoracic breathing), your stomach area (abdominal breathing). Consider the abdomen as a divider, a wall. We can take this meditation far deeper using the words of this midrash, thinking about the upper body and lower body as representing the two firmaments of creation, or the upper waters and lower waters that are described in Kabbalah.

FESTIVE SUTRA #6: *'In the Tabernacle there was fire and wind and water: the offspring of the heavens is fire, the offspring of the air is the wind, the offspring of the earth is water. The first is above and the water below, and the wind holds the balance between them. And in the body, the head is fire, the heart is wind (spirit) and the stomach water'*[13].

YOGA PRACTICE: Sun Salutes

Despite the intensity of the long fast day on Tisha B'Av - which occurs in the heat of the summer - we can still practice some gentle sun salutes to move our *pranic* energy. One idea is to do a series of four sun salutations, each one focusing on a different element. Earth, wind, air and fire all constitute different energies within our body, and balance our subtle energies is a gateway to better health, peace of mind and spiritual development.

---

[12] Ibid.
[13] *Man and Temple*, p114-5. Footnote on p135, Midrash Rabbi Shema'ua Hashoushani, ed. A. Berliner, *Monatschrift fur die Geschichte und Wissenschaft des Judentums*, xiii (1864), pp. 227, 229, 230, 262.

There are many ideas still to be explored within the context of *Tisha B'Av* and this is purely intended as an introduction. The traditional prayers and readings of the day focus on the destruction of Jerusalem and yearning for the Temple to be rebuilt, and we can sincerely attempt to find a yogic equivalent within our body. We are made in the image of God but also in the image of the Temple, and by relating to the temple within we fulfil the words of the Torah, 'Make for Me a Sanctuary and I will dwell within *them*'[14]. You are a sanctuary, you are a living temple, and through raising your consciousness and awareness, your body can be a dwelling place for the Divine.

---

[14] Exodus 25:8.

TU B'AV

TU B'AV: VALENTINE'S DAY FOR THE SOUL

FESTIVE SUTRA: 'The daughters of Jerusalem used to go forth to dance in the vineyards' *Mishna Ta'anit, 4:8*

YOGA PRACTICE: Dancing or free-flow *vinyasas*

The ancient festival of *Tu B'Av*[1] has received a modern revival. Rebranded as the 'Jewish Valentine's Day' it is often celebrated with singles parties, people dressed in white clothes and no religious ritual or ceremony (because there is none). We might go back to the original text and take a yogic approach to connecting with God through our body, breath and movement:

> 'Rabbi Shimon ben Gamliel said: *There were no happier days for the people of Israel than the Fifteenth of Av and Yom Kippur, since on these days the daughters of Jerusalem used to go out dressed in white garments which were borrowed in order not to shame the one who had none. All the garments required immersion. And the daughters of Jerusalem used to go forth to dance in the vineyards. And what did they say?* – "Young man, lift up your eyes and see what you will select for yourself; do not set your eyes on beauty but fix your eyes on family; for Grace is deceitful and beauty is vain, but a woman who fears God shall be praised;" and it says further, "*Give to her the fruit of her hands and let her deeds praise her in the gates…*"'[2].

---
[1] The fifteenth day of the month of Av. This usually occurs in July or August.
[2] *Mishna Ta'anit, 4:8*

When practicing yoga we are looking with more than just our eyes. Mr Iyengar taught the importance of cultivating the sensitivity with our skin[3], using the sensory information in our muscle tissues and nerve systems so the entire body's intelligence can work together. In a yoga workshop with Max Strom we were taught the importance of using our skin in all poses, being aware of what we are 'seeing' with our skin, keeping it alert and active. When the maidens of Jerusalem told the men to look with more than just their eyes, to move beyond lust and consider if the girl they liked would be a good partner for family, this demanded deeper *in*sight rather than just sight alone.

The song *Aishet Chayil*, a woman of valour, is taken from Chapter 31 of King Solomon's *Book of Proverbs*. It is traditionally sung by men to their wives on Friday night, shabbat evening. The penultimate line is quoted above: *'False is grace and vain is beauty, but a God-fearing woman, she should be praised'*[4]. On what is traditionally the most romantic night of the week, which the rabbis decreed was the opportune time for husband and wife to be together, the man is effectively saying: 'I love you. You are beautiful, but I see beyond your beauty. I see your heart, your connection with the Divine. When we grow old and looks fade, you are still beautiful to me for I see your Divine Consciousness'[5].

---

[3] *Light on Life*, pp33-36.
[4] Proverbs 31:30. Translation from *The Complete Artscroll Siddur*, p359.
[5] I made that up, but as one of my teachers says, "you get the principle".

THE SHABBAT SUTRAS

LOTUS POSE/PADMASANA

'All my bones will say, "God, who is like you?"'

PSALM 35:10

SHABBAT

TANTRIC SHABBAT: WEEKLY ENERGY CONNECTIONS

SHABBAT SUTRA: 'The Sabbath is one-sixtieth of heaven'
Babylonian Talmud, Brachot 57b

We might view Shabbat as a 25-hour yoga or meditation practice. By observing the basic principles of switching off phones, refraining from spending money, cultivating rest and connection with God, we create a meditative space to elevate our thoughts and spirit. Every 'don't do', each negative commandment which tells us not to drive or spend or create, can also be seen as a positive pathway to reach the Divine. God is all around us, within us, in the fabric of creation at all times, and Shabbat is a practice through which to continuously and consciously raise this awareness.

The shabbat afternoon *mincha* prayer, includes a simple statement: "You are One". We may spend our weekdays forgetting that God runs the world and pretending that we are in charge, that we entirely create our reality and that we are responsible for everything that happens to us. Whilst there are some serious truths in here, Shabbat reminds us that we are a partner in creation, us and God. That we are made in the image of God and that we are never alone. Loneliness, stress and fear are symptoms of duality, of being separated from the Creator. One intention for this 25-hour practice is to be able to fully say, with all of our body, mind and soul, "You are One".

SAMADHI & ENLIGHTENMENT

The ultimate intention for any yoga practice is *Samadhi*, or enlightenment[1]. It is the result of all the meditation, the asana, vinyasa and pranayama practices. In some ways, *Shabbat*, the Sabbath, is a 25-hour yoga practice during which we aim for this taste of enlightenment.

This all-inclusive meditation, or super yoga practice, runs from sundown on Friday until sundown on Saturday and has proven so powerful that it became the key focal point of several religions. Christianity may have moved their Sabbath to Sunday and Islam to Friday, but its appeal remains the same, even if the name and specific details differ.

The journey to enlightenment begins with boundaries and restrictions. Traditional Jews will begin on Friday afternoon by lighting candles and saying blessings over bread and wine. Boundaries are established within which the Sabbath is protected. These include switching off televisions, computers, mobile phones and all other communication or entertainment devices that use electricity. All the food for the 25-hour period is cooked in advance. Arrangements for socialising during the meals have already been made (hence no need to use the telephone – 'where are you?' 'I'm late!' 'I can't find it' etc) and many people have their house lights on a time-switch so that the lights turn on and off automatically. In this 'light', everything can become an intentional practice, right down to the way we use the lights in our house. This particular issue is an extension of the biblical commandment not to light a fire on the seventh day, but the implication is far more profound than not lighting a metaphorical fire. The whole exercise is a spiritual practice and a powerful metaphor.

---

[1] Samadhi may also be translated as 'ecstasy'.

FREEDOM WITHIN BOUNDARIES

Freedom happens within boundaries. A state can only allow its citizens to have civil freedoms when there is an established rule of law. When there are no boundaries, there is the greater potential for anarchy. On the other hand, if there are only boundaries, there is no freedom at all. It is a subtle balance. On a Torah or Kabbalistic level, this is the blend between Abraham who represents *Chesed* (lovingkindness), Isaac who represents *Gevurah* (Discipline or Restriction), and these two qualities are synthesised in Jacob who represents *Tiferet* (Compassion, Balance or Harmony)[2].

We experience the principle of freedom-within-boundaries when working on a yoga mat. By keeping within the four boundaries of the mat, I am able to practice freely without impinging on my neighbour's space, and vice versa. This also applies in large workshops, where over 100 people or more can do a long yoga sequence without ever bumping into one another or getting into one another's space. It seems obvious, but this only happens when keeping to the discipline that is imposed by staying within the four edges of a rectangular mat.

There are rules for yoga postures with regards to correct alignment. These allow for the muscles to be engaged, the body to be supported, the breath to penetrate more deeply into the body, improved stance, healthier physical functioning and a deeper sense of relaxation once we have explored the limits of our being.

A lotus posture, *padmasana*, has specific rules and can be performed incorrectly. The thighs need to be rotated upwards, which opens the hips and allows for the ankles to be placed across the opposite leg. The ideal is for our knees to be relatively close together and the outsides of the upper legs to be parallel with one another. This creates a firm base. The root lock (*mulah bandha*) is engaged, the spine is straightened and a line of energy is created upwards from the anus/perenneum through to the crown of the head.

---

[2] For a more in-depth and practical exploration of these concepts, and to discover how they directly relate to your life, please refer to *The Kabbalah Sutras - 49 Steps to Enlightenment*.

When carried out incorrectly, the lotus can damage our knees. If practiced without focus, or with a slouched spine and curved shoulders, breathing becomes obstructed and it can be painful. A continued slouching posture can even make you feel depressed or sad. On the other hand, by keeping within the guidelines of the posture, respecting it and holding it correctly, it becomes a powerful meditation position that is energising, grounding and uplifting.

The notion of Shabbat as a 25-hour meditational practice, is not always easy. One day a week we choose to stop activity and commit to living within a conscious, spiritual space.

Pausing your life for a yoga session can also be challenging. Perhaps there is a telephone call to make, a friend to meet or some more work to be done. Yet honouring the space, marking out the time and committing to the activity, brings its own rewards. These might not always seem immediately apparent, but bit by bit we can glimpse a tiny taste of something almost other-worldly.

TAKING A BREATHER

SHABBAT SUTRA: 'For in six days the Creator made the heaven and earth, and on the seventh day He rested and took a breather' *Exodus 31:17*

The essence of Shabbat, the very point of Shabbat in general, is to recreate or re-enact part of the process of creation and to plug into the energy of the original seven day cycle. We are not concerned at this stage by the literal interpretation of the first part of Genesis and whether the seven days actually correspond to seven sets of twenty-four cycles. Science suggests that the earth is 4.5 billion years old, there are dinosaur remnants from the Jurassic age and other overwhelming evidence to suggest that the first seven 'days' were much longer than the ones we have now, making a literal reading quite unhelpful or historically inaccurate. Nonetheless, we are humans and have a 24-hour clock. That is the length of our day, and that is what we are working with.

TANTRIC SHABBAT

The account of creation describes mankind as being made "in the image of God" and there is something God-like in our yoga practice during the seventh day as we tap into this energy.

The Hebrew word for 'resting' is *Va-yinafash* which is a kind of soul-break, or in-spiration. My friend Joel Lurie Grishaver explains in one of his teachings that the root of the word is *nefesh* – meaning 'soul' – and that Shabbat is an opportunity for self renewal. As we will see elsewhere, Nefesh can also be read as *nashaf*, meaning 'to exhale' or 'to breathe'. There is a sense of God taking a moment for breath at this point, and pausing for renewal and for refreshing the soul connection.

It makes practical sense to pause once a week, to take time out and reflect on our lives: *Shabbat as an extended yoga practice*. When we go to a yoga class or do a self-practice we might stop for an hour or two during which time we will focus on the notion of physical Oneness, before returning to 'real' life with the rush of normality and switching on the cell phone. Shabbat begins and ends with the ritual of lighting candles and takes us into a space of conscious living, where we are in a space of perpetual yoga-unity, aware of our Creator, aware that we are created, and aware that this day is elevated through our actions. There are continual reminders of the need for mindfulness and keying in to the consciousness of the day. This verse from Exodus appears in the *Kiddush* blessing over the wine to remind us to *Va-yinafash* – to connect to our soul and breathe.

Shabbat is a time for a longer, deeper yoga practice because the space and rhythm of the day is very much directed towards experiencing total unity. It is a time for taking the lessons and experiences of yoga into the world and to create a space to stop, reflect and slow down. The yogic principle of *ahimsa*, non-violence, loosely corresponds to the idea of being *rodef shalom*, or pursuing peace. Peace, *Shalom*, is the theme of the day. We greet everyone with the words *Shabbat Shalom*, as if to continually remind ourselves that this is a rest-day to experience peace.

Our aim is for conscious, mindful living at all times and while Shabbat is a longer experience of unity, we can take this awareness into our daily lives, framing our sunrise practice with the context of Shabbat. Just one day a week to stop, reflect and find that deeper connection.

It can be difficult to maintain 'good yoga' whilst living the hustle of everyday life. The pressure to earn a living, pay the bills, commute around a busy city, run a car and manage a busy calendar mean that despite one's best efforts to complete a regular and committed Hatha Yoga practice, the sense of physical and spiritual elevation/connection can easily be lost as we leave our home. Shabbat-awareness is something which can elevate the week and be carried over into a mindfulness throughout the other six days. By performing a doubly-intensive yoga practice on the seventh day, we can stage an awesome ending to the week and beginning to the next.

Let's look at some ways of elevating the 'seventh [day] practice'.

SHABBAT – ONE BIG YOGA POSTURE

SHABBAT SUTRA: 'Remember the Sabbath and sanctify it. Do all of your work over six days, and the seventh day shall be Shabbat to the Lord, your Creator [on which] you refrain from all of your labour, you, your son or daughter, your male or female workers, or your cattle, or the stranger who is within your estate. For in six days the Lord made heaven and earth…'[3]

The renowned yogic writer Georg Feuerstein commented that 'all forms, branches of Yoga, have the same goal. [These are] liberation, enlightenment, freedom, the transcendence of the human condition, or the fulfilment of our highest potential'[4]. We might approach yoga with a desire to free ourselves of the 'monkey mind' phenomenon that plagues daily thought and makes extended concentration into something difficult. Perhaps we are looking for physical freedom, to change our body image or body shape into something more desirable. For many people, there is just a strong desire, however conscious or unconscious, to escape from the stress and demands of life for a period of time and to become totally absorbed in the vibe of a yoga studio. Maybe it is the low lights,

---

[3] *Exodus 31:16-17*
[4] He writes more about this in *The Deeper Dimension of Yoga*.

the sweet-smelling incense, the gentle music, the deep and demanding physical engagement or the nurturing voice of the teacher. Either way there is a framework for tapping into a sense of freedom by completely committing and giving oneself over to the process and in doing so, leaving all worldly cares behind.

The ideal situation is to be able to take lessons learned during asana and vinyasa practice and carry them into life after the session, so that we are always 'doing' yoga. Put another way, this could be described as living mindfully and consciously. Put another way still, it could be interpreted as living with a constant awareness of the Divine; that we are always connected to the Creator. For example, a yoga class might explore the principle of non-stealing, perhaps with regards to not 'taking' a posture that our body is unprepared for and thereby putting ourselves at risk of injury. We try to experience the principle whilst on the yoga mat, take it into every part of our body and be mindful to challenge ourselves in postures without damaging ourselves. We then try to incorporate this principle into our general behaviour, whether it is being careful not to take any items of our property that do not belong to us, not to copy music that we have not paid for, or not to 'steal' people's goodwill. The challenge is not to be underestimated: yoga may appear easy to teach or practice, but it can be ongoing work to keep it present in every area of our lives.

How can we 'live' this ideal of liberation and ongoing freedom? In this sense, Shabbat is one continual yoga posture. The psychologist Erich Fromm and former British Chief Rabbi Lord Jonathan Sacks both talk about the mindset that we are encouraged to move into throughout the entire seventh day. They stress how Shabbat presents a great principle of humanity, accessible to everyone and certainly not the exclusive domain of one religion:

> *'It is more than a 'day of rest'…it is a symbol of salvation and freedom. This is also the meaning of God's rest; this rest is not necessary for God because he is tired, but it expresses the idea that great as creation is, greater and crowning creation is peace…he must really 'rest' not because he is tired but because he is free and fully God only when he has ceased to work. So is man fully man only when he does not work,*

when he is at peace with nature and his fellow man; that is why the Sabbath commandment is at one time motivated by God's rest and at the other by liberation from Egypt. Both mean the same and interpret each other; 'rest' is 'freedom'[5].

Erich Fromm

'All relationships of hierarchy and dominance are temporarily suspended, one day in seven....the Sabbath is thus the most compelling tutorial in humandignity, environmental consciousness, and the principle that there are moral limits to economic exchange and commercial exploitation. It is one of the great antidotes to consumerisation and commodification'[6].

Rabbi Jonathan Sacks

To discuss a Sabbath yoga practice is almost a tautology because as mentioned, Shabbat *is* a yoga practice, but this connection can be easily lost or forgotten. Ironically the rhythm of a traditional Jewish Sabbath tends to result in disassociation from the body, with an emphasis on long communal prayer in the synagogue, large and often unhealthy meals where overeating is the norm, and the all-essential Shabbat afternoon sleep. This pattern leaves little room for physical connection that results in a feeling of alertness and vigour, but tends towards a sense of heaviness and dullness through inactivity. With high calorie intakes of frequently starchy foods and the lethargy-inducing mix of protein and heavy carbohydrates, a typical Shabbat lunch is often (but not always) the equivalent of a big Christmas dinner every week. This is not the ultimate breeding ground for mindfulness but it does have the potential depending on how we experience it.

Shabbat is about experiencing freedom, but it is liberation within boundaries and not just a case of relaxing in front of the television or mindlessly 'switching off' from life during the 25 hour cycle. The injunction to refrain from work encourages us to stop performing *malacha*, which is specifically creative tasks that are usually linked with economic

---

[5] *The Forgotten Language: An Introduction to the Understanding of Dreams, Fairy Tales, and Myths* by Erich Fromm.
[6] *To Heal A Fractured World*, p169.

functions. These include writing, driving, spending money and everything that fits Rabbi Sacks' description of the Sabbath as "freedom from commercialisation".

Just as we have specific guidelines for yoga postures, there are rules and recommendations for optimising the Shabbat space, through the commandments to *Zahor* (remember) and *Shamor* (observe/guard) the seventh day. Shabbat is a dynamic relaxation that cannot fail to lead to a sense of freedom when observed with commitment. Although there are many customs and laws which are specifically kept by Jews, the general principles are universal which is why the notion of a Sabbath has become so central to Jewish and Muslim life. Our Sabbath yoga practice can lead towards a much deeper soul connection and really set the tone for the week.

SHABBAT AND EXERCISE AS PRAYER

SHABBAT SUTRA: 'And let me be my prayer to you, God' *Psalm 69:14*

The Bible can be viewed as a healing text, a piece of wisdom literature that continues to offer strength, consolation and inspiration. One question we might ask, while observing *Shabbat*, and keeping the Sabbath laws; what is the role of exercise on the seventh day?

In the past many students have asked me about the question of whether it is halachically (i.e. Jewish law) acceptable to exercise during Shabbat. This is a grey area in terms of *halacha*. When I began teaching a spiritually-integrated yoga practice during Shabbat seminars back in 2001, I asked my rabbi, Dovid Ebner, and he suggested that there is no problem on Shabbat as it is not exercise, but a form of prayer.

PROHIBITION & POSSIBILITY

The prohibition of work on Shabbat is based around 39 categories of creative activity, all of which were used in the building of the Temple in Jerusalem over 2000 years ago. These are archetypes which include many areas of contemporary work. Although they are phrased in fairly agricultural terms – sowing, ploughing, binding sheaves, building, pulling down, baking, lighting a fire, carrying an item from one domain to another, they translate to specific actions in our everyday life. 'Lighting a fire' corresponds to switching on electrical items, which is why Orthodox Jews will have lights in their homes on a time-switch. 'Baking' is fairly self explanatory, hence the custom of preparing all of the Sabbath food before the event so that no cooking needs to be done on the day. There is no prohibition against exercising, although it is often considered as 'not in the spirit' of Shabbat. From the perspective of yoga or other physical meditation, we might view Shabbat as the perfect time for an extended practice. It is a day of peacefulness and yoga is the practice of unity, but how can we balance this with the fact that *halacha* (rabbinic law) effectively forbids extreme exercise?.

One approach around our intention is to remember that yoga is not exercise but meditation. Although there are various classes where yoga is presented as a keep-fit solution, whether it is 'yoga for weight loss', 'yoga for thighs and bums' or 'yoga for runners', these are usually just marketing gimmicks that lead people through asana and vinyasa sessions. The power of Hatha yoga is that the physical body is kept healthy as a result of postures and movement, and the tangible benefits are almost secondary. If we were to turn the music up loud and go through rounds of sun salutes with the sole intention of losing weight and getting a cardiovascular workout, it may look like yoga but would just be physical exercise. Rather, we are concerned with internal 'yoking', unifying our body and soul, integrating with the Divine, and experiencing God in our body. Yoga reminds us of our infinite nature, our eternal soul, and in doing so we refresh the connection with our physical nature. Some forms of yoga minimise physicality altogether, such as mantra yoga, transcendental meditation and Jnana Yoga.

There have been occasions where I have not been allowed to teach physical meditation during Shabbat in a synagogue setting. In almost all cases it was either prior to the main service or as an alternative (rather than as a replacement) but attitudes are gradually changing in the religion as a whole.

Measured breath is an essential part of the physical practice of yoga, and it is considered ideal to be able to breathe smoothly and eventually reach a level where you can go through extreme *vinyasas* without even breaking into a sweat. Ancient yogis would focus on maintaining a regular heartbeat throughout, even lowering the rhythm of their heart at will. These are the hallmarks of advanced meditation rather than exercise as we know it.

KOSHER KARMA SUTRA

One expression of Kabbalistic unity on Shabbat is for married couples to have conjugal relations on Friday night. The process of sexual intercourse, where two people literally join as one flesh, is seen as reflecting the unity of God, and when a child is born, that is a further expression of the oneness. There are various kabbalistic allusions here[7]. Yoga is a similar expression of this unity, where separate elements (body, breath, concentration) all join towards one focused point, becoming one. There are yogic practices for sexual union, most notably The Karma Sutras, but that discussion is way beyond the scope of this modest little volume!

---

[7] One Kabbalistic description of Shabbat is the synthesis of the Divine spheres of *Yesod* (connection) and *Malchut* (mastery). These two qualities represent the masculine and feminine, and when a husband and wife join together they are physically representing this union of Divine energies. For extended essays and sources, please see the relevant chapters in *The Kabbalah Sutras*.

SHABBATASANA/SHEVA-ASANA/DYNAMIC RELAXATION

'For in six days God made heaven and earth, and on the seventh day he rested and was refreshed'

EXODUS 32:17

SHABBAT POSE

SHABBATASANA/SHEVA-SANA: DYNAMIC RELAXATION

The ultimate yoga *asana* is *Shavasana*, Corpse Pose. It is the perfect symbolic posture to explore the concept of Shabbat, but also one of most difficult poses. It appears to be relatively simple: lie on your back with your eyes shut, hands by your sides, palms turned upwards and keep your mind present. If you can stay present and keep your mind focused during this complete physical relaxation, you are some way towards mastery in the pose.

We might say the same of Shabbat. Can we fully step out of the demands of the world, taking time off from working, shopping, creating, cooking and cleaning but still be present, conscious and mindful?

The fifteenth-century Hatha Yoga Pradipika explains that 'lying on the back on the ground like a corpse is Shavasana. It removes fatigue and gives rest to the mind'[1].

Although Shavasana is usually presented as a 'relaxation posture' which involves lying on one's back, loosening most of the muscles, 'sinking into the floor' and allowing our minds to wander, this completely misses the point of the posture. Some teachers describe how it can take several months to learn shavasana, which combines an inner concentration

---
[1] *Hatha Yoga Pradipika*, p14.

with outer stillness. The internal focus is on the breathing and bringing a conscious awareness to the entire body. Although this is one the most comfortable postures in the spectrum of Hatha Yoga, it is also one of the most challenging because people can easily fall asleep in the pose. There are plenty of yoga classes where the sound of snoring begins to fill the room during this 'final relaxation', although this misses the opportunity of the mental concentration within the pose. Can we keep our consciousness present during Shavasana?

Not everybody likes the word 'corpse pose' and some have even sought to rename it, with terms like *shanta-asana* ('tranquil posture'), *prashrita–asana* ('lying down posture') or even *shatithilya-asana* ('relaxation posture'). This misses the asana's objective. As mentioned earlier, Talmud describes in various places how earthly experiences can give a hint of things to come, with the Talmud referring to dreams as *'one-sixtieth of prophecy'* and Shabbat as *'one-sixtieth of the future world'*[2]. One aspect of Shavasana is that we are preparing for the eternal rest – death – as we lie in the position that our body will take when we have breathed our final exhale and our soul has exited our body. Nonetheless the corpse posture can achieve the precise opposite of death when performed with full concentration, because it can be used as a restorative pose, a healing remedy for stress and hypertension that leaves us reinvigorated. Just as a fully-observed Shabbat will take the participant away from aspects of the material world for a short space of time before returning them with full energy and renewed motivation, Shavasana has a similar effect.

Rabbinic wordplay makes great use of puns, allusions and linguistic similarities and there is one too obvious to go unmentioned. The Hebrew word 'shabbat' (Sabbath) comes from the root word *Sheva* meaning seven. Whether we practice Shavasana, *Shabbat*-asana or *Sheva*-asana (the seventh-day pose), it can provide a gateway for us to reach a higher consciousness.

Shabbat Shalom.

---

[2] "Five things are a sixtieth part of something else: namely, fire, honey, Sabbath, sleep and a dream. Fire is one-sixtieth part of Gehinnom. Honey is one-sixtieth part of manna. Sabbath is one-sixtieth part of the world to come. Sleep is one-sixtieth part of death. A dream is one-sixtieth part of prophecy". - *Babylonian Talmud, Shabbat 57b.*

SABBATH VINYASA

NISHMAT KOL CHAI: PRAYER PRACTICE SEQUENCE

There is a yoga sequence hidden in the middle of the Shabbat morning prayers. For years it has struck me that people will read through this prayer which describes an intimate physical sequence, but not connect with the words they are saying. Often we will not notice something until somebody brings attention to it, so these *Shabbat Sutras* are an opportunity to connect with a physical prayer that is hidden in plain sight.

Nishmat Kol Chai is one of my favourite prayers. A part of the Shabbat morning service (*Shacharit*), it features at the end of the psalms of praise (*Pesukei d'zimrah*), which are a series of poetic meditations. The Kabbalists teach that the four parts of the morning prayer service correspond to the four Kabbalistic worlds, or four levels of vibrational energy. This prayer is a transition point, to inspire and lift us from one world to the next.

Although this prayer has relevance to everyone and is a universal tool for meditation and contemplation, it is worth noting exactly what it covers and how it fits into the Shabbat service. Read at the end of a selection of psalms, it forms a climax that involves the entire body, as if to focus our energy; it is followed by the *Shema* prayer which is an expression of unity. *Nishmat Kol Chai* can be read as a prayer for stilling the mind and body, and preparing ourselves for a declaration of oneness.

SABBATH VINYASA: AN INTEGRATED YOGA PRACTICE

Saturday morning, *Shabbat*, is a time for an extended, deeper meditation. There is more time for stillness, reflection and concentration. This may be more difficult to achieve during moments of stress, but the circumstances are set up to optimise the possibility of peacefulness. *Nishmat Kol Chai*, translated as "*the soul of all living things*" or "*the breath of all living things*", is a tribute to the Creator.

We now begin a text-and-practice yoga sequence to physicalise the prayer.

SHABBAT SUTRA 1: *'The soul breath of every living being shall bless your name, Endless One, Creator'*

נִשְׁמַת כָּל חַי תְּבָרֵךְ אֶת שִׁמְךָ ה׳– אֱלֹקֵינוּ

YOGA PRACTICE: Lotus or Easy Pose (cross-legged). Focus on grounding.

The usual translation of *Nishmat Kol Chai* is *'the soul of all living things'*, but a more accurate way of understanding it is the 'soul-breath' as the word *neshama* (soul) and *neshima* (breath) both share the same spelling. This wordplay suggests something akin to the yogic concept of *pranayama*. Similar to *Chi* in the Chinese systems, *Prana* is the life force that is measured and stimulated by the external breath but is actually much more subtle than the process of air being drawn into the lungs and the oxygen being absorbed into blood for the body's use.

Yogis learn to direct their pranic energy to achieve extreme postures and balances. Concentrating this energy makes more easy work of more complicated manoeuvres such as handstands and other inversions because once the breath is engaged and the body is aligned, energy is free to flow. As I have written about in the earlier books, one of the first moments which hooked me into studying yoga was watching my teacher Edward Clarke slowly raise his feet into a handstand, which was the result of his many years' practice of both asana, vinyasa and pranayama[1].

'The soul of every living thing shall bless your name' is a somewhat esoteric prayer and hard to literally put into practice because our soul is intangible, at least according to traditional interpretations. Perhaps one way to bless the creator with our 'soul breath' or 'life force' is through concentrated breathing. Certain Kabbalists include ways to physicalise mystical meditations by combining the breath and movement. Two examples are the *Yichud* meditations of Rabbi Yitzhak Luria and the breath meditations of Rabbi Abraham Abulafia. Both explored how we can use physical actions to unify the name of God through our body, which also happens to be a perfect definition of the word 'yoga'[2]. are based around this notion of combining physical actions with our soul in order to unify God's name.

SHABBAT SUTRA 2: *'[Endless One, Creator] the spirit-breath of all flesh shall constantly glorify and exalt, remembering your Nobleness/Divinity'*

וְרוּחַ כָּל בָּשָׂר תְּפָאֵר וּתְרוֹמֵם זִכְרְךָ מַלְכֵּנוּ תָּמִיד

YOGA PRACTICE: *Ujiya* breathing - count 10 deep breaths.

Ruach is also associated with healing. The word first appears at a time of chaos and destruction, when the world was in total disarray, prior to the creation of humans, animals or vegetation. The appearance of *Ruach Elohim*, the spirit of God, is immediately followed by the first utterance 'Let there be light'[3].

---

[1] An introductory way to experience the handstand is to practice whilst leaning against a wall. To find out more about Edward's teachings, see www.tripsichore.com.
[2] See Rabbi Aryeh Kaplan's *Meditation & Kabbalah*, especially the chapters on the Ari z"l and Rabbi Abraham Abulafia. I have explored various practical applications of this in my book *The Kabbalah Sutras*.
[3] Genesis 1:3.

The seventh day is more than just rest and relaxation. It is a spiritual recharge that can be reached through withdrawing ourselves from some acts of creation and reconnecting with our true nature – our breath – on a profound level. The joy of Shabbat is the essence of *Shavasana* (corpse posture) when we find a stillness that is outwardly immobile but inwardly dynamic. Through stepping out of our busy activity and returning to our centre, finding our balance, we can then go back into the world with a renewed energy. This is what happens at every 'successful' yoga class: we leave our car keys, cellphone and worldy worries outside the room so that we can focus and enter a state of deeper relaxation.

The final stage of *Nishmat Kol Chai* is engaged breathing. These two phrases – 'the soul-breath of all living things' and 'the spirit breath of all flesh' are meditations to remind us both of our own breathing and the fact that we are part of a larger organism, the planet Earth, which is 'breathing' on a much larger scale. Our breath does indeed permeate all living things because we share the same air with birds, trees, animals and streams.

The 21st century is a time for humans to remember the vast interconnectedness that binds together everyone and everything on the planet. In previous centuries we took what we wanted from the land and dropped our waste materials into the sea and skies, but the onset of manmade ecological disasters has brought everything into a new light. We are all part of the same planet and the ecological systems are joined. A nuclear disaster in Russia can cause damage in England and a tidal wave in the Pacific can have economic repercussions in North America. We can all ignore the fact that some Africans are starving but eventually nature finds a way to remind us of our connection and our overall responsibility. A tiny hole in the ozone layer can cause problems for everyone, no matter where it is and who caused it. A melting ice cap may have a long-term consequence for everyone, wherever they are.

The Midrash tells a story of man who was on a boat and started drilling a hole beneath his seat. His companions asked *"why are you doing this?"*. He replied, *"Why do you care? Aren't I drilling under my own place?"*. They said to him *"but you will flood the boat for all of us!"*[4].

During this yoga practice, consider your own body. If you stub your toe, you will become aware of the pain throughout the rest of your body. Our bodies are like small planets, full of vast amounts of activity and consisting of many smaller organisms, but maintaining an overall sense of wholeness. With every yogic breath we take, we can bring our awareness to connect with the wider world. *The soul breath of all living things, the spirit breath of all flesh;* we breathe deeply, synchronise with the breathing of everyone else in the room and turn our thoughts towards the Higher Being, of whom we are all a part. We are now invited to deepen our breathing. The *ruach* is another part of the soul that is mentioned here. Often translated as spirit, it relates to the quality of water because it is first mentioned in Genesis when God's spirit-breath hovers above the surface of the water[5].

SHABBAT SUTRA 3. *'[You], who rouse the sleepers and awaken the slumberers'*

הַמְעוֹרֵר יְשֵׁנִים

YOGA PRACTICE: Bring your awareness to your skin and the sensations you feel, and listen closely to all of the sounds around you.

Breathing is an unconscious act but we can use it to bring us into consciousness so that we are mindful of our thoughts, our actions, our communications and living as part of God. The metaphor of waking up is evoked in the Friday night song *Lecha Dodi* which includes the words *Uri Uri Shir Daberi* - 'Wake up! Wake up! Sing a new song!' and is sung just as Shabbat is coming in and precisely when people may be falling asleep after a long week.

The process of becoming more aware of the esoteric part of our lives is often called a spiritual awakening. Although we were not physically

---

4   *Midrash Rabbah, Vayikra/Leviticus 4:6.*
5   *Genesis 1:2.*

asleep, the metaphor holds true in that people can be asleep to the possibilities around them. The patriarch Jacob experienced this when he 'awoke from his sleep and said "surely God was in this place and I did not know"'[6]. As we gradually awaken we can become aware of the spiritual light, the *Or Ein Sof* that is around us on a moment-by-moment basis.

SELF-KNOWLEDGE & CONSCIOUS AWAKENING

Jacob's awakening can also be translated with a more new-age twist: the Hebrew words for 'I did not know' are *'anochi lo yadati'* which might be more translated as 'I, I did not know'. Or rather 'God is in this place and myself, I did not know'. In other words, Jacob senses the Divine presence and that leads him to immediate self-knowledge and conscious awakening.

One of the biggest challenges of today's culture and lifestyle is to get enough sleep when our bodies need it, and in turn, to become fully awake. Whereas agrarian ages were bound to a rhythm of waking at dawn and sleeping at dusk, we have 24-hour supermarkets, on-demand entertainment and all-hours communications. Everyone has enough personal digital devices to ensure that we can receive an endless chain of instant messages and almost never be out of contact, but as a result it can be much harder to get in contact with ourselves. There are coffee chains on every street of every major city to ply us with caffeine and keep our energy up. What about inner calm and stillness?

CAFFEINE & CONCENTRATION

Whilst caffeine might have its place, the nature of the drug is to increase alertness at the cost of inner calm. While it stimulates our concentration, the accompanying rush of adrenaline heightens activity within the brain and makes it that much more difficult to achieve inner stillness. Instead, a powerful breathing technique, when combined with engaged physical movement, is a far more effective force to rouse us from our slumber.

---

[6] *Genesis 28:16.*

With the introductory framing elements in place, we can now focus our attention on moving through the Nishmat sequence, bringing consciousness to every part of the body, stimulating our attention and focus. The Nishmat body-review is an extended version of the morning blessings, expanding the concept of how every single part of the body can be brought together as one.

SHABBAT SUTRA 4: *'He who makes the mute speak'*

הַמֵּשִׂיחַ אִלְמִים

YOGA PRACTICE: Seven chants of the word *'Shalom'*, elongating the *'om'*.

The use of mantras in yoga is fairly widespread and many classes begin with chants such as the invocation to Lord Patanjali, author of the Yoga Sutras[7], and a typical Ashtanga vinyasa class will begin with the traditional chant. This is complex from a Jewish perspective because of the commandment not to worship any other gods[8] (even though from a Hindu perspective all of their deities are expressions of one unified God). Nonetheless, there is a soothing and wakening quality to chanting and the very act of humming or softly singing sends vibrations through our body, touching us on a deeper level at the start of the practice.

Making the 'mute speak' is relevant because if we are practicing at the inception of a new day, we have been effectively mute overnight whilst asleep. Following on from this, when we later say 'all my bones shall say "Endless one, who is like you?"' we are giving our body a further

---

[7] This is the translation of the invocation: "Let us bow before the noblest of sages Patanjali, who gave yoga for serenity and sanctity of mind, grammar for clarity and purity of speech and medicine for perfection of health. Let us prostrate before Patanjali, an incarnation of Adisesa, whose upper body has a human form, whose arms hold a conch and a disc, and who is crowned by a thousand-headed cobra" (from http://bksiyengar.com/modules/IYoga/sage.htm).

[8] Exodus 34:14.

opportunity for expression as the bones have also been 'silent' over night and now begin to move for a new day and singing their unique song.

When teaching a yoga practice I will usually begin the class with three chants of Shal-om, which engages the vocal chords and allows the resonance of the primal sounds to reverberate throughout all of our cells. I encourage students to find a place of deep peace within their body and allow that to reverberate throughout their cells during the chant.

SHABBAT SUTRA 5: *'[He]...who releases the bound'*

וְהַמַּתִּיר אֲסוּרִים

YOGA PRACTICE: Hip openers and twists.

The phrase refers to how God releases slaves from their captivity, but we can read it on other levels. First there is the early morning muscular tightness that most people experience in their limbs, and the liberating stretches that release this tightness. We must use muscles or they will eventually atrophy. People who never exercise certain muscles tend to experience tightness and stiffness that just becomes part of their status quo. They just get used to it and as they grow older, yoga becomes a valuable and essential tool for physical liberation on a daily basis. The Hebrew phrase for 'freeing the bound' is *matir assurim* and the *assurim* can be read as the natural restrictions that our body imposes on itself when it is not being used. If our muscles are ignored, they will eventually wither and stop working altogether. We see this atrophy throughout nature, whether it is a pond that begins to stagnate when waters stop moving for too long, or a hospital patient who is bedridden for an extensive period and requires physiotherapy to regain working use of a limb. We see this with cars which are left unused for a few months, as rust sets in and corrodes their bodywork while the engine gradually seizes up.

A key part of the Biblical narrative is how the Hebrew slaves leave Egypt. Much has been taught about the significance of *Mitzrayim*, the Hebrew word for Egypt. Another translation for mitzrayim is 'from narrow straights' or 'out of the bound place' and Egypt can be understood as a metaphor or code for narrow thinking or pessimistic attitudes. Rather than beginning our day from a place of anxiety or negative thinking, as we combine body, breath and movement, our thoughts go straight to the breathing and free themselves from the shackles of an over-active mind. The worries or stresses that can accompany a new day are therefore healed and on their way to being set free.

SHABBAT SUTRA 6: *'[He] who supports the fallen'*

וְהַסּוֹמֵךְ נוֹפְלִים

YOGA PRACTICE: *Vinyasas*/Sun salutations and leg-strengthening postures.

'*He who supports the fallen*' can be read from an emotional or psychological perspective, as we consider how God elevates people who are depressed, downhearted or suffering. People who are in pain are being lifted up, supported or 'held' by the Universe and Divine love. The phrase also appears in the sequence of morning blessings, at which point we can think of how we are being supported to physically stand up once again after a night's sleep.

This would be an appropriate verse to match with standing yoga postures, or a vinyasa/sun salutation sequence. Meditating on *Someach Noflim*, supporting the fallen, we focus our attention on the ground beneath us and strengthen our legs which hold us up.

SHABBAT SUTRA 7: *'and straightens the bent'*

וְהַזּוֹקֵף כְּפוּפִים

YOGA PRACTICE: *Mulah bandah*/Root lock, mountain pose and forward bends.

Zokef Kefufim, straightening the bent or folded, is a moment to become conscious of aligning our spine. *Kafuf*, meaning bent or out of alignment, can be similarly approached from a metaphorical perspective. How have we allowed our life direction to bend away from our goals and ambitions? Where are we off-track? How have we turned from the path of justice and doing what is right, and are there places where we can be more truthful or honest? Rabbi Chaim Luzzato's 18th century book was called *Mesillat Yeshiarim*, the Path of the Upright, and explores opportunities for straightening out one's behaviour.

Zokef Kefufim brings our attention to our physical alignment, straightening the lines of energy throughout our body. Asana practice aims at achieving a clear flow of energy. You can experience this by holding your hand out in front of you; notice if your elbow is slightly bent, and what that feels like within your body. Now straighten your arm, reach your hand out, and become aware of the energy pulsing along your arm, from the shoulder through to the tips of the fingers and beyond. Explore the difference between a straight arm and a bent arm, which feels stronger and how your energy differs between the two.

Yogis view this energy as emanating from the perineum at the base of the pelvis. The central point is referred to as the *mulah bandah*, or 'root lock', and every single asana is related back to this place. The mulah bandha, or groin area, is the centre point in Da Vinci's portrait of a man, and it is also the point of physical creation as it houses the reproductive organs. One of the most drastic effects of ageing is to become stooped and doubled over as the spine begins to weaken and space between the vertebrae starts to diminish. Although there are days when we all feel old, by regularly straightening and opening the spine in this action of *zokef kefufim*, we can engage our energy and improve our posture – both physically and morally.

PRAYER PRACTICE

SHABBAT SUTRA 8: *'To you alone we give thanks…Were our mouths as full of the song as the sea, and our tongue as full of joyous song as its multitude of waves'*

לְךָ לְבַדְּךָ אֲנַחְנוּ מוֹדִים: אִלּוּ פִינוּ מָלֵא שִׁירָה כַּיָּם, וּלְשׁוֹנֵנוּ רִנָּה כַּהֲמוֹן גַּלָּיו

YOGA PRACTICE: Inhale through your nostrils and exhale through your mouth, with the 'Ocean breath' *ujiya* breathing sound.

The previous verse has left us in an upright standing position and we now engage our mouth to invoke the sound of the sea. We can experience this using a full *ujiya* breath. Yogic breathing is louder than normal respiration because it relies on drawing the air through the nostrils, directly to the back of the throat and keeping the glottis open. "Closing your glottis is like holding your breath" explains Ashtanaga teacher John Scott. "If this happens, the energy flow stops and your muscles become starved of oxygen and pranic energy, and therefore tighten up". Some teachers refer to ujiya breathing as the 'ocean breath' because of the sound it makes, which is very similar to the rushing of waves.

Water is central to the Biblical exodus story, beginning when Moses, the redeemer figure, is initially placed in a basket which is put into the River Nile. The name *Moshe* (Moses) is given to him by the Egyptian princess who draws him from the water, and the translation of the Egyptian name Mo-she means 'to withdraw from the water'. He later performs the first miracle of the ten plagues at the waters of the Nile, leads the slaves to escape by parting the waters of the Red Sea, subsequently sings a song at the Sea, deals with complaining hordes of people at the place of the 'bitter waters' and eventually causes his own downfall by hitting a rock to withdraw water, rather than speaking to it as commanded.

We can meditate upon the water element during a yoga practice, aiming for the fluidity of a water-like movement as we move through vinyasas, and keeping this flowing approach with our breath. There is also a connection between water and liberation. Human beings are carried by waters at every stage of creation, from the male fluids at the point of conception to the fluid in the amniotic sac, to the waters which part at the point of our birth. The Red Sea parting is a metaphor for the parting of the waters prior to birth. As Moses led the people through the parting of these waters, the Children of Israel went through a rebirth, en route to Mount Sinai where they received the Torah.

Yoga is a liberation practice. The Hebrew word for liberation or freedom is *herut* and the Sanskrit is *moksha*. We are continually practicing the process of freedom through the physical yoga practice, as we release tension and tightness from limbs. This is then extended to releasing emotional and psychological constrictions. The water element is referred to in the second, defining verse of the Yoga Sutras where it says that the 'state of yoga is achieved when we calm the vacillating waves of the mind'[9].

The Biblical verse 'Our mouth as full of the song of the sea and our tongue as full of joyous song as its multitude of waves' can be practiced literally when we use an ujiya (ocean) breath, filling our mouth and throat with what sounds like a 'song of the sea'. The ujiya technique is also a helpful monitoring device as we listen for the smoothness of our breath whether practicing a fluid vinyasa or a still asana. When the song of our breath is smooth and regulated, our thoughts are calm and flowing like the waves on the shore.

SHABBAT SUTRA 9: *'Our lips as full of praise as the breadth of the heavens'*

וְשִׂפְתוֹתֵינוּ שֶׁבַח כְּמֶרְחֲבֵי רָקִיעַ

YOGA PRACTICE: Lion pose.

The mouth tends to receive minimal focus within yoga because for the majority of postures it is kept closed. Nevertheless our faces can easily store tension and it is easy to end up betraying stress and pressure through a clenched mouth and over-intense gaze. The key to regular ujiya breathing is to have the mouth relaxed, maintaining a calm state at all times.

---

[9] *Yoga Sutras* 1:2. This is my own free translation based on various existing translations.

PRAYER PRACTICE

'*Get out of bed like a lion*' advised the Shulchan Aruch[10], a manual for living. The yogic lion pose, *simhasana*, involves opening one's mouth like a roaring lion, and pushing out the tongue. The experience of expansiveness spreads across our face, making the lips wide and awakened for the day.

This verse, that 'our lips [should be] as full of praise' raises another question, namely, what if we are not feeling positive, not feeling connected with God, and not feeling in the mood to express this praise? One thing I have found over the years is to attempt my yoga practice nonetheless. If I wake up one morning and do not feeling like praying, I still do my best. The same with my physical practice or my meditation practice. I have heard a variation of this teaching from different angles. One of my Roshei Yeshiva,[11] Rabbi Shlomo Riskin, once taught that it was on the days that he did not feel like going to pray that he made the extra effort: "I don't even know what a lie-in feels like", he said. Similarly my first yoga teacher Edward Clark used to say that the most difficult yoga pose was putting on his shorts and standing at the front of the yoga mat in the morning.

We are humans, we can be strong and our minds can overcome our emotions. We do not have to be held ransom to our feelings and when we are not in the mood, we can do it anyway.

SHABBAT SUTRA 10: *'and our eyes as brilliant as the sun and moon'*
וְעֵינֵינוּ מְאִירוֹת כַּשֶּׁמֶשׁ וְכַיָּרֵחַ

YOGA PRACTICE: *Tadasana*/Mountain pose with your eyeline fixed on a point in front of you, slightly raised.

The process of becoming more conscious involves every part of our body. The focus of our eyes is a sometimes overlooked aspect of asana practice, and every posture has a *drishti*, or

---

[10] The Shulchan Aruch (compiled by R. Joseph Karo (1488-1575 C. E.) is the standard code of Jewish Law. Its opening lines reads: "Arise like a lion to serve your Creator in the morning" (1:1).
[11] i.e. one of the heads of the *yeshiva* (rabbinical seminary) where I studied.

point of focus, on which to place our gaze. The *Shema* prayer mentions the dangers of 'straying' after the desires of our eyes 'do not follow after your heart and after your eyes'[12], and there is a sense that our eyes can be used to illuminate our minds or to lead us astray. The yogic concept of *drishti*, i.e. choosing where we are going to place our focus, seems a key way to take command of our sight.

There are a variety of postures and yogic meditations which benefit the eyes and these include shoulder stands, headstands, forward bends (standing and seated) and there are specific sequences which will also help the eyes[13]. All of these will send blood flowing in the direction of the eyes and can increase healing. Many people will carry out an entire yoga practice with closed eyes to focus the mind away from sensual distractions. The yoga sutras call this *pratyahara*, for sensory deprivation during the practice. It allows us to 'see' things differently as we respond to the space around us with closed eyes. It can be enlightening to realise how much we are able to experience without the use of our eyes, quite literally 'seeing' with our other limbs.

The Book of Psalms says: 'For with you is the source of life, in Your light we see light'.[14] Turning our gaze upwards there is a sense of gratitude and connection with the Ultimate Light, but also a strong sense of opening the energy channels and letting light burst forth from within. Elsewhere in the Book of Proverbs, the soul is compared to a candle and our eyes are seen as the interface between our soul and the world.

There are various ways to physicalise the verse 'our eyes as brilliant as the sun and moon'. One approach might be to remind ourselves that Hatha Yoga – the practice of physical yoga – translates as follows; the vowel 'Ha' represents the sun and 'tha' the moon – we connect these two primordial forces through our spiritual and physical practice. From a textual perspective, we can look at King Solomon's proverb that the human soul 'is the flame of God'[15], and our eyes are the gateway to the soul.

---

[12] Numbers 15:39.
[13] B.K.S. Iyengar developed a lot of remedial postures which support the healing of specific body parts. See *Light on Yoga* for a comprehensive and well-referenced resource.
[14] Psalm 36:10.
[15] Proverbs 20:27.

PRAYER PRACTICE

SHABBAT SUTRA 11: *'and our hands as outspread as the eagles of the sky and our feet as swift as hinds...'*

וְיָדֵינוּ פְרוּשׂוֹת כְּנִשְׁרֵי שָׁמָיִם, וְרַגְלֵינוּ קַלּוֹת כָּאַיָּלוֹת

YOGA PRACTICE: *Garudasana*/Eagle Pose

We can take this verse as a cue for physical choreography, with 'hands outspread as eagles of the sky' as the first stage in Eagle pose, *garudasana*, move into a high arch position with your hands above your head. The movement is accompanied by drawing your shoulder blades downwards and creating more space across the ribcage, enabling a deeper breath. As we use our hands, arms and shoulders to deepen the breath, we quieten the mind and remind ourselves of the non-corporeal part of ourselves – the soul. The phrase 'wings of eagles' appears elsewhere in the Bible, reminding us of how we are being supported by the Eternal, and how we are all part of God. We spread our hands towards the sky and although our body stays on the ground, our exhaled breath does indeed fly to the heights and the expanses of the planet.

Similarly we can meditate on the phrase 'our feet as swift as hinds' and consider how we can bring a light and supple quality to our movement. As we breathe and stretch we open lines of energy that flow through our body and bring energy to our limbs and down to our feet.

Some systems of Kabbalah point to the fingers and toes as representative of the 10 *sefirot*, the Divine spheres. 10 is a natural number for human beings because we are decimal creatures by design, with 10 fingers and 10 toes. Other 'tens' include the 10 commandments and the 10 plagues, both of which are easy to count on two hands. The 16th century Kabbalist Rabbi Joseph Tzayah (1505-1573) described how each of the 10 sefirah-energies sit within the hand, corresponding to the lines of the palm.

SHABBAT SUTRA 12: *'Therefore, the organs You set within us, and the spirit-breath and soul-breath that You breathed into our nostrils and the tongue that You placed in our mouth, all of them shall thank and bless, praise and glorify, exalt and revere, sanctify and declare the sovereignty of Your Name, our King'.*

עַל כֵּן, אֲבָרִים שֶׁפִּלַּגְתָּ בָּנוּ, וְרוּחַ וּנְשָׁמָה שֶׁנָּפַחְתָּ בְּאַפֵּינוּ, וְלָשׁוֹן אֲשֶׁר שַׂמְתָּ בְּפִינוּ. הֵן הֵם: יוֹדוּ וִיבָרְכוּ וִישַׁבְּחוּ וִיפָאֲרוּ, וִירוֹמְמוּ וְיַעֲרִיצוּ, וְיַקְדִּישׁוּ וְיַמְלִיכוּ אֶת שִׁמְךָ מַלְכֵּנוּ

YOGA PRACTICE: *Sirsasana*/Headstand

The rabbinic choreography of *Nishmat Kol Chai* moves towards a crescendo, a spiritual climax where all of our body joins together in a unity that is the essence of yoga. The 'spirit-breath and the soul-breath that you breathed into our nostrils' sounds like an echo of the creation story in Genesis where God breathed the 'spirit of life' into Adam,[16] as if to say that we are being created afresh with every new day, every breath, in every moment. This is a powerful meditation in itself.

As the strains of everyday living seep through our mind and our ego does its work of reminding us what we have not achieved, where we have failed and how we have missed opportunities or are going to lose out on something in the future, the soul-breath in our nostrils awakens us to every moment and reminds us that we are continually being 'born' every second. There is no past, no future, only the present moment. Our bodies praise and celebrate God because when we are in this state of Oneness, we are part of God, at least in the sense that everything is God and we are reconnecting with that Divine perspective of ourselves. Ultimately there is no personal success or failure because we are connected to the Source: everything is a spiritual lesson intended for our personal development.

---

[16] *Genesis 2:7.*

PRAYER PRACTICE

SHABBAT SUTRA 13: *'For every mouth shall offer thanks to You, every tongue shall vow allegiance to You, every knee shall bend to You, every erect spine shall prostrate itself before you'*

כִּי כָל פֶּה, לְךָ יוֹדֶה: וְכָל לָשׁוֹן לְךָ תִשָּׁבַע: וְכָל עַיִן לְךָ תְּצַפֶּה: וְכָל בֶּרֶךְ, לְךָ תִכְרַע: וְכָל קוֹמָה, לְפָנֶיךָ תִשְׁתַּחֲוֶה

YOGA PRACTICE: Forward bends and Child's pose

The English name of this prayer can be translated as *'The Song of the Soul-breath of All Living Things'* and it describes a sun salute of sorts. Taking these verses literally and joining the actions will move us through a traditional *surya namaskar* (sun salute). Beginning with a gently-closed mouth to enable a full ujiya nostril-breath, the tongue is lifted to the palate, the knees are bent as part of the sun salute, we fold towards the ground and our heart space is opened. Another interpretation of 'every knee shall bend to you and every erect spine shall prostrate itself to you' is to take child's posture, or something similar to the prayer position seen in mosques, which is a natural human expression of submission. The body language of this bowing position is clear, as if to say *'You are greater than me'*.

This sense of submission continues throughout all of our yoga practice as we recognise there is a Higher will, a superior being of whom we are all a part. Our ego is the source of the majority of pain we experience within life. There is occasional physical pain, but the body excels at self-healing when we allow it.

Often we can prolong our own pain, especially through internal negative voices. The pain that stays with us is the voice inside the head telling us what we lack, how life should be different, how other people have it better, how/what/why/when/would/could/should – a cacophony of noise and distraction. In submitting ourselves to something greater, to recognise that we are part of something much bigger, that we are God, we are pure light, we are the love that is creation, we begin to lose ourselves and become aware of the presence of God. As the Baal Shem Tov taught, to meditate on the phrase *Shiviti Hashem l'Negdi Tamid*, 'I will continually be aware of the presence of God'.[17] This is an accurate description of the state of yoga.

One way to practice this awareness of God is through chanting, even silently. There is a yogic mantra *So Hum,* meaning 'I am that', and it can be said during a vinyasa practice. As we breathe in we would imagine the word 'so', and we would focus on the word 'hum' during the exhale. Similarly we could substitute the Hebrew *Ehad* (One); 'E' on the inhale and 'chad' on the exhale.

The intention here is to move into a state of heightened awareness and approach a place of eternal healing.

SHABBAT SUTRA 14: *'All hearts shall fear you/be in awe of you'*

וְכָל הַלְּבָבוֹת יִירָאוּךָ

YOGA PRACTICE: Backbends (e.g. *Dhanurasana*/Wheel Pose)

The theme of unity continues. The Book of Psalms describes how we might *"unify our hearts to be in awe of Your name"*.[18] Although the heart is often referred to in a metaphorical sense, in our yoga practice we can literally focus on our heart.

Our pulse rate will initially increase through vinyasa movements, as the body is ensuring that enough oxygen gets to the blood. The eventual aim of any yoga practice is to maintain a regular pulse, almost to match the regularity of our breath. Even though we are engaged with relatively active movements, in theory we should eventually maintain a deep sense of calm beneath it all. There are tales of yogis who were able to speed up and slow down their pulse at will, demonstrating control over the heartbeat.

We can choose where we feel awe and fear. We can be in fear of the political cycles or have this awe for God. This practice can take cultivation. Many people will only feel a deep connection to God when they

---
[17] Psalm 16:8.
[18] Psalm 86:11.

are confronted with a serious illness or loss of a loved one, but we do not need to wait until that point.

King David wrote, 'Do not rely on nobles, nor on a human being, for he holds no solution. When his soul-breath departs he returns to the earth, on that day his plans all perish'[19]. He puts a repeated emphasis on trusting in God rather than in humans, and recognising which parts of life are Eternal and which are transient.

This said, it can be challenging to maintain a steady pulse. Modern life is filled with anxiety and stress-inducing situations. There is a biological predisposition to speed up our pulse when we need it, to run from situations. The 'fight or flight' mechanism recognises when we are in danger, such as being chased by a wild animal, and ensures that more oxygen is being pumped through our system so that we can run to safety. The problem is that our bodies might react the same way when we are becoming anxious over a credit card bill, but rather than dispelling the oxygen-fuelled energy that is created from a rapidly beating heart, we just internalise it. This is where stress sets in. Where it would have been appropriate to run away from an imminent physical threat, and the body would calm down naturally, instead we might just feel pain.

One of my teachers explains that this is purely a matter of maintaining perspective and choosing our responses. A credit-card bill is not a knife being held at our throat. We have the power to control how we are going to respond.

Part of our practice is staying connected with God, continually reminding ourselves that we are souls wrapped in bodies and that our soul-breath is the eternal part of us while our body will eventually decay and perish. Eventually everyone's story remains the same, when 'the dust shall return to the earth as it was, and the spirit shall return to God who gave it'[20]. In recognising the transience of life we can move into this place of surrender, opening our body and heart to allow a powerful, soothing breath that reconnects us with the source. An ideal state of being is to

---

[19] Psalms 146:3-4.
[20] Ecclesiastes 12:7.

reach the place where our nerves, depression and anxiety dissipate and we confront the daily pressures of life with equanimity and peace. Rather, our hearts are directed towards the Great Energy and any *yirah* (fear/awe) is reserved for the Eternal rather than the credit card company and the challenging boss. At a higher level, rather than feeling any fear, we are moving towards a state of perpetual awe.

SHABBAT SUTRA 15: *'All the innermost organs shall sing to your name'*

וְכָל קֶרֶב וּכְלָיוֹת יְזַמְּרוּ לִשְׁמֶךָ

YOGA PRACTICE: *Marichyasana*/Twist (to stimulate the 'innermost' organs)[21].

As mentioned earlier, it is easy to speed through these prayers without paying conscious attention to the body parts mentioned, and not to physicalise every component of these prayers or just to treat them as metaphor (e.g. So it is 'as if' my bones are singing to God, rather than really making them move and sing, and *"praise God through dance/movement"* as it says in Psalm 150).

How can we be mindful in this practice? There is little rabbinic apparatus for truly experiencing these phrases on a specific, phrase-by-phrase basis. My intention with this "Bibli"yoga methodology is designed to unpick and unlock these Hebraic clues, and the innermost organs, the *Kerev V'Haklayot*, is a perfect example. Rather than just gloss over the phrase, we can specifically consider the inner organs, whether it is the liver, kidney or digestive system.

Postures that focus on these areas are usually associated with cleansing and support against illness. The liver is the body's filtration system, removing toxins from the blood, producing proteins and storing iron and vitamins, not to mention several other vital processes. The kidneys form a central part of the urinary waste system. The stomach is underrated as

---

[21] There are various twists that massage the kidneys and liver. The stomach and digestive system can be stimulated through *uddiyana* breathing sequences. .

a food processing unit, because when there are problems with our digestive system, the rest of the body will inevitably suffer. In the 12th century, Rabbi Moses Maimonides (Rambam) wrote about the importance of a healthy stomach and how poor digestion can be a major cause of illness[22].

A body which 'sings' to the Creator is one which has clear channels of energy, feels open and healthy, free from pain and is able to function well. On a practical level, this may be when you get into the kind of state where you just want to sing or dance. Children are especially good at being in tune with their feelings and living in this state of play, and we love seeing children who just break into song in a public place, completely free from inhibition. Like a bird at dawn that is just doing its job and singing out, they are in a very natural state that enables. As we unblock the fear, pain or sadness that resides within the tight places of our body, we can open up to gladness and joy so that *'all [our] innermost organs shall sing to Your name'*.

SHABBAT SUTRA 16: *'As it is written; All my bones will say: Endless One, who is like You?'*

כַּדָּבָר שֶׁכָּתוּב, כָּל עַצְמוֹתַי תֹּאמַרְנָה

YOGA PRACTICE: *Vinyasas* /Sun salutations

This verse jumped out at me right at the beginning of my Jewish-spiritual-yogic journey around 2003. This verse 'all my bones...', written by King David, suggests a full-body prayer. One traditional interpretation is the to-and-fro swaying motion used by Jews during prayer, known as *shockelling*[23]. What if we could use our entire body as a prayer? What if we were to find a way to use all of our bones as a full-body spiritual connection? We can do this by strongly focusing our intention, or we can borrow the movements of yoga, specifically a *vinyasa* (sun salutation) with the intention that all of our bones will be 'speaking' to God during the practice.

---

[22] *Hilchot Deot, Chapter 4*, halachas 12-14.
[23] It is also taught that this swaying motion is reminiscent of the flickering of a candle, as our soul is often compared to a candle.

Yoga can be excellent for our muscular-skeletal system, whether we are looking to create flexibility or strengthening. We can approach the practice purely from the standpoint of physical exercise, or with a continual Divine consciousness - *Shiviti hashem L'negdi tamid* - 'I will keep Hashem/the Divine name before me always'[24].

SHABBAT SUTRA 17. *'Bless the Eternal, my soul-breath, and let all my innermost organs bless his Holy Name'*

בָּרְכִי נַפְשִׁי אֶת ה'- וְכָל קְרָבַי אֶת שֵׁם קָדְשׁוֹ

YOGA PRACTICE: *Savasana*/Shabbat Pose - lying flat on your back, stay fully conscious as if you are on an altar and offering your entire practice as a sacrifice or gift to Hashem.

This verse comes from the opening of Psalm 103, and reminds us to engage our soul-breath once more and connect with the innermost parts that we were exploring just a few lines earlier. the repetition is similar to being in a yoga class where you are practicing postures, mentally focused on correct alignment and foot placement, and your teacher reminds you to 'keep breathing!'. The phrase *'bless my soul-breath'* refocuses us and reconnects everything together. It could also be a reminder of Psalm 103 in its original context which refers to the body within its spiritual-Godly framework: *'Bless the Eternal, my soul, and let all my innermost organs bless his Holy Name. Bless the Lord, o my soul, and do not forget his benefits. Who forgives all our wrongdoings, who heals all your diseases...He satisfies you with good things...so that your youth is renewed like an eagle's'*[25]. As the yoga works through our bodies, the renewal happens so that over time we regain the key elements of our youth. There can then be a lightness within our body and the ability to see the endless potential within each of us.

---

[24] *Psalm 16:8.*
[25] *Psalm 103:1-5.*

PRAYER PRACTICE

SHABBAT SUTRA 18: *'O God, in the omnipotence of Your strength, great in the glory of Your name, mighty forever and awesome through your awesome deeds, O King who is sitting upon a high and lofty throne'*

הָאֵל בְּתַעֲצֻמוֹת עֻזֶּךָ, הַגָּדוֹל בִּכְבוֹד שְׁמֶךָ, הַגִּבּוֹר לָנֶצַח, וְהַנּוֹרָא בְּנוֹרְאוֹתֶיךָ הַמֶּלֶךְ הַיּוֹשֵׁב עַל כִּסֵּא רָם וְנִשָּׂא

YOGA PRACTICE: Seated meditation: The God Posture!

The concluding line of *Nishmat Kol Chai* has a direct hint as to how we might end this sequence. *B'tatzumat Uzeha* may be translated as 'in the omnipotence of your strength' but can also be understood as 'in the *bones* of your strength'. We are all expressions of God, all part of the Creator, and we might use this to bring attention to our bones as a part of God.

God is described as 'sitting upon a high and loft throne' in a posture, which sounds like an invitation to attempt something similar on our yoga mat, at least in *sukhasana* (easy posture) or *padmasana* (lotus).

Shabbat Shalom.

THE SHABBAT SUTRAS

SHABBAT MEDITATIONS

SHABBAT MEDITATIONS

Shabbat is a yoga mat. There are four sides to the mat, representing the boundaries of the space in which I practice. These are artificially-constructed outlines that I can step over at any time. But if I transgress the boundaries and move beyond my mat or walk over the mats of others, it can reduce or weaken everyone's experience. I need to stay on my mat until the end of the class, see it through (even if I am tired or distracted) and only then will I experience the full benefit.

Shabbat is the asana. A *trikonasana* (triangle posture) might strengthen my legs, send energy from my foot through to my hand, a lotus can open my hips and a backbend can invigorate my spine. But when I only go halfway towards the pose or do not fully commit to the posture, it does not yield its full benefits to me. It cannot, because the ideal shape of the posture is one of ideal alignment where the energy flows freely through one's limbs. We do not have to create a perfect shape because our bodies are not perfect and they may not be ready to visit that place yet, but we do have to do the very best that we can do.

Shabbat is Shavasana. The pose of stillness, of focus and of peaceful contemplation. Lying flat on my back, I stay fully alert. Bristling with aliveness, feeling my heart beating and my breath flowing. To everyone else it might look like I am doing nothing, but inside I am reinvigorated. This is Shabbat, the seventh day.

ETHICS OF THE YOGIS

EASY POSE/SUKHASANA

'Be among the disciples of Aaron, loving peace and pursuing peace'

ETHICS OF THE FATHERS 1:12

ETHICS OF THE YOGIS

INTRODUCTION

The Torah gave the command to 'circumcise your heart'[1], which is a practical impossibility. We might understand it as a metaphor for character refinement. Also translatable as 'cut away the barriers of your heart'. The Hebrew word for barriers is *orlah*, and the commentator Rashi explained that this is about removing blockages from our hearts. Like leaves that have fallen in a drain and stop water from flowing through, the blockages in our hearts are the things which stop us connecting with other people, and prevent the free flow of love between us. These blockages can take many different forms and each of them are variations of the ego. Selfishness, jealousy, dishonesty, pride, self-centredness, violence and every other negative behaviour are all manifestations of ego that arise when we try to assert ourselves. None of these things can exist when we are in a state of pure presence. When we understand that our lives are perfect, whole and complete, and that we have everything we need to live our life and fulfil our Divine mission, we no longer feel that we lack anything.

10 COMMANDMENTS OF YOGA - YAMAS & NIYAMAS

There are 10 ethical principles described in the Yoga Sutras, a set of moral codes known as the *yamas* and *niyamas*. These two aspects of

---
[1] *Deuteronomy 10:16.*

character refinement are considered the first two 'limbs' of the eight-limbed system of Ashtanga Yoga described in the sutras (*ashto* means eight, *anga* means limb, and this is the classical name for the fully integrated yoga practice, not to be confused with modern Ashtanga-vinyasa yoga as taught by the late Sri Patthabi Jois).

The Yamas are described as ethical ideas that 'indicate how individuals should respond and relate to other people and all living beings and to the environment, in order to achieve a peaceful and harmonious world'[2]. In principle, by engaging with the physical practice of yoga we will grow and strengthen in character.

The yamas and niyamas might be seen as the ten yogic commandments, and are a core part of a yoga practice that is often overlooked, but absolutely essential to the practice. There are different approaches to studying them. Some teachers will teach the texts, others believe that the asana practice will lead you to the moral refinement mentioned in the sutras, and many teachers will overlook it entirely. I heard of one respected teacher who was said to have improved his character and absorbed the essence of these teachings as a direct result of his physical yoga practice[3].

The first five yama principles are based on abstinence and are; non-violence, truthfulness, non-stealing, non-lust and non-possessiveness. These are followed by the niyama ideas of purity/cleanliness, contentment, austerity/sacrifice, study of the sacred texts/self and living with an awareness of the Divine.

ETHICS OF THE FATHERS

I am interested in the conversation between the Yoga Sutras and Ethics of the Fathers *(Pirkei Avot)*, a Jewish moral code that is explained over six chapters in the *mishna*, part of the Oral Law. *Ethics of the Yogis* is designed as a short introduction to each of the yamas and niyamas, to

---

[2] *Ashtanga Yoga*, by John Scott.
[3] Although I have studied with this teacher and have great respect for him, I did not hear it from him directly so will not mention his name for the sake of discretion.

explore how they integrate with Jewish teachings and how we can contextualise them within a Torah perspective. This is by no means exhaustive but a beginning to the conversation.

The 10-part system has been a natural model for spiritual systems for thousands of years. Apart from anything else it is practical - we are decimal creatures, with ten fingers and ten toes, and correspondingly there are ten commandments, ten *sefirot* (Divine Spheres) and more 'tens' to be found.

SMASHING THE SHELLS

The Kabbalah talks about the continued need for stripping away the levels of negative energy that surround us, which it calls *klipot*. These are also described as 'shells' by the Zohar, and we might picture them as dark shells which contain light - our job is to smash the shells through positive thoughts, actions and behaviours. The shells/klipot can manifest as disharmony, desire, jealousy and all of the other negative emotions that stay with us and get stuck in our body. There are various methods for clearing emotions from the body and one approach is to achieve this clearance through the body. B.K.S. Iyengar wrote that people 'try to solve their emotional problems through intellectual understanding. Emotional issues can, however, be resolved only through emotional understanding'. Jews may find this refinement through the performance of *mitzvot* (commandments or connection points) and the *mitzvah* of keeping the body healthy paves the way towards emotional clearance. Iyengar explains that 'yoga is about channelling and transforming [negative] energy to higher purposes...in our spiritual quest, it is required of us that we develop our body in such a way that it is no longer a hindrance, a drag, but becomes our friend and accomplice. Similarly, our emotions and intellect must be developed for divine purposes'[4].

The Ethics of the Yogis are intended to help create a holistic experience where we learn, integrate, heal and purify at the same time. The

---
[4] *Light on Life*, pp82-83.

sages described how it is ideal to learn so that we put the teachings directly into practice: 'Rabbi Ishmael the son of Rabbi Yossei would say, "One who learns in order to do, is given the opportunity to learn, teach, observe and practice"'[5].

---

[5] *Ethics of the Fathers 4:5.*

PEACE

ETHICS OF THE YOGIS 1: PEACE

KOSHER SUTRA: 'Hillel said: "Be like the disciples of Aaron, loving peace and pursuing peace"' *Pirkei Avot - Ethics of the Fathers 1:12*

YOGA SUTRA: *Ahimsa*/Non-Violence, *Yoga Sutras 2:35*

The first principle of yoga, *ahimsa*, is the absence of violence, or 'non-violence'. This is immediately at odds with Jewish philosophy which teaches that 'there is a time for war and a time for peace'[1] and if we know that somebody is planning to attack us - a *rodef* (pursuer) - we are commanded to get up early and strike them first if there is no alternative[2]. Nonetheless, how can we relate to and practice the principle of non-violence? We are prone to internal wars, a barrage of self-criticism where we criticise ourselves, hold anger against ourselves and refuse to forgive ourselves for years on end. There is immense power in forgiving ourselves for all the things we did or didn't do, and

---

[1] Ecclesiastes 3:8.
[2] Babylonian Talmud, Sanhedrin 73a - 'And these are the ones whom one must save even with their lives [i.e., killing the wrongdoer]: one who pursues his fellow to kill him [rodef achar chavero le-horgo], and after a male or a bethrothed maiden [to rape them]...'.

permanently ceasing hostilities towards ourselves and others.

In the Yoga Sutras, Patanjali taught that 'in the presence of one firmly established in non-violence, all hostilities cease'[3]. This is powerful when we consider it: he is not saying that it is the words, preaching, sermons or slogans that cease hostilities, but being in the *presence* of the non-violent person. We might imagine somebody who is so cultivated and who radiates such an energy of peace that we automatically want to put down our 'weapons' (be they literal weapons or weapons of harmful thoughts and words).

Hillel, the head of a great rabbinic academy, taught that we should 'be like the disciples of Aaron, loving peace and pursuing peace'[4]. He chose Aaron the High Priest as his role model. Aaron was the brother of Moses and was famous for his ability to reconcile warring parties. Aaron, we are told, would deal with disputes by privately visiting both parties individually, and telling them that the other side wanted to make peace – 'Bob…did you know that Jim is really be sorry about what he said to you?' 'Jim..I saw Bob today and he wishes this whole thing had not happened and that there's some way to make amends'. Having convinced each of them separately he would swiftly bring about a reunion. Aaron was so well-liked amongst the people that after his death the entire nation of Israel mourned for him[5]. He was even more popular than his brother Moses.

The Hebrew phrase for 'pursuing peace' is *rodef shalom*, and implies someone who actively seeks situations for harmony and reconciliation. The Hebrew word 'rodef' appears elsewhere in the Bible, as in our earlier example of an enemy who is planning an attack (in which case a pre-emptive strike is allowed)[6]. It is as if Hillel is suggesting that we

---

[3] Yoga Sutras 2:35.
[4] Pirkei Avot, Ethics of the Fathers, 1:2.
[5] 'The whole congregation saw that Aaron had died, and the entire house of Israel wept for Aaron for thirty days', Numbers 20:29.
[6] The word 'rode' is also used in halachic (Jewish legal) terminology in the case of a foetus whose growth threatens the life of its pregnant mother. In certain cases this foetus is considered a 'rodef', e.g. pursuing the life of the mother, which can lead to a legally-allowed abortion.

should actively pursue situations to make peace and to go after it with vigour.

We have plenty of opportunities to pursue peace. For example, every time we visit our families there are usually some occasions to seek peaceful thoughts and words. Or when we find ourselves criticising the way we have behaved, or judging another person, we can become conscious of these thoughts and choose the peaceful path.

We might read Hillel's teaching another way as the word Shalom is also a greeting, used for both 'hello' and 'goodbye'. We can pursue peacefulness every time we say hello to someone…and we also might pursue peace by looking to say goodbye to certain situations that are not harmonious and helpful to us. The question is available right now: where would you experience more shalom (peace) by saying shalom (so long, farewell) to certain situations or people? (Immediate family does not count).

The yogi can take this principle onto the yoga mat. Our asana/vinyasa practice presents many opportunities for pursuing peace. Many of us have caused damage to our bodies through an over-rigorous yoga practice (I speak for myself), and it is essential to enter the mat in peace and leave it in peace - *'nichas b'shalom v'yotzeih b'shalom'* to quote Rabbi Akiva[7]. Many people have injured themselves through pushing their limbs into an over-ambitious posture that their bodies were not ready for. I once heard a teacher say that 'the ego is in the knees', as a hint to all yoga students who were forcing their knees into lotus pose when their hips were not open enough, causing knee-pain as a direct result. So much for enlightenment. These temptations can be greater in group classes when we see other people who are more physically flexible, or perhaps want to impress the teacher. These motivations are all the result of the ego, and become a source of pain and disharmony. Pursue peace.

The word shalom holds another secret for us. Its three root letters (*shin*, *lamed* and *mem*), also spell *shalem* which means wholeness. We are

---

[7] The 'Pardes' story teaches about the four Rabbis who entered into the mystical Orchard. 'Ben Azai gazed and died..Ben Zoma gazed and went insane, Aher became an apostate..Rabbi Akiva entered in peace and exited in peace'. *Babylonian Talmud, Hagigah 14b.*

actively seeking to become whole, to recognise that we are whole, and to look for a holistic balance and harmony in everything we do.

PEACEFUL YOGA PRACTICE: Keep this idea in mind as an intention at the start of your yoga practice, actively pursuing a state of peace and wholeness, and embodying Shalom. Every posture should be peaceful from start to finish. If you are doing a more energetic or strenuous practice, still maintain a sense of peace in your thoughts and be careful to keep your face relaxed, only using the energy that is required and avoiding excessive strain. In time, we may help bring our society into a state of pure shalom 'when swords will be beaten into ploughshares and all war will cease'[8]. Until then, we have our work cut out.

---

[8] Isaiah 2:4.

TRUTH

ETHICS OF THE YOGIS 2: TRUTH
SEEKER OF TRUTH

KOSHER SUTRA: Rabbi Shimon Ben Gamliel said: "the world stands on account of these three things – righteousness, truth and peace" *Ethics of the Fathers/ Pirkei Avot 1:18.*

YOGA SUTRA: *Satya*/Truthfulness, *Yoga Sutras 2:36*

The Yoga Sutras state that 'upon being established in truth, there is surety in the result of actions'[1]. Mr Iyengar translates it as 'When abstention from stealing is firmly established, precious jewels come'[2]. Truth is considered a foundation for yoga postures and wisdom for life in all situations. Rabbi Shimon Gamliel taught that the world stands on account of truth, and there are many ways to explore this teaching. We could consider how the Hebrew word for truth, *Emet*, contains the first, middle and last letters of the Hebrew alphabet (*Alef*, *Mem* and *Tav*), as if to hint that the word 'truth' is the foundation for the alphabet and every word that is spoken. At its most basic level, there is no spiritual refinement or cultivation without truth. We want

---
[1] *Yoga Sutras 2:36.*
[2] *Light on the Yoga Sutras of Patanjali*, p.150.

people to be truthful to us, we want our leaders to be truthful, and we want to think of ourselves as truthful. The question is: are we completely truthful, and if not, what can we do about it?

TRUTH & TRIKONASANA

In every yoga posture we aim to establish the 'truth' of the pose. There is an ideal form for every position, for example triangle posture, *Trikonasana*, has a specific placement for the feet, spine, hips, hands, and gaze. If we find ourselves cheating in a pose, perhaps missing out a certain part of it so that we can look more flexible or graceful, even though we are sacrificing the foundation of the pose, we might ask: am I being completely honest in this pose? Can I align more clearly with the classical version of the posture, or at least be honest with myself as to where I am cutting corners? Can I be honest in my dishonesty?

Telling the truth is skill and can take cultivation. Children are routinely encouraged to tell the truth by parents who are often living a life of inconsistencies. As soon as the child, with their innocent detachment and fresh perspective, is able to ask the question "but Mummy, you said *this* and you're doing *that*. Why?", the answer is often the same: "because I am: you'll understand when you're older". And so, the child learns to mould the truth, to cover the truth, to squash the truth into what is convenient. They are told to speak the truth but see a lie, so they too learn to lie. And so the cycle continues. In the end, many of us are living lies to some degree or other. Not necessarily big lies, but lots of small ones that add up to a larger whole.

ADMITTING UNTRUTHS

Living little untruths appears to be easier and less painful than making the decision to speak truth and live truth. One person might say, "*My partner and I are not really suited but we may as well get married now because it's a good time to do so and I'm sure things will get better in the end*" (even though, deep down, they know that the relationship will not improve but they would rather avoid the truth, even if that means facing the consequences later. Another person may say, "*I really should change my diet and get more exercise, but the winter holidays are coming up so it will be easier to start the fitness routine in January. I am absolutely going to start my diet in the new year. Now could you please pass the doughnuts?*". This may be occasionally true but for many people it is another lie, as they have no intention of starting the diet - that too is fine, this is not about judging people's eating habits, our concern here is speaking the underlying truth. From a holistic perspective there is always a price to pay. Sometimes people manifest an illness when they do not listen to their inner voice of truth. Or maybe they receive a harder lesson later on.

TRUTH & NATURE

'The world stands on account of truth' said Rabbi Shimon ben Gamliel. Nature lives a simple truth, with every flower and plant living according to the real circumstances around it. If it rains a little, the flower is nourished. If it rains a lot, the flower dies. If the wind blows, the stalk may bend, but either way the flower will not get stressed and start talking about not being happy with itself, complaining about how it finds the wind just too much to deal with, how it wishes it was born in another flowerbed and brought up with the advantages that some other flowers had – good alkaline soil, fertiliser and more love and attention from the gardener. The flower just grows, and if the surrounding flowers are cut by a florist, it does not wither into a depression but keeps on growing until its time is done. It lives with the truth, responds to the truth, does not start fabricating stories around itself. Of course, the human mind is far more complex than the structure of a flower, but the same principles apply.

1. Where am I being untruthful in my life?
2. Where can I be more truthful in my life?
3. Where am I being untruthful about being untruthful? (In other words, where have I convinced myself that I am telling the truth, perhaps with regards to social situations, career choices, activities am I doing. Where am I not admitting to myself that I would rather make other choices?)

TRUTH ON THE YOGA MAT

Back to the yoga mat and our earlier question. Can we be truthful as to where our body is 'at' on any one day? Self-honesty is critical within an asana practice because if we lie about how capable we are and force ourselves into a posture, we can cause ourselves pain and injury. I have done this many times, as the 'truth' about our bodies can change from day to day. Some days we may feel flexible and open but other days our muscles are more tight or perhaps recovering from over-stretching. 'The world stands on account of truth' taught Rabbi Shimon, and so must the yogi. When I force myself into a deep forward bend without being properly warmed up and open, I can injure my lower back muscles. It may be frustrating when the rest of the class is doing the splits but if the pose is beyond my capability at this moment then I will only cause injury by failing to accept that basic truth. In other words my legs would respond with their truth as if to say "you have just pushed us too far".

LAZY TRUTH

Truth also works the other way: "*I am tired, hungover, I'm not up to yoga today. Maybe I have a virus coming on*". Is that true? Really? On those mornings when I lay in bed ignoring the impulse to get up and practice, I often felt a pang of regret when I finally arose having pressed the snooze button for the eighth time. The moment has been lost and by then it may be too late to fit in a decent practice. Regret is fine if we use it positively and allow it to be a guide and show us how to respond truthfully on the next occasion (rather than staying in bed out of laziness). Continual regret, however, is just a sign that we are ignoring a big truth.

TRUTH STANDS

There are a couple of other rabbinic commentaries that can fuel our journey to internalise *Emet* (truth). A midrash says that 'truth rests on two legs whilst falsehood stands on one'[3], inferring that truthful living is

---

[3] The Talmud asks 'why are the letters of Sheker (falsehood) close together while those of Emet (truth) are far apart?' (this refers to their place in the Hebrew alphabet) 'because Falsehood is frequent, truth is rare. And why does falsehood

a more stable base. Perhaps you are a great yogi and can hold a one-legged balance for 20 minutes, but this will be the exception rather than the rule. The midrash is suggesting that truthful behaviour creates lasting results whilst falsehood-based actions are a weak foundation. This is visually represented through the Hebrew letters, as those spelling *Emet* (the Hebrew word for truth) each have a firm base and two 'legs' : [אמת]. Meanwhile the letters spelling Shequer (falsehood) each appear to stand on one leg: [שקר].

GOD'S SEAL

The Talmud tells us that 'God's seal is truth'[4]. Yoga deals with the energetic seals, or bandhas, where we are encouraged to keep a firm flow of energy in certain directions and 'lock' the flow at various points around the body rather than allowing the energy to leak out. When taking a standing posture this can be achieved by bringing awareness to the various energy seals around the body, and creating strong, powerful standing postures.

There is much more we could discuss about being truthful, but ultimately it comes back to the same simple message: stand in truth.

May the truth be with you.

[stand] on one foot, whilst truth has a brick-like foundation?' [on two feet, referring to the two-legged shape of the Hebrew letter Aleph - א - 'Truth can stand, while falsehood cannot stand', BT *Shabbat 104a*.

[4] 'Rabbi Chanina said: The seal of the Holy One, blessed be He, is Truth', Babylonian Talmud, *Shabbat 55a*.

ETHICS OF THE YOGIS

ABUNDANCE

ETHICS OF THE YOGIS 3: ABUNDANCE WEALTH BEYOND MEASURE

KOSHER SUTRAS: 'Do not steal' *Exodus 20:13*. 'Do not steal [You, plural]' *Leviticus 19:11*

YOGA SUTRA: *Asetya*/Non-Stealing, *Yoga Sutras 2:37*

"You shall not steal" says the ten commandments[1]. Although most people are not shoplifting or engaging in Grand Auto Theft, there are subtle ways of stealing, whether it is taking somebody's time, taking excessive breaks whilst at a job or rounding up hours on a timesheet. The Talmud explores the nuances of stealing, as we shall see later, whether it is stealing with our words, our energy or our intention. There are also ways of stealing whilst on a yoga mat, taking a posture that is not ours because our body is not ready for it.

The Yoga Sutras says that 'all wealth comes to one who is established in non-stealing (*asetya*)'[2]. Patthabi Jois taught that asetya/non-stealing begins with not stealing material property but extends to not cheating

---
[1] *Exodus 20:13.*
[2] *Yoga Sutras 2:37.*

people with 'sweet words' or achieving selfish ends when pretending to be truthful.

Ethics of the Fathers reveals yet another angle in not stealing, when it says that we should 'say something in the name of the person who said it' and this will 'bring redemption to the world'. In other words, when you share an impressive or inspiring quotation, do not 'steal' it and pretend that you created it, but rather share the name of the person who taught it[3]. This action alone, of stealing other people's creativity for personal gain, has been the cause of many court cases. From a spiritual angle, the sages went so far as to say that by not stealing the words of others, we can raise the spiritual consciousness of the planet.

WHAT'S MINE IS MINE

When do we first develop an ego and begin claiming ownership over material possessions? I remember the day one of my nephews discovered the word 'mine'. He was two years old at the time and until that point would become happy with almost anything. He was happy if given a cuddly toy. He was happy if it was moved away from him and would then find something else to focus on and be happy with that. Simple things would delight him. Then one day his will became stronger and he developed an idea of *ownership*. It all began simply enough – he wanted to hold on to a conker[4] during a car journey. It was a fresh, shiny hazelnut-coloured conker that he had picked up during an autumn walk in the park but my brother-in-law was concerned that he would put it in his mouth during the journey home, so the conker was taken away from my nephew. He started to cry (my nephew, not my brother-in-law). The attachment to objects had begun and rather than feeling he had enough things, he was suddenly experiencing a sense of lack. And so the ego had

---

[3] 'One who says something in the name of its speaker brings redemption to the world, as is stated *(Esther 2:22)*, "And Esther told the king in the name of Mordechai."' *(Ethics of the Fathers 6:6)*.

[4] For non-British readers, a conker is the fruit of the horse-chestnut that falls from trees during the English autumn. They are brown, shiny and prized possessions amongst schoolboys who traditionally stick a shoelace through them and start bashing them against one another in 'conkers' tournaments to see who has the strongest conker. It is an English thing...

been born. Of course, I say *my* nephew but there really is no 'my'. We enter the world naked and leave it with the same amount of possessions we started with. So how does everything get so complicated in between?

ABUNDANCE & LACK

It is natural to have an ego. The sages were fully aware of humans' complex and differing relationships to things. Although it is natural for children to develop strong attachments to objects, the sages question this approach with adults who continue to insist that "what's mine is mine"[5], without looking to share. We can inquire more deeply into where we feel strong attachments in life, where we feel there is a sense of lack, and where this might lead us to steal, even on a minuscule level.

STEALING TIME, THOUGHTS & HEARTS

The Talmud taught that we are forbidden to steal people's time by misleading them[6], such as pretending to a shopkeeper that you are interested in an item when you are not, inviting a friend for dinner when you know they will refuse or opening a barrel of wine for someone and pretending it is in their honour when you were planning to open it anyway. The Book of Samuel recounts how King David's wayward son Absalom 'stole the hearts of all the men of Israel'[7]. These forms of thought-theft are known as Geneivat Da'at, literally 'stealing someone's knowledge'. In short, don't do it!

---

[5] 'There are four types of people: One who says, "What is mine is yours, and what is yours is mine" is a boor. One who says "What is mine is mine, and what is yours is yours" – this is a median characteristic; others say that this is the character of a Sodomite. One who says, "What is mine is yours, and what is yours is yours" is a *chassid* (pious person). And one who says "What is mine is mine, and what is yours is mine" is wicked'(*Ethics of the Fathers*, 5:10, translation from Chabad.org).
[6] 'It is forbidden to mislead people' - *BT Chullin 94a*.
[7] *2 Samuel* 15:6.

MEDITATIONS ON ABUNDANCE

We might focus on abundance, that we have been created in the image of God, with pure abundance. There is a daily blessing said every morning that acknowledges and thanks the Creator with the words *she'asa li kol tzarchi*, that all of our needs are taken care of. What if we do not feel we have everything we need? One spiritual practice is to look harder. To explore how this in itself may be a lesson and an area of growth for our soul.

ON THE YOGA MAT

Yoga is a practical way to explore non-stealing. *Lo Tignov*, do not steal, applies on the mat as mentioned earlier. We should not 'steal' a posture that does not belong to us, or we will have to pay the price. If our hips are not flexible and we push ourselves into the splits, what might happen? Equally if our shoulders are flexible to the point of weakness and we over-contort ourselves, what could be the result? Sometimes our bodies need flexibility and sometimes they need strengthening. This is about you knowing your body and being truthful with where your body is at on any given day. If we stop to listen, our bodies will quickly inform us of their truth, telling us which muscles are open, which want to be stretched, and which want to be left alone.

Another nuance to the practice of non-stealing can arise in a group yoga class. We might compare our practice to that of another student, envy their flexibility or accomplishment and try to do the same. There is a balance to be struck between being inspired and motivated by what somebody else is doing, and not recognising that our bodies are different. This process of learning is often about trial and error.

The subtleties of non-stealing may even escape our attention. How often do we try to get the teacher's attention during class, perhaps for an extra adjustment in a posture, or just so that we are given that extra energy? Rather, if we can apply absolute truth to every moment, only asking for the help we genuinely need, going as far into a posture as we are able to and not allowing ourselves to release from a posture before we really need to, then we cannot help but progress.

When outlining the punishments for stealing, the Mishna (oral law) explains that under certain circumstances, a thief is liable to return the stolen object along with a penalty payment of up to four or five times the object's original value[8]. This principle can be accurate when experienced with our own bodies. Anyone who has injured themselves through indulging in an over-energetic sports session without being properly warmed up or after a long period of rest, will testify that a moment's ego-driven actions can have a real cost. One day's exertion can easily result in four or five days' worth of recovery time, which is far from fun.

Abundance is all around and our challenge is to recognise that we have enough to satisfy our needs, whilst being prepared to work for the things we want. Spiritual and material wealth is everywhere. The art is to see it and realise it, moment by moment.

---

[8] *Mishna Bava Kamma 7:1.*

SCORPION IN HANDSTAND/VRSCHIKASANA II

'Who is strong? The person who can focus their desires'

ETHICS OF THE FATHERS 4:1

POWER

ETHICS OF THE YOGIS 4: POWER HOLDING BACK & FOCUSING ENERGY

KOSHER SUTRA: 'Spiritual accomplishment (Torah) is acquired by means of forty-eight qualities, which include...limited business activity, limited sexual activity, limited pleasure, limited conversation, limited laughter' *Ethics of the Fathers/ Pirkei Avot, 6:6*

YOGA SUTRA: *Brahmacharya*/Non-Lust/Energetic Focus, *Yoga Sutras 2:38*

Moderation and abstinence are seemingly at odds with the predominantly secular culture which teaches that you can have anything whenever you want it. After all, what else was the purpose of the sexual revolution if we are to be held back? The Torah feels differently, as did the Yogis. Just as the sages taught that Torah or spiritual accomplishment is achieved through limiting our energetic output, whether it is business, sex, pleasure, conversation or laughter, so too the Yoga Sutras which teaches that 'upon being established in non-lust there is attainment of vital energy'[1].

---

[1] *Yoga Sutras 2:38.*

Put in very straightforward terms, if we limit our sexual output, we maintain more life-force. This topic has been written about extensively by Mantak Chia in *Taoist Secrets of Love: Cultivating Male Sexual Energy*, and he specifically looks at how men lose their chi or core energy through ejaculation, which is why it should be done sparingly[2]. The Yoga Sutras principle extends this to excessive lusting, which is another way we might lose our chi if our mind over-dwells on fantasy situations. The rabbinic sages in Ethics of the Fathers extend this principle to all-round energy management, seeing how we can potentially lose energy through over-exertion in various other areas as well.

ENERGY MANAGEMENT: YOUR 100 UNITS

We might look at this as energy management. Imagine you have 100 core units of energy each day[3]. You can use these for eating, sleeping, talking, sex, healing and other activities. You can also use this for spiritual accomplishment. If you use up all your energy units on physical endeavours, there will be no power left for raising your vibration and elevating your soul.

THE ECONOMY OF ENERGY

A mindful yoga practice can also teach us to be economic with our energy. My teacher Edward Clark would encourage us to ask this question: "how can I achieve this posture with the minimum of effort? What is the most simple and effective way of getting there?". We are trying to conserve and increase our levels of energy, which is why the aim is to move through vinyasa sequences with grace and style rather than with flailing limbs which cause exhaustion and energy loss. Although some yoga classes are advertised as an opportunity to sweat and lose weight, the ideal is to carry out a practice without sweating, hence this idea of

---

[2] I have written about this extensively in the eight chapters about Yesod in my book *The Kabbalah Sutras*.
[3] I borrowed the '100 units' idea from Dr Caroline Myss who teaches it in the specific context of healing, and discusses how people stop themselves from healing because so much of their mental energy is wrapped up in anger or regret.

the 'retention of vital fluids'. Another friend of mine who is a masterful business coach will be careful to give clients exactly what they need, nothing more and nothing less. Whilst this is an art rather than a science, the energetic principle of focusing our energy, what the Kabbalists call *Gevurah*[4], leaves us with enough energy to pursue our goals.

INTIMACY

The Torah's laws of Family Purity, *Taharat Mishpaha*, outline how a married couple can have sex at specific times and are encouraged to refrain from marital relations whilst the woman is menstruating. In his book *Yoga Mala*, Patthabi Jois expressed an almost identical idea, stating that 'the menstrual cycle should be considered [and sexual activity] should take place in accordance with the menstrual periods'.[5] He also said that 'union with one's lawful wife should be undertaken for the sake of begetting good progeny', which is very similar to the words of Maimonides who taught that 'when procreating, one should set their intention' on bringing down the soul of a great sage[6]. Although the Rabbis have no problem with recreational intimacy between a married couple - it is positively encouraged - this is all within boundaries and limits.

'*Limited business activity, limited sexual activity, limited pleasure…*'. This principle is about keeping our lives in balance. This is not a treatise of abstinence but moderation. It is also about fulfilling our true potential through leaving ourselves with sufficient bandwidth. When our energy is focused in one direction we can be a lot more effective than if we are distracted and lacking focus. We stay connected to our soul, connected to our calling and connected to God.

---

[4] For more information about this principle, please see the relevant chapters in *The Kabbalah Sutras*.
[5] *Yoga Mala: The Original Teachings of Ashtanga Yoga Master Sri K. Patthabhi Jois*, p11.
[6] The direct Hebrew translation is '[when procreating] one should set their heart on having a child who will be a sage and great person in Israel' (Maimonides *Sefer Mada, Hilchot Deot*/Laws of Knowledge 3:3). Although Maimonides explicitly talks about setting one's intention at that specific moment, the Kabbalists (e.g. in *Sefer Bahir*) discuss how it is possible to affect the reincarnation cycle at that time and draw down a particularly elevated soul to be your child.

NON-ATTACHMENT

ETHICS OF THE YOGIS 5: NON-ATTACHMENT
YOU CAN'T TAKE IT WITH YOU

KOSHER SUTRA: 'In times of trouble, why should I fear the negative forces around me? People who trust in their earth, who glory in their riches? It cannot redeem someone or pay his ransom to God....Do not be afraid when a man becomes rich, when his household goods increase, for when he dies he cannot take any of it along; his goods cannot follow him down' *Psalm 49*

YOGA SUTRA: *Aparigraha*/Non-Attachment/Non-Greed, *Yoga Sutras 2:39*

The principle of non-attachment is rarely taught in a Jewish context although both the Book of Psalms and Kabbalistic teachings stress the immortality of our soul, and the temporary nature of life on earth. We may understand the principle from an academic perspective, that when we die we 'cannot take any of it along' but can we embody this and make it real in our life?

The yogic principle of *aparigraha* teaches non-greed, as if to free oneself from desire. The Yoga Sutras says that 'upon the foundation of freedom from greed (*aparigraha*), one gains insight into the reasons for the cycles of birth and death'[1]. BKS Iyengar translates it as 'Knowledge of past and future lives unfolds when one is free from greed for possessions'[2]. This suggests that when we can free ourselves from earthly wants, this opens up the doorway to higher levels of intuitive insight, revealing the reasons for why people are incarnating, and why they are being born and dying. Perhaps it reveals the secrets of Divine justice and karma, for example why some die young, others die old, some are born into difficult family situations and others are born into luxury. Maybe it provides spiritual answers as to why the Holocaust happened[3].

We might easily get lost in the nuances here. A Torah perspective does not suggest getting free of earthly desires but rather channelling our desires for a higher purpose. Another example would be if someone has a strong sexual drive, can they channel that to create a beautiful family that will help elevate the planet? The Talmud brings the example that someone who has a strong desire to kill might become a *shochet*, a ritual slaughterer, and focus their desire in that direction: *'He who is born under Mars will be a shedder of blood. Rabbi Ashi observed: "Either a surgeon, a thief, a slaughterer, or a circumciser". Rabbah said: "I was born under Mars!"'*[4]. This is a great example of how we can choose where to focus our energy. Rather than quenching or quashing desires[4], our question is around how we manage these desires.

ABUNDANCE

A God-conscious spiritual practice will ideally led us to an awareness of abundance. We have everything we need right now, everything

---

[1] Yoga Sutras 2:39.
[2] *Light on the Yoga Sutras of Patanjali*, p.152.
[3] Tragedies from a human perspective may have a very different meaning from a spiritual perspective, for example if a soul has to go through a certain level of cleansing to reach a higher level, it may have to experience pain in the earthly realm. This level of theology is however beyond the scope of this book.
[4] There is even a role for the Yetzer Hara, the 'evil' inclination that may push one towards lust or jealousy. Rabbi Moshe Cordovero taught that "the yetzer Hara was created for the sake of [a person's] wife" (Tomer Devorah p.103). In other words, a person might take that inclination for physical connection, and channel it towards their spouse.

we need to complete our spiritual mission, and if we feel we are lacking something, then maybe our spiritual mission is the process of getting it or coming to terms with not getting it! The rabbis taught 'true wealth is being happy with your lot'[5], but really feeling it, thinking it and living it is an ongoing practice.

The Book of Job might be read as a meditation on non-attachment. Job is a man who loses his home, his business, his spouse and children, but maintains an overriding faith and belief.

Every aspect of yoga practice presents an opportunity for non-attachment through acceptance of the present moment and choosing what you have. This ranges from the mode of transport we use to class (how nice is your car, if you have one?), to the cost of the workshop (it cost *how much?*), to the mat you are using (what do you mean you haven't got a double-thickness organic rubber fibre yoga mat?), to the postures you are practicing (are you comfortable with your body? Can you accept your level of ability? Can you rejoice in the moment as it is?).

YOU CAN'T TAKE IT WITH YOU

The ancient world placed a great emphasis on burial customs. Egyptians, Romans, Greeks - many excavations of great civilisations have revealed that people were buried with a number of carefully chosen possessions, whether it was household idols, jewellery or a bag of coins to pay the ferryman across the river Hades in the journey to the mythological underworld. The Kabbalah presented an alternative view where an individual's soul is effectively rejoining the great Eternal Soul, and Jewish burial customs reflect this fact in the lack of fanfare. Everyone is buried in a very simple wooden casket, all of the body is wrapped in a bland garment and possibly a prayer shawl, and the whole event is an opportunity for the mourners to focus on the greater meaning of life, in which everything passes and worldly wealth is transient. The Mourner's prayer celebrates the eternity of God and solace is found in the fact that although our bodies pass away, there is a part of all of us that is eternal.

---

[5] *Ethics of the Father 4:1.*

AN INCONVENIENT TRUTH

Material riches *'cannot redeem'* someone, according to the Psalmist. Whilst money has the possibility of making life more comfortable, it does not have the inherent power to bring happiness. We see plenty of examples of wealthy people who are depressed. A highly inconvenient truth is that happiness doesn't come 'when' (I am rich/married/retired/successful/powerful etc.), but 'now' or not at all. Happiness, along with all other emotions and events, is a present-tense phenomenon. More importantly, money has no power or value for spiritual accomplishment, despite what certain institutions might have us believe. There is no sense of 'paying a ransom to God' in terms of buying ourselves an eternal life on earth. However sophisticated your private healthcare plan is, or however much money you give to charity, all of us are destined to eventually die.

'In times of trouble, why should I fear?'. The Psalmist recognised that fear and pain comes from our deep attachment to things outside oneself. Freedom comes from non-attachment. The difficulty is that as soon as we become aware of self, which may be around 8-12 months old if not sooner, we also learn words like 'mine' or 'yours'. We begin to experience a sense of lack and we find ourselves trapped in an ego-based cycle of longing and desire. Death is the great leveller as it reveals we all come into the world with no physical possessions, and cannot take them with us. What we can take with us, according to some of my teachers, is our consciousness. If we refine our way of thinking and elevate our thoughts during our lifetime, those 'riches' do remain with our soul and can be carried over to the other side and beyond.

MONEY & SPIRITUAL PERSPECTIVE

There are many teachings from Biblical and rabbinic sources that can remind us to keep money in a bigger spiritual perspective.

The laws against bribery recognise that our emotions can be directly affected by money, hence the Torah implores us to *'not take a bribe because a bribe blinds those who have sight and perverts the words of the righteous'*[6].

---
[6] Exodus 23:8.

The sages teach one of the dangers of excessive ownership, saying 'the more possessions, the more worry'[7], and as a safeguard there is the well-known notion of giving 10% of our wealth to charity[8]. We are reminded time and again not to get caught up with the transient things in life and to stay focused on our spiritual growth, remembering that we are an eternal soul with a temporary body. Our body will eventually die. If we can maintain that perspective then we have the possibility of living our life with far less pain, greater pleasure and experience truer freedom by staying connected to the deeper truth.

JUST A TRAVELLER

The legend is told about the 19th Century rabbi known as the Chofetz Chaim (whose name literally means 'keeper of life'). Some wealthy tourists visited him at home and saw that his one-room apartment was sparsely furnished with no accoutrements of wealth and a tired old sofa. "We would love to buy you some new furniture", said one of the tourists. "We will arrange it for you when we get back to the States – please accept it as our gift". The rabbi turned to him and smiled. "Thank you, but no. I have a question. Why are you only carrying one possession with you – where is your sofa and household furniture?". The baffled tourist replied, "well, I am just travelling at the moment. I don't need much – I'm not staying for that long!". The Chofetz Chaim looked him the eye. "Me too. I am also just a tourist in this world".

NON-GRASPING ON THE MAT

Our minds are used to yearning, chattering and wanting things that we do not have right now. This can be brought to the fore on the yoga mat, wanting our body to be younger, stronger, more flexible, more beautiful or a list of other desires.

---

[7] *Ethics of the Fathers* 2: 7.
[8] Equally we are not to push ourselves into hardship so that we would become a recipient of charity, and as such Maimonides prohibited that we give away more than 20% of our wealth.

One way to embody this principle is as follows: Practice a yoga pose, do your best and then let it go. Move onto the next one. Practice a third posture and then let that one go. Do not judge it. Before we accept a breath into our body, we release a breath into the world. There is no storing of spare breaths – that would be absurd. We do not have a 'breath bank'. We have what we need on a moment-by-moment basis and this is arguably the most useful substance of all: life itself. Yoga brings us into present-moment awareness, acceptance of the now and the knowledge that everything we currently see will pass away.

'Do not be afraid when a person becomes rich, when his household goods increase, for when he dies he cannot take any of it along; his goods cannot follow him down'[9]. Enjoy and accept every pose and every breath. As we release our desires and welcome the current breath, we relinquish the pain of not having and experience the ultimate wealth – the joy of life itself.

The second half of Ethics of the Yogis turn our focus to internal principles for harmonious living. These are the third part of the eightfold system of yoga, which are called the *niyamas*. They are; cleanliness/purity (*sauca*), contentment (*santosha*), austerity (*tapas*), study of the self and sacred texts (*svadhyaya*), and devotion, or living with an awareness of God (*Isvara pranidhana*). These are also described as 'spiritual disciplines'[10], and they continue to train us in practices for physical refinement, spiritual elevation and continuous awareness of God.

---

[9] Psalm 49:16-17.
[10] Light on the Yoga Sutras of Patanjali, p.30.

PURITY

ETHICS OF THE YOGIS 6: PURITY
CLEAN HANDS & PURE HEARTS

KOSHER SUTRA: 'Who may ascend the mountain of the Lord? One with clean hands and a pure heart' *Psalm 24:3-4*

YOGA SUTRA: *Sauca*/Cleanliness, *Yoga Sutras 2:40*

There is a direct connection between spiritual cleanliness and physical cleanliness. King David makes the connection in the Book of Psalms, in a chapter which is read at the end of the morning prayers every Sunday. It is not enough for us to ascend the mountain of God with 'clean hands' alone, just paying attention to our physicality, nor is it enough to focus on clean thoughts and a spiritually 'pure heart', but rather we must integrate our bodies and our souls. This takes us away from duality, seeing our body and soul as separate or in conflict, and brings us back to unity, harmony or oneness.

FREEDOM FROM DESIRES

The Yoga Sutras teach that 'cleanliness of body and mind develops disinterest in contact with others for self-gratification'[1]. Patanjali suggests

---
[1] Ibid., *Yoga Sutra 2:40*, p. 153.

that cleaning our body and our soul will bring us closer to God and remove physical desires. This is a deep level of work, keeping our body physically free from dirt and keeping our mind and emotions similarly clean. In doing so we can harness our core sexual energy, transform it into a spiritual energy and elevate our body, mind and soul. The Jewish yogi is not encouraged towards celibacy or abstinence but rather towards a continual channelling of his or her energy.

CLEAN & PURE

The Torah refers to at least two kinds of cleanliness, *naki* (physically clean) and *tahor* (spiritually pure). Cleanliness and Godliness go hand in hand. The prophet Isaiah exhorted spiritual seekers to *"Turn away, turn away from there and touch nothing unclean as you depart from there. Keep pure as you go forth, you who bear the vessels of the Lord"*[2]. There is a play on words here, as he refers to the physical vessels of the Temple, such as the Menorah, wash-basin or other ritual objects, but our bodies are also 'vessels of the Lord' as they are receptacles of our soul[3].

There is a major role for purity within marriage and *Taharat Mishpacha*, the laws of Marital Purity, define the times when a couple may and may not be physically together[4].

CLEAN FOOD

We can also consider our relationship to food, and whether the food is sufficiently 'clean' for our body and our soul. The notion of kosher food means that it is fit for consumption. The Torah has specific rules for spiritually clean animals (e.g. cows) and unclean animals (e.g. pigs), as well as methods of slaughtering that render them clean (*kosher*) or unfit (*treif*). We might extend the principles of kashrut to the following questions: Is the food we are about to eat going to be nourishing and good for us? Is our food from sustainable sources? Are the crops bathed in poisonous pesticide chemicals? Were the farm workers treated ethically? If we

---

[2] Isaiah 52:11.
[3] This is more of a Kabbalistic interpretation, alluded to in many places.
[4] E.g. a husband and wife may not touch during her period or for seven 'clean' days afterwards.

are eating meat then are we aware whether the animal was treated well during its life and given a peaceful death? This is an entire field of study and there are organisations dedicated to raising awareness and ethical standards to broaden our understanding of kashrut, like *Uri L'Tzedek* ('rise up for justice'), an organisation who give a special certification to kosher restaurants who treat their workers fairly[5].

CLEAN THOUGHTS

The Rabbis frequently teach the importance of watching our thoughts, and the Shema, Judaism's most central prayer, tells us to 'not explore after your hearts or after eyes you use to stray'[6]. The 'food' that goes into our mind also has a profound effect on the way we see, think about and relate to the world[7].

From a kabbalistic perspective, this state of mental and physical cleanliness is essential for achieving higher levels of meditative connection and ultimately, prophecy. Rabbi Aryeh Kaplan explained that 'a person has to go through the ten stages of purification mentioned in Ramchal's *Path of the Just* before becoming worthy of Divine Inspiration, *Ruach HaKodesh*, or prophecy'[8]. Indeed the original process of revelation, of receiving the teaching at Mount Sinai, was preceded by three days of cleansing and purification[9] and to this day there is a rabbinic law that states a Torah teacher should ensure their clothes are neat and clean, and not torn or stained[10].

KRIYA YOGA

Our yoga practice moves us into a state of purity and cleanliness in the three arenas of body, mind and spirit. A clean body leads to a clean

---

[5] See more about the *Tav HaYosher*, the 'Ethical Seal' at http://utzedek.org/tav-hayosher/tav-hayosher-restaurant-list/
[6] Numbers 15:39.
[7] Mr Iyengar suggests that 'as we stop watching pornography and violence and stop having nightmares and become more self-aware, then the mind is cleansed', *Light on Life*, p259.
[8] *Inner Space*, p.135.
[9] Exodus 19:14-15.
[10] Rambam, Hilchot Deot 5:9.

mind and a clean soul. *Kriyas* are yogic processes that cleanse the body and *uddiyana kriya* is performed as a rolling motion through the stomach that massages the abdominus rectus. Recommended at the start of the day because of its power to cleanse the organs in the stomach, it is a movement that purifies the digestive process by helping to strengthen the abdominal muscles and cleanse the various parts of the digestive tract.

Beginners to yoga may often sweat quite a lot as they learn postures and vinyasa, but this can eventually reduce as we replace our frenzied energy with a more calm and measured approach. Sweat is a natural form of purification as the moisture washes through our pores and yoga allows us to purify our bodies from the inside out.

The Hasidic master Rabbi Nachman of Breslov wrote about the spiritual need for physical purification: *'it is necessary to show great compassion for the body, to see to purifying it so as to be able to inform it of all the insights and perceptions which the soul perceives. This is because the soul of every human being is continuously seeing and comprehending very exalted things. But the body knows nothing of them. Therefore every person…should see to purifying the body so that the soul will be able to inform it of all that she is always seeing and comprehending'*[11]. This takes us back to the Yoga Sutras' teaching that cleaning and purifying our bodies can lead us to a great clarity, connection with God and freedom from physical desires. Rabbi Nachman takes it further, explaining how our purification will essentially lead to deeper intuition and the development of psychic powers so that we can improve our perception.

As we improve our yoga practice we become more aware of the subtle energies within our bodies and the subtle changes from day to day and moment to moment. This increases our natural vocabulary, as we approach similar postures on a regular basis and see how our bodies react differently. Our internal cleansing enables us to relate to the outer world with greater clarity, helping to keep our life in harmony and balance.

---

[11] *Likutei Moharan*, 22:5 – translation in Vol 3, Lesson 22, p240, NY: Breslov Research Insitute, 1990.

CONTENTMENT

ETHICS OF THE YOGIS 7: CONTENTMENT
GET SATISFACTION

KOSHER SUTRA: "Ben Zoma taught...Who is wealthy? The person who is happy with what they have" *Ethics of the Fathers 4:1*

YOGA SUTRA: *Santosha*/Contentment, *Yoga Sutras 2:42*

The Rabbis taught that the pinnacle of wealth is being *sameach b'chelko*, happy with what you have[1]. The Yoga Sutras conveys a similar principle with *santosha*, contentment, saying that 'from contentment and benevolence of consciousness comes supreme happiness'[2]. We are currently at a point in history when the business of marketing is an art and science that perpetually seeks to destabilise people's happiness in order to sell them products, to make us feel a yearning for that which we do not have, telling us that the only path to joy is to spend money and buy things. Vast amounts of money are spent researching our preferences and the psychology and emotions of effectively selling to us. The practice of being content is more essential

---
[1] *Ethics of the Fathers 4:1.*
[2] *Yoga Sutras 2:42., Light on the Yoga Sutras..p.155.*

than ever before. Contentment is a rabbinic practice, a yogic practice and arguably the most reliable pathway to true inner wealth.

Humans naturally gravitate towards pleasure and away from pain. Freud called it the 'pleasure principle', describing how we have a natural tendency to take the shortest route to a pleasurable outcome[3]. Although there is a certain level of physical luxury that may bring more happiness, the path to joy can ultimately only be an internal route. If a couple are desperately unhappy and yearning for a child but have $50 million in the bank, are they truly wealthier than a family with four children who are living month-to-month but have a house full of love and laughter? The rabbis and yogic sages teach us that inner contentment precedes external luxury and is ultimately the only true wealth we have.

Who is wealthy? The person who is happy with what they have. This can be easy to say, but hard to put into practice if our minds are thinking of everything we do not have. Ben Zoma's prescription locates happiness within ourselves. True contentment can never be reached through an external source. No amount of possessions can give us deep-seated, everlasting joy. Happiness which depends on an external source is ultimately very fragile and liable to be overturned when the circumstances change.

Rabbi Moshe Chaim Luzzato (17th century) taught that the only reliable external source of joy is God, saying that humans were 'created for the sole purpose of rejoicing in God and deriving pleasure from the splendour of His Presence; for this is the true joy and the greatest pleasure that can be found'[4]. Maimonides suggested that contemplating these wonders of creation is are a sure-fire method for transforming our mood into a state of joy. He wrote that when we stop and reflect upon everything that is around us, really engage with it and notice what is there, this process can lead us into a state of gratitude and awe.

Often we do not help ourselves. Parents unwittingly instil messages of discontent into children, confusing messages of ambition with

---

[3] On Metapsychology - The Theory of Psychoanalysis: "Beyond the Pleasure Principle", "Ego and Id" and Other Works (Penguin Freud Library, London, June 1991).
[4] The Path of the Upright, *Messilat Yesharim*, Chapter 1.

happiness, e.g. 'You will be happy when you have a big house, a great career and build a life for yourself' rather than 'be happy now..and also aim for these goals'. Proverbs states that 'a lover of money will never be satisfied with money'[5]. However exciting the new toy/computer/car/boat/house, our initial enthusiasm always wears off and the ego eventually rears its head and asks "nu? So what's next? This model is already outdated…". It is an effective parent who turns to their child and says "work hard but be happy with where you are at. Thank the Universe every day. The greatest riches in the world are feeling happy right now". This does not mean avoiding ambition or striving to improve conditions for ourselves and our family, but when we can let go of the need for those desires to be fulfilled, we automatically experience rewards.

A lack of happiness can lead to illness. This is another discussion, exploring how blame, complaining, regretfulness and unresolved anger can cause major illnesses like cancer[6]. The Book of Proverbs teaches that 'a joyful heart makes for good health and despondency dries up the bones'[7]. The healing qualities of a contented lifestyle can keep our heart light and body healthy.

YOGA & MEDITATION PRACTICE

The practice is being happy and content. Finding reasons to be happy and content. On the yoga mat this can look like striving for an asana, doing the best we can to reach a posture or maintain our stamina during a practice, but being content with whatever we achieve. There is a continual tension between working at our yoga practice and not becoming frustrated if our ability fails to meet expectations. The possibility for happiness lies inside us. This moment is absolutely perfect..until we say it isn't.

---

[5] *Ecclesiastes 5:9.*
[6] See Brandon Bayes' book *The Journey* or Caroline Myss' *Why People Don't Heal*
[7] *Proverbs 17:22.*

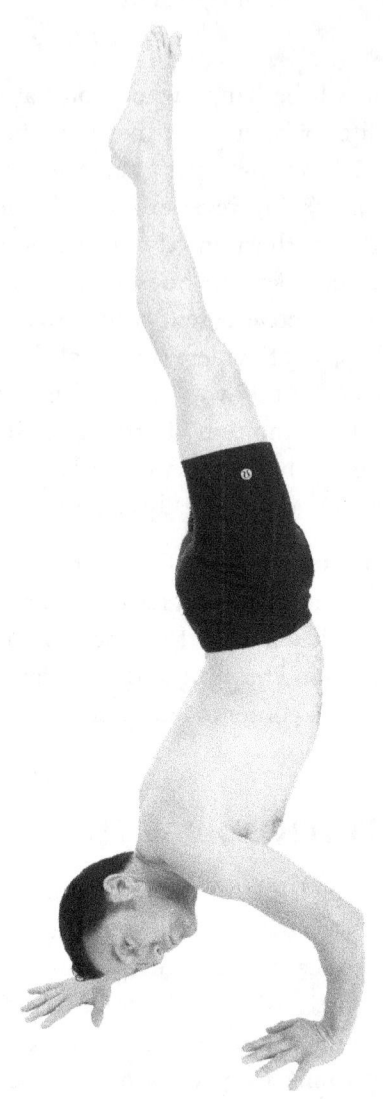

SUPREME

'A continual fire shall you keep burning on the altar'

LEVITICUS 6:6

DISCIPLINE

ETHICS OF THE YOGIS 8: DISCIPLINE
BURNING DESIRE

KOSHER SUTRA: 'A continual fire shall remain burning on the altar; you shall not extinguish it' *Leviticus 6:6*

YOGA SUTRA: *Tapas*/Sacrifice/Austerity, *Yoga Sutras 2:43*

Most ancient religions had their fire rituals and almost everyone still lights candles as part of a ceremonial practice. The core element of fire is essential to human survival for light, heat, cooking and healing. *Tapas* is the yogic quality of discipline, sacrifice or austerity. Similar to the sefirah[1] of *Gevurah* (discipline, strength, focus), tapas can be applied directly to our yoga practice as it represents inner focus, inner fire and inner discipline.

Patanjali wrote that 'through the intensity of self-discipline and purification comes the dwindling of all impurities and the perfection of the body and senses'[2]. Another translation reads that 'Self-discipline (*tapas*) burns away impurities and kindles the sparks of divinity'[3]. Tapas is an

---
[1] Divine sphere in the Kabbalistic Tree of Life system.
[2] *Yoga Sutras 2:43*.
[3] *Light on the Yoga Sutras of Patanjali*, p156.

important principle in our yoga practice to use our inner fire as we burn away negativity and cultivate a burning desire for that which we want to achieve. It is a heat arising within and a self-discipline that can spur us towards our goal.

The idea of sacrifice is deeply powerful even though it may sound antiquated and anachronistic and irrelevant to modern life. Jews stopped sacrificing animals when the Temple in Jerusalem was destroyed over 2000 years ago. Nevertheless the principle of a sacrifice lives on. The Hebrew word for sacrifice, *korban*, means 'bringing close' as by intentionally giving up something precious (e.g. our money, time, energy), we can feel a nearness to God.

Most of the ancient Jewish sacrificial ceremonies would involve an element of fire, usually to cook the offering. Fire can be used as a means of purification and transformation: cooking and heating food so that it is safe to eat, transforming wood into heat energy that will keep us warm, creating tools to farm crops or weapons to defend our communities, or even to turn raw metals into jewellery that will make us feel beautiful.

A samurai sword must be heated and cooled many times, tempering the steel for battle. The weapon gets stronger by going through the fire, and when we look back over difficult or heated times in our life, we too can see how many of those 'hotter' challenges strengthen us. One skill is to recognise that we are being strengthened during a difficult time.

INNER FIRES & BURNING THROUGH THE CHALLENGE

The yogis talked about the internal fires that arise through yoga practice and many people experience heat within their body when involved with a vigorous practice or a hard class. One of my teachers described the 'inner fires' and there are many yogis who will not drink water during their practice lest they extinguish these fires and cool the body. These inner fires can be likened to a sacrificial process as they burn away at our ego and the parts of us that would rather avoid doing the physical and meditation work. Those moments when we would like to relax, take it easy and not have to deal with holding a pose for a few more seconds are exactly when the inner firepower can take over. This internal heat takes on a motion of its own and can help us to 'burn through' challenging postures.

PERSONAL GOALS

Tapas may be seen as a firepower that helps us to achieve our goals. Mr Iyengar taught it was a complementary balance to *ahimsa*, non-violence. We can take the inner violent energy and channel it towards a positive goal. He gave the example that 'Mahatma Gandhi would never have been able to summon up the implacable peacefulness which moved an empire, without his ruthless attitude toward his own self'[4]. We too can take our fire and direct it like a laser.

SACRIFICIAL FIRE

When the children of Israel left Egypt they were commanded to slaughter a sheep, and 'eat meat that same night, making [it] ready over a fire'[5]:

> *'You will find that when the Children of Israel were in Egypt, they served idols, which they were reluctant to abandon, for it says: They did not every man cast away the detestable things of their eyes (Ezekiel 20:8). God then said to Moses; "As long as Israel worship Egyptian gods they will not be redeemed; go and tell them to abandon their evil ways and reject idolatry". This is what is meant by: "draw out and take yourselves lambs"' [for the Passover sacrifice]*(Exodus 12:21).

---

[4] "Ahimsa cannot be properly understood without reference to tapas. Tapas is the inner *himsa* (violence) by which we create the possibility of the outer ahimsa. Ahimsa cannot exist alone. A complementary force must necessarily exist. Mahatma Gandhi would never have been able to summon up the implacable peacefulness which moved an empire, without his ruthless attitude toward his own self. Violence is perhaps too strong a word for *tapas*, but it is a burning inner zeal and austerity, a sort of unflagging hardness of attitude towards oneself which makes possible compassion and forgiveness towards others", Light on the Yoga Sutras of Patanjali, pp155-156.

[5] Exodus 12:8.

That is to say: '*Draw away your hands from idolatry and take for yourselves lambs, thereby slaying the gods of Egypt and preparing the Passover; only through this will the Lord pass over you*'[6].

In other words, burn away the ego. 'False gods' are the things that we put in a place of great importance but ultimately cause us pain and discomfort. This is the essence of God – the ultimate truth that all is one. The way we are able to deny god, to create unhappiness and cause 'blockages' in the spiritual flow is through false gods that we set up. If we keep the fires burning on a continual basis, we can gradually move ourselves towards a place of clarity and oneness.

Keeping the fires burning isn't easy to do at first. Our egos will present all kinds of resistance to a regular disciplined yoga practice, just as they will distract us from keeping a hastily-made New Year's resolution. As the adage goes, we might do 'little and often'. 10 minutes' yoga every day is better than 60 minutes once a week, because our body learns, grows and develops as a result of regular discipline and practice. This produces results on a physical and emotional level, our body becomes strengthened and our mind becomes more prepared for reducing the turbulence of daily living.

---

[6] Midrash: precise source unknown.

STUDY

ETHICS OF THE YOGIS 9: STUDY
BURN THE EGO

KOSHER SUTRA: 'Spiritual study[1] is equivalent to everything' *Mishna Peah 3:4*

YOGA SUTRA: *Svadhayaya*/Self-Study, *Yoga Sutras 2:44*

Accept a teacher for yourself', taught Rabbi Yehoshua ben Perachyah[2]. The Hebrew phrase *Oseh Lecha Rav* is also translated as 'make a rabbi for yourself' or something similar. In our context of embodied spirituality we might also translate it as 'make yourself your teacher' (*aseh* - make *lecha* - (to) yourself *rav* - teacher). In other words, how can we use our own bodies to teach us?

The Sanskrit word *svadhyayat* means 'by study which leads to the knowledge of the Self, Self-study or reading the scriptures'[3]. Yoga Sutra 2:44 outlines the penultimate principle of the *niyamas* (yogic spiritual

---

[1] The original hebrew for this is the word *Torah* which can be translated as 'the instruction'. I have used a more free translation in this context for spiritual study, which although not normative is still faithful to the root of the word.
[2] *Ethics of the Fathers 1:6*, translation from Artscroll Siddur p547.
[3] Yoga Sutra 2:44. Iyengar translation, *Light on the Yoga Sutras*.p156.

disciplines), explaining that 'through study of spiritual books comes communion with one's chosen deity'[4].

There is some freedom of interpretation, but whether it is the study of scriptural books, study of self or study of others, the intention is that we find communion and unity with God. This is not an academic discipline for the sake of advancing knowledge without action. Rather it is study that leads to action. The final Sanskrit word in the sutra, *samprayogah*, means 'union' or 'coming into contact with the Divine'[5]. Here we very clearly see the word yoga in connection with God (so..any class that promises to teach 'yoga without spirituality' is not technically practicing yoga...).

The yogis and the rabbis place a high value on spiritual study. *Talmud Torah K'neged Kulam*, "studying Torah [or spiritual study] is the equivalent to everything"[6]. More than just stimulating the mind on an academic level, the aim of Torah study is to be transformative. Nowadays there is something of a cult of learning for intellectual prowess, almost for the sake of gathering information rather than focusing on transforming it into practical effect. The Talmud extols the virtue of learning *Torah lishma* - Torah for its own sake - but unless we become better people then it is purely an exercise for the mind. In 1998 a *Beit Midrash* study hall was being opened in North London and then Chief Rabbi Lord Jonathan Sacks said that if people left the room after Torah learning and were not inspired to do something to improve the world around them, then the exercise had failed to improve its potential[7].

There is another approach for people who do not enjoy the process of reading and studying with books. Many schools of yoga purely teach *asana* and *vinyasa*, the postures and flowing movement sequences, and yogic writings do suggest that this in itself is a complete and valid path to reaching God. Like the Roman soldier who was said to have 'merited

---

[4] Swami Satchidananda translation.
[5] Ibid.
[6] *Mishnah Peah* 3:4.
[7] Talk given at the Beit Midrash study hall that was opened at the London School of Jewish Studies (formerly known as Jews' College London) in Hendon, London, 1998.

the World to Come in a single moment'[8] because his actions were so open-hearted and spiritually aligned, there is every reason to suggest that perfecting yoga postures in their correct alignment will lead to this result[9].

BODY AS A TORAH SCROLL

It is sometimes taught that every Jew is a *Sefer Torah*, a Torah scroll, so studying oneself and one's actions *is* a form of studying the Torah. This being said it is essential that almost everyone[10] studies under a teacher and learns from a tradition, but the focus of this chapter is on self-study.

LEARNING FROM THE ENTIRE BODY

The sages asked, 'who is wise? The person who learns from everyone'[11] The Hebrew phrase for 'everyone', *MiKol Adam*, can also be interpreted as 'from the entire person', in other words, the wise person can learn from their entire body. How might we do this? There are many ways to observe our reactions to events so we can learn from our emotions. We can watch and learn how our bodies respond to different foods (e.g. Coffee and sugar may promote anxiety or raise the pulse). We can look at our emotional responses, become aware of our interactions with other people, be conscious of where we would like to refine our personalities. Other forms of biological self-study will reveal our state of physical and emotional health. These might include: studying our breath, our pulse, or eye colour (iridology), or body's output (e.g. urine, which will say if we are dehydrated) and many more physical clues or biomarkers.

---

[8] The midrash about the Ten Martyrs recounts the execution of Rabbi Chanina ben Teradion, whose executioner helped him and promptly threw himself into the fire, and 'a divine voice exclaimed' that both of them 'have been assigned to life in the world to come'. Quoted in The Book of Legends, *Sefer Ha-Aggadah*, p240.
[9] The majority of contemporary Iyengar yoga studios will focus purely on alignment rather than going into yoga philosophy.
[10] There are some people who are enlightened and reincarnate fully conscious, so they possibly will not need a teacher. Though in the case of Moses, he learned directly from God.
[11] *Ethics of the Fathers 4:1.*

SELF STUDY ON A YOGA MAT

On a yoga mat we can see our attitude towards poses, where we are seeking shortcuts, or how our bodies behave under certain conditions. Our bodies are another 'text' in this sense, here to teach us along the way.

Self-study can be a spiritual discipline as a source for cultivation, learning and refinement. Our physical bodies can be the ultimate teachers, for this lifetime at least.

SURRENDER

ETHICS OF THE YOGIS 10: SURRENDER & TRIUMPH

KOSHER SUTRA: 'Surrender, cast your burden on God and He will sustain you (He will never let a righteous person collapse)' *Psalms 55:23*

YOGA SUTRA: *Isvara pranidhana*/Surrender/Devotion to God, *Yoga Sutras 2:45*

The final principle of Ethics of the Yogis is surrender. The Yoga Sutras refers to *Isvara pranidhana*, complete surrender to God that will lead to joy and peace. King David referred to *Hashlech*, or casting oneself forth as a process of letting go. The rabbis also spoke of *Bitachon*, a trust in God that leads to liberation because we know that above everything there is a greater power that will protect us.

Samadhi, enlightenment or ultimate bliss, is the eighth and final rung on the eightfold path of Ashtanga yoga. Here are four translations of this sutra:

ETHICS OF THE YOGIS

'By total surrender to God (Isvarapranidhama), enlightenment and joy is attained'[1]

'From devotion to the Supreme Being comes the attainment of Samadhi'[2]

'From devotion to the Lord, one is given perfect absorption into Spirit'[3]

'Surrender to God brings perfection in Samadhi'[4]

The Baal Shem Tov, the founder of the modern mystical Chassidic and Kabbalistic devotional movements, was fond of the phrase *Shiviti Hashem L'Negdi Tamid* which we have explored earlier, 'I will keep God before me at all times' or 'I will continually remain conscious of Hashem' or 'I will perpetually stay aware of The Divine'. I could continue to re-translate this but there is only one question that matters here.

When all is said and done, can we stay conscious of God? Can we keep this consciousness of Hashem at all times, that we are all connected and that all is one? As the Alter Rebbe taught, can we unify our thoughts, speech and actions?[5] (As a reminder, yoga means 'unify' so we can consider our yoga practice as a practical application of the Alter Rebbe's teaching).

'Do not rely on nobles, nor on a human being, for he holds no salvation. When his breath departs he returns to the earth. On that day his plans all perish'[6].

---

[1] Yoga Sutras 2:45
[2] *Ashtanga Yoga - Practice & Philosophy*, by Gregor Maehle, p225.
[3] *Yoga Sutras of Patanjali - As interpreted by Mukunda Stiles*, p28.
[4] *Light on the Yoga Sutras of Patanjali*, p.157.
[5] Discussed by Rabbi Shneur Zalman of Liadi, the *Alter Rebbe*, in *Sefer Tanya* (See the beginning of Chapter 4. Lessons in Tanya, Vol 2, p74).
[6] Psalms 146: 3-4

The Kosher Sutras trilogy is now complete.

May our hearts be uplifted

May our bodies be healed

May our minds be enlightened

May our souls be elevated

May our spirituality be strengthened

NEXT YEAR IN JERUSALEM!

לְשָׁנָה הַבָּאָה בִּירוּשָׁלָיִם

APPENDIX 1: IS YOGA KOSHER?

A major concern brought by Jewish practitioners of yoga is the question of how the practice fits in with halacha, Jewish law. This is a much broader study that is far beyond the scope of the book but I would like to mention some of the issues as these questions are raised with some frequency, especially within Orthodox circles.

IS YOGA KOSHER?

There are many answers to this question and the first question is to define yoga. My teacher Edward Clark wrote that 'the idea behind yoga is one of unity: the search for oneness, or *eka grata*'[1]. This definition, which aligns with that of the Yoga Sutras, is completely attuned with the Jewish pursuit of oneness as mentioned in the *Shema* prayer, that all is One, or Echad.

On the other hand, when yoga is practiced in front of statues of various deities, this can create unease for a Jewish practitioner. One might argue the *halacha* both ways, namely, that it is forbidden or *ossur* to prostrate oneself in front of an idol, based on the commandment *'Thou shalt have no other gods before me. Thou shalt not make a graven image..*[2]. There are further counter-arguments: from a Hindu perspective the statues are all representative of one singular God, or from a Buddhist perspective the Buddha statues represent more of an idea rather than something to which you are praying.

IDOLS & STATUES

My personal preference is to avoid the situation of being in front of an idol. Whenever I was attending a class in a yoga studio where there were statues I would be careful not to place my mat directly in front of them. If I was teaching a workshop in a studio then I would take blankets and cover them up - I could have followed Abraham's Biblical example

---

[1] 'Welcome to Tripsichore Yoga' essay, in the *Tripsichore Yoga DVD*, '*Uniquely Advanced Vinyasa*' with Edward Clark, by Pranamaya Inc, 2006.
[2] Exodus 20:2-3

of smashing all the idols but in this context it did not seem so polite, especially if I wanted to get invited back.

FURTHER READING

I have included a longer essay on the topic of why yoga is kosher at the start of my book *The Kosher Sutras*, and my suggestion for the concerned practitioner would be to consult your local Orthodox rabbi. Soon after I began practicing yoga, I took advice from my teacher Rabbi Dr Dovid Ebner[3], with whom I studied at Yeshivat HaMivtar back in the '90s, and Rabbi Ebner gave me the encouragement to start offering my own interpretations of yogic-based Torah teachings.

---

[3] Rabbi Ebner is the *Rosh Yeshiva* and *Mashgiach Ruchani* at Yeshivat Eretz HaTzvi in Jerusalem.

APPENDIX 2:
HALACHA, SHABBAT & EXERCISE

CAN I DO EXERCISE ON SHABBAT?

Shabbat observance is a kind of mindful practice that includes the avoidance of *melacha*, which are the 39 categories of work that were associated with the Temple in Jerusalem. Some of the issues involved with exercising on Shabbat are that we can cause the body to sweat, and the Shulchan Aruch[4] forbids exercise for this reason[5].

HALACHIC SOURCES

As yet I have been unable to find any rabbinic responsa that specifically discuss yoga on shabbat, and the closest sources relate to jogging. Rabbi Howard Jachter wrote that "*The Mishna Berura (328:130) explains that this is part of the rabbinical decree forbidding the taking of medicine on Shabbat. The Mishna Berura (301:7) forbids jogging on Shabbat for this reason. He even cites authorities that forbid one from taking walks on Shabbat if the intention is to stay healthy and the walk is not merely for pleasure. "Speed walking" for exercise is undoubtedly forbidden on Shabbat. Rav David Zvi Hoffman (Teshuvot Melamed L'Hoil 1:53), Rav Eliezer Waldenberg (Teshuvot Tzitz Eliezer 6:4), and Rav Gedalia Felder (Yesodei Yeshurun 4:297-299) forbid exercising on Shabbat based on this Halacha*"[6].

This approach would be further supported by the prophet Isaiah who said 'restrain your foot on shabbat'[7], and the corresponding Talmud that says 'your walking on Shabbat should not be like your walking during the week'[8], however the Rema taught that one may walk leisurely on shabbat

---

[4] O.C 328:42
[5] Quoted in http://www.koltorah.org/ravj/medicONshabbat2.htm by Rabbi Howard Jachter.
[6] Ibid.
[7] Isaiah 58:13.
[8] Babylonian Talmud, Shabbat 113b.

APPENDIX

if that is part of their enjoyment, the *Oneg Shabbes*[9]. This, however, is a legal disagreement, a *machloket*, and the Elya Rabbah argues that such a walk is forbidden[10]. The Magen Avraham[11] says that you can walk for health reasons on shabbat, and *halacha* (Jewish law) follows this opinion. We could reasonably argue that all yoga is for health reasons, for the mind, body and soul.

EXERCISE OR PRAYER?

One of the key questions around practicing yoga on Shabbat is whether your intention is to do it for exercise or for prayer. There are various halachic prohibitions against exercise[12], for example, "One should not, as a rule, perform physical exercises on Shabbath or Yom Tov"[13], "One is not allowed to swim"[14], and "One may not do strenuous physical exercise on Shabbath"[15]. From a halachic standpoint we might argue that as yoga is not being done for exercise but rather for connection with God, and the exercise benefits are a *p'sik reisha* (an unintended outcome), the laws of prohibited exercise do not apply.

My teacher Rabbi Dovid Ebner said that on the basis you accept yoga is allowed [from a Jewish standpoint], it is fine to practice on Shabbat[16].

DANCE

There are various other permitted forms of movement on Shabbat, and many synagogues today will include people who are dancing during prayers and breaking a sweat, so the previous issue seems more about whether you are exercising rather than sweating.

---

[9] The Rema, Rabbi Moshe Isserles, lived in Poland 1525-1572. This was written in his glosses to *Orach Haim 301*, quoted in 'Running on Shabbat', dailyhalacha.com.
[10] The Elya Rabbah was Rabbi Eliyahu Shapiro of Prague, 1660-1712, quoted ibid.
[11] The Magen Avraham was Rabbi Abraham Gombiner who lived in Poland, 1637-1683, quoted ibid.
[12] Shemirath Shabbath Kehilchathah, 14:38, 16:39 & 34:22
[13] Ibid., 14:38
[14] Ibid., 16:38.a.
[15] Ibid., 34:22
[16] Rabbi Ebner mentioned Rabbi Shlomo Zalman Auerbach, who warned against excessive exercise on shabbat that might lead one to sweat.

APPENDIX 2

YOGA AS PRAYER

I approach yoga as a form of fully-integrated embodied prayer. The intention is in keeping with the original intention of yoga, namely to unite our spirit with God. From a halachic perspective we might argue that the exercise benefits are a by-product that happen as a result of the action, a *psik reisha*. For our purposes, however, **yoga is both kosher and permissible on shabbat**. Phew. Now, go and practice.

APPENDIX

BIBLIOGRAPHY

JEWISH

Bialik, Hayim Nahman and Ravnitzky, Yehoshua Hana (Editors), *The Book of Legends: Sefer Ha-Haggadah. Legends from the Talmud and Midrash*, Translated by William G. Braude, New York: Shockhen Books: 1992. Originally published in Hebrew in Odessa, 1908-1911.

Blackman, Phillip (commentary & translation) *Mishnayoth, Vol II, Order Moed*. Judaica Press: Gateshead, 1990.

Caro, Rav Yosef, *Shulchan Aruch*, 1565.

Cordovero, Rabbi Moshe, *The Palm Tree of Devorah/Tomer Devorah* translated by Rabbi Moshe Miller. New York: Targum/Feldheim, 1994.

Hashem, *JPS Hebrew-English Tanach*. The Jewish Publication Society: Philadelphia, 1999.

Kaplan, Rabbi Aryeh, *Inner Space - Introduction to Kabbalah, Meditation and Prophecy*. Edited by Abraham Sutton. Jerusalem: Moznaim, 1990.

Kaplan, Rabbi Aryeh, *Meditation and Kabbalah*. New York: Weiser Books, 1989.

Kaplan, Rabbi Aryeh, *Sefer Yetzirah*, translation and commentary. San Francisco: Weiser Books 1997.

KiTov, Rabbi Eliyahu, *The Book of Our Heritage, Vol III*. Feldheim: NY, 1978.

Luzzato, Rabbi Moshe Chaim (Author), Kaplan, Rabbi Moshe M. (Translator), *Path of the Upright (Mesillat Yesharim)*. JPS: 2010.

Melton, *FMAMS Teacher's Guide for 'Rhythms of Jewish Living'*. Jerusalem: 2002.

Neuwirth, Rav Yehoshua Y., Shemirath Shabbath - *A guide the practical observance of Shabbath*. Feldheim Publishers, New York: 1989.

Patai, Raphael, *Man and Temple: In Ancient Jewish Myth and Ritual*. New York: Ktav 1967.

Sacks, Rabbi Jonathan, *To Heal A Fractured World*. Shocken: London, 2007.

Sacks, Rabbi Jonathan, *The Jonathan Sacks Haggada*. Maggid Books, Koren Publishers: Jerusalem, 2013.

Stern, Rabbi Yosef, *Days of Our Joy: Sfas Emes*, Artscroll Mesorah: New York: 1995.

Sherman, Rabbi Nosson, *The Complete Artscroll Siddur - Yom Kippur*, translation and anthologised commentary. Mesorah Publications: NY 1984.

Sherman, Rabbi Nosson, *The Complete Artscroll Machzor - Rosh Hashanah*, translation and anthologised commentary. Mesorah Publications: New York, 1985.

Weinberg, Rabbi Matis, *Patterns in Time, Vol 1: Rosh Hashannah*. Feldheim: 1988.

YOGISH

Akers, Brian Dana (trans.) *Hatha Yoga Pradipika*. Woodstock: Yogavidya.com, 2002.

Bays, Brandon, *The Journey: A Practical Guide to Healing Your Life and Setting Yourself Free*. Atria Books: 2001

Chia, Mantak, *Taoist Secrets of Love: Cultivating Male Sexual Energy*. Aurora Press: 1984.

BIBLIOGRAPHY

Coulter, David H., *Anatomy of Hatha Yoga – A Manual for Students, Teachers, and Practitioners*. Motilal Banarsidass: Delhi, 2001

Eliade, Merce, *Yoga: Immortality and Freedom*, (Mythos: the Princeton/Bollingen Series in World Mythology), Willard R. Trask (Translator), David Gordon White (Introduction). Princeton University Press, 2009.

Ferris, Tim, *The 4-Hour Work Week: Escape the 9-5, Live Anywhere and Join the New Rich*. Ebury Press: 2011.

Feuerstein, Georg, *The Deeper Dimension of Yoga: Theory and Practice*. Shambhala Publications: 2011.

Freud, Sigmund, *Beyond The Pleasure Principle (1922)*. Kessinger Publishing: 2010.

Freud, Sigmund, *On Metapsychology - The Theory of Psychoanalysis: "Beyond the Pleasure Principle", "Ego and Id" and Other Works*. Penguin Freud Library: London, 1991.

Fromm, Eric, *The Forgotten Language: An Introduction to the Understanding of Dreams, Fairy Tales, and Myths*. Grove Press: NY, 1951.

Kripalani, Krishna (compiled by), *Gandhi's Life in his own words - My Life is my message*. Navajivan Trust, India, 1983

Iyengar, BKS, *Light on Life: The yoga journey to wholeness, inner peace, and ultimate freedom*. Emmaus, Pa.: Rodale, 2005.

Iyengar, BKS, *Light on Yoga*. New York, Schocken: 1995.

Jois, Sri K Pattahabi, *Yoga Mala*. New York: North Point Press, 2002.

Maehle, Gregor, *Ashtanga Yoga - Practice & Philosophy*. New World Library: February 2011.

Myss, Caroline, *Anatomy of the Spirit: The Seven Stages of Power and Healing*. Harmony: 1996.

Myss, Caroline, *Why People Don't Heal & How They Can*. Three Rivers Press: 1997.

Scott, John, *Ashtanga Yoga: The Essential Step-By-Step Guide to Dynamic Yoga*. Stroud: Gaia, 2000.

Stiles, Mukunda (translation), *Yoga Sutras of Patanjali*. Boston: Weiser Books, 2002.

GLOSSARY

HEBREW

Alef
First letter of the Hebrew alphabet. Kabbalistically, the letter *Alef* contains the secrets of Creation.

Amidah
The standing prayer that is said three times every weekday, and in different formats on the Sabbath and Festivals. Also known as the *Shemonei Esrei* ('Eighteen Blessings', it actually contains nineteen blessings).

Avodah Zarah
Idol Worship, a Biblical prohibition.

Bet
The second letter of the Hebrew alphabet.

Binah
Understanding. Also, of the upper *sefirot*, or energetic qualities of God that reside within the body.

Daat
Knowledge.

Ein Sof
'Without end', a Kabbalistic term and name for God that refers to His vastness and endlessness.

Gevurah
Strength or discipline. The *sefira* that is associated with the left arm.

Halacha
Jewish Religious law. The root, *holech*, means 'walking'.

Hanukkah
or *Chanukah*. The festival of lights, commemorating the rededication of the Holy Temple in Jerusalem at the time of the Maccabean revolt in the 2nd Century BCE.

Hesed
Lovingkindness, or giving. Also the *sefira* that is associated with the right shoulder and arm.

Hochma
Wisdom. One of the upper *sefirot*.

Hod	Humility or Glory. The *sefira* which is associated with the left leg.
Kabbalah	The Jewish mystical tradition. *Kabbalah* means 'receive'.
Keter	Crown: one of the upper sefirot, that resides on the top of the head.
Ketuvim	Writings. The third and final part of the Biblical canon that includes Psalms, Proverbs, Ecclesiastes and the Megillot (Esther, Ruth etc).
Ma'ariv	The evening prayer service.
Malchut	Kingship (from *Melech*, King). The sefira which is connected to the hands, feet, mouth and womanhood.
Midrash	Rabbinic commentaries, often told in the form of stories.
Minha	The afternoon prayer service.
Mishna	The oral law. Redacted by Rabbi Yehuda HaNassi c.220 CE. The mishna is written in short, memorable sentences, similar to sutras.
Netzach	Endurance. The sefira which is connected to the right leg.
Nevi'im	Prophets (singular: *Navi*). The section of the Bible which contains the major prophetic writings including the Books of Joshua, Kings, Isaiah, Jeremiah and the 12 'minor' prophets.
Or Ein Sof	A kabbalistic term to describe the endless light of the creator (*Or* – light, *Ein* – without, *Sof* – end).
Pesah	The festival of Passover, commemorating the exodus from Egypt.
Pirkei Avot	Ethics of the Fathers, a tractate of the Mishna that contains moral and ethical precepts.

GLOSSARY

Purim	The Festival of Lots that remembers the survival of the Jewish people through the earthly actions of Queen Esther, Mordechai.
Rabbi	Teacher or religious leader.
Rabbi Akiva	Rabbi Akiva ben Joseph (c.40–c.137 CE) was the leader of the generation. He is considered one of the major founders of rabbinical Judaism, and was eventually martyred by the Romans.
Rabbi Shimon Bar Yochai	The first century sage who is attributed with authoring *The Zohar*, the major work of Kabbalah. Also known by his acronym, Rashbi.
Rabbi Shimon Ben Gamliel	The leader of the generation (c.10 BCE – 70 CE) and head of the Sanhedrin (court), just prior to the destruction of the Second Temple. He was martyred by the Romans.
Rav	Alternative term for Rabbi.
Rosh Hashannah	The Jewish New Year festival that occurs at the 'head' of the year (*Rosh* - head) (*Hashannah* – the year).
Sefira	The mystical qualities of God that are manifested throughout creation, including within the body.
Sefirat HaOmer	The 49-day period between the festivals of *Pesach*/Passover and *Shavuot*/Pentecost. Originally an agricultural process, it was later revealed to contain Kabbalistic qualities that lead people from the state of impurity to liberation.
Shaharit	The morning prayer service.
Shavuot	The festival of Pentecost, during which the first fruits of the year's crops were brought to the Temple as offerings.
Shema	The most important Jewish prayer. *Shema* means 'Hear' or 'Actively Listen'.

SANSKRIT

Ahimsa Non-harming or non-violence, one of the moral disciplines (*yamas*).

Asana A physical yoga posture (lit. 'seat'). The third limb of Patanjali's eightfold path.

Ashtanga The eightfold or eight-limbed (*ashto*, eight) (*anga*, limb) path of yoga described by Patanjali in the *Yoga Sutras*.

Ashtanga Vinyasa Yoga The form of yoga developed by Sri K. Patthabi Jois which has become the basis of 'flow' and 'power yoga'.

Bikram Yoga Bikram Choudry's yoga system consisting of a fixed sequence of 26 asanas, performed in a room that is heated to 95-100 degrees.

Niyama The self-restraint aspects of Patanjali's eightfold path which includes purity/cleanliness (*saucha*), contentment (*santosha*), austerity/heat (*tapas*), study (*svadhyaya*) and surrender to God (*Isvara pranidhana*)

Dharana Inward-focused meditation and concentration. The sixth limb of Patanjali's eightfold path in the *Yoga Sutras*.

Dhyana Outward-focused meditation, the seventh limb of Patanjali's eightfold path.

Hatha Yoga The most prominent branch of yoga practised in the West, that is centred around physical postures (*asana*), breath control (*pranayama*) and focused on physical transformation.

Iyengar Yoga The system of yoga based on the teachings of B.K.S. Iyengar, which are primarily focused on strengthening and healing the body through improving alignment.

GLOSSARY

Kirtan	Call-and-response form of yogic chanting.
Kosha	The five 'envelopes' or 'energetic sheaths' that make up our physical, energetic, mental, psychic and spiritual bodies.
Kundalini	The spiritual energy or serpent power that must be awakened through the central column of the body.
Kundalini Yoga	A form of yoga that focuses on using the kundalini energy as a path to freedom.
Om	In yogic and Hindu teachings, Om or Aum is the sound which symbolises Absolute Reality.
Prana	Life force or breath that sustains our body.
Pranayama	The practice of breath control, and the fourth limb of Patanjali's eightfold path.
Satya	Truth or truthfulness. An aspect of moral discipline (*yama*).
Sivananda Yoga	A form of Hatha Yoga based on the teachings of Swami Sivananda.
Samadhi	The ecstatic, unified state of enlightenment and self-realisation. The culmination of Patanjali's eightfold path.
Sutra	A short phrase or aphorism in Sanskrit literature. Famous collections include the *Karma Sutra* and the *Yoga Sutras*. A Kosher Sutra is a Biblical phrase or verse that is used within the Bibliyoga context.
Vinyasa	A flow of yoga postures that are connected with steady breath, as with a Sun Salutation.

Yama	The moral aspects described in the *Yoga Sutras*, that form the first limb of Patanjali's eightfold path. They consist of non-violence (*ahimsa*), truthfulness (*satya*), non-stealing (*asteya*), abstinence or restraint of sexual energy (*brahmacharya*) and absence of greed or jealousy (*aparigraha*).
Yoga	Union or discipline. The path to achieve inner freedom, self-realisation and connection with God.

BOOK CLUB QUESTIONS

Here are some discussion questions for your book club.

1. Choose an essay from one festival in The Festive Sutras section and meditate on its teachings. Which idea has the most resonance for you? Why? If you had to take the idea further, what questions would you ask about this festival? (As we were taught in yeshiva - seminary - 'a great question is better than a good answer').

2. The Shabbat Sutras explores physical metaphors for connecting with the Sabbath. After you read this section, how can you take these concepts into your daily life? The daily prayers name each day after Shabbat, i.e. Sunday is referred to as 'the first day of Shabbat', Monday is 'the second day of Shabbat' and so forth. How else can you expand this practice so that you can experience a sense of calm and grounding throughout your week?

3. Ethics of the Yogis introduces a conversation between a well-known section of the Oral Torah, The Ethics of the Fathers (Pirkei Avot), and a central yogic set of teachings, The Yoga Sutras. How do you feel about this inter-textual dialogue? What is your response to the synthesis of ideas? If you could only take one of the essays with you, which one would it be? Why?

4. I genuinely hope you enjoy these teachings and that your learning leads to a greater revelation of light, peace and healing in your life. As Rabbi Shimon Ben Gamliel taught, 'the essence is not the learning, but the practice' (*Ethics of the Fathers, 1:17*).

MORE RESOURCES

To get more resources, sign up for Marcus's regular email teachings at www.marcusjfreed.com. There are many video teachings at Marcus's Youtube channel ('Marcus Freed'), including a free library of over 100 videos for his books *The Kabbalah Sutras* and *The Kosher Sutras*.

INDEX

A

Alter Rebbe, 11, 36, 62, 111, 218, 225, 263, 265

Anger, 8, 10, 48, 113–114, 116, 118–119, 175, 192, 207, 225, 263

Asana, ix, xxi, xxiii, 11, 18–19, 30, 64, 79, 130, 135, 138, 141–142, 145, 152, 154–155, 167, 172, 177, 182, 207, 214, ix, 225, 234

Ashtanga, 55, 64, 149, 172, 193, 217–218, 225, 234

B

Baal Shem Tov, 7, 36, 159, 218, 225, 263

baseless hatred, 114, 116, 118, 225, 263

Bitachon, (trust), 217, 225, 263

Body, xiii–xvii, xx, 4–5, 8, 11, 14–18, 20–21, 23–27, 30, 32, 34–35, 37–38, 48–49, 51, 60–64, 67, 72, 74, 80–81, 84–85, 87, 92, 104–105, 107–108, 112, 114–116, 120, 123–126, 130–131, 134–136, 138–139, 142–145, 147, 149–152, 155–164, 173, 182–183, 185, 188, 197, 199–204, 207, 209–210, 212, 215, 223–224, 242, 223–225, 231, 233–235, 245

Brahmacharya, 111, 191, 225, 236

breath, ix, xx–xxi, xxiv, 4–7, 11, 17, 19, 21, 24–25, 27–29, 35, 40, 55, 59, 79–81, 93, 115, 121, 125, 131, 133, 139, 144–147, 151, 153–154, 157–161, 164, 168, 200, 215, 218, ix, 225–226, 228, 234–235, 263

C

Chagim, (festivals), xiv, 225

Chevruta, (friend), xiii, 105, 225

chi, 14, 49, 144, 192, 225

Clark, Edward, 70, 155, 192, 221, 221, 225, 263

cleansing, 14–15, 111, 162, 196, 203–204, 225–226

D

discipline, (see Gevurah, strength), 37, 92, 131, 209–210, 212, 214, 216, 225, 227, 231, 235–236, 263, 265

drishti, 67, 155–156, 225

E

Ecclesiastes, (see also Kohelet), xiv, 27, 39–41, 67, 83, 85, 161, 175, 207, 225–226, 232, 263

Echad, (one, oneness), xv, 17, 19, 61, 221, 221, 225

Edward Clark, 70, 155, 192, 221, 221, 225

Egypt, xviii, 32, 54, 84–85, 87–90, 94, 99–100, 111–112, 136, 150–151, 211–212, 225–226, 232

Emet, (truth), 62, 74, 80, 179, 182–183, 225, 227

Ethics of the Fathers, (see Pirkei Avot), xiv, 20, 72, 105, 172, 174, 176, 186–187, 192, 199, 205, 213, 215, 235, 225–226, 232, 263

Etrog, 23–25, 29, 225

F

Feuerstein, Georg, 18, 33, 110, 114, 134, 225

Forgiveness, 118–119, 211, 225

G

garudasana, (Eagle Pose), 157, 225

Gevurah, (see strength, discipline), 18, 37–38, 92, 94, 131, 193, 209, 225, 227, 231

God, (see Hashem), ix, xiii, xv–xvi, xxiii, 3–4, 6–7, 10–11, 15–19, 21, 23–25, 27–29, 32, 35, 49, 58–63, 69, 74, 76, 80–81, 84, 87–89, 92, 98, 110–114, 117–119, 124–126, 129, 133, 135–139, 145, 147–151, 155–163, 165, 183, 188, 193, 196–198, 200–202, 204, 206, 210–212, 214–215, 217–218, 221, 224, ix, 221, 224–225, 231, 233–234, 236, 263

H

Hagaddah, xv, 39, 90, 225

halacha, xv, 137–138, 221, 223–224, 221, 223–225, 231

Hashem, (see God), 10, 17, 19, 35, 60–61, 111, 159, 164, 218, 225, 264

heart, ix, 8–10, 15, 23–25, 80, 87–88, 114, 116, 119, 121, 126, 139, 156, 159–161, 168, 171, 193, 201, 207, ix, 225, 264

I

Isaiah, 11, 13–14, 53, 61, 63, 178, 202, 223, 223, 225, 232

Israel, xviii, 17, 24, 29, 47, 49, 61, 69, 75, 90, 103–104, 109, 125, 154, 176, 187, 193, 211, 225, 264

Iyengar, 18, 126, 156, 173, 179, 196, 203, 211, 213, 215, 225, 234, 264

J

Jealousy, 104, 171, 173, 196

K

Kabbalah, (see also Yichudim), ix, xiv, xviii, xx–xxi, xxiii, 7, 17, 32, 35–38, 85, 92, 104–105, 116, 123, 131, 139, 145, 157, 173, 192–193, 197, 235, 242, ix, 1, 225, 232–233, 245

King David, ix, 24, 34, 36, 161, 163, 187, 201, 217, ix, 225, 264

King Solomon, xiv, 27, 39–41, 62, 83, 126, 156, 226

klipot, (negative energy constructs), 173, 226

Kohelet, (Ecclesiastes), 27–28, 39, 225–226

INDEX

korban, 210, 226

kosher, xiv, xx, xxiii, 59, 84, 139, 202–203, 219, 221–222, 224, 235, 242, 221–222, 225–226, 235, 245

Kriyas, (yogic cleansing rituals), 204, 226

Kundalini, 4, 226, 235

L

Lecha Dodi, 147, 226

Love, 10, 18, 40–41, 49, 67–68, 89, 114, 116–117, 119, 126, 151, 159, 163, 171, 181, 192, 199, 206, 226, 264

M

Mahatma Gandhi, 211, 226

Maimonides, 20, 163, 193, 199, 206, 226–227, 264

Mantak Chia, 48–49, 192, 226

midrash, (rabbinic commentaries), 15, 24, 109, 116, 120, 123, 146–147, 182–183, 212, 214–215, 226, 232

mincha, (afternoon prayer), 17, 19, 129, 226

Mishna, (oral law), xiv, 58, 125, 172, 189, 223, 223, 226, 232

Mitzrayim, (Egypt), 112, 150, 226

Mitzvot, (commandments), 15, 67, 116, 173, 226

Mo'ed, (Festivals), xix, 226

moksha, (freedom), 154, 226

Moses, 16, 20, 34, 36–37, 54, 81, 85, 88–89, 99, 111, 113–114, 121, 153–154, 163, 176, 211, 215, 226–227, 264

Moshe, (see also: Moses), 153, 196, 206, 223, 224, 226–227

Mount Sinai, xviii, 16, 32, 80–81, 84, 113, 121, 154, 203, 226

mulah bandah, (yogic root lock), 152, 226

N

Neshama, (soul), 17, 27, 35, 63, 144, 226, 264

Neshima, (breath), 27, 35, 144, 226

Nishmat Kol Chai, 24, 143–144, 146, 158, 165, 226

Niyamas, xxi, 65, 171–172, 200, 213, 226

O

Or Ein Sof, (Endless Light), 148, 226, 232

Orlah, 171, 226

P

Patanjali, ix, 18, 64–65, 149, 176, 179, 196, 200–201, 209, 211, 218, ix, 226, 234–236, 264

Parsha, (weekly Torah reading), xiv, 226

Patthabi Jois, 172, 185, 193, 226, 234

Peace, 30, 35, 39, 70, 116, 123, 133, 135–136, 150, 162, 175–178, 217, 235, 242, 226, 245, 264

Pesukei d'zimrah, 143, 226

Pharaoh, 87–88, 91, 226

Pirkei Avot, (see also Ethics of the Fathers), xiv, 20, 172, 176, 235, 225–226, 232

power, 10, 60–61, 63, 80, 83, 94, 98, 104, 112, 138, 161, 175, 191–192, 198, 204, 217, 226, 234–235

practice, ix, xiii–xiv, xvi, xx, 3, 6, 8, 10–11, 13–15, 17, 19–20, 23–25, 27, 29, 31–33, 35–41, 43, 47, 49, 51, 53, 55, 59–61, 63–65, 67–72, 74–75, 79, 83, 87, 90–94, 98, 103–104, 106–107, 109–116, 118, 120–121, 123, 125, 129–139, 142–145, 147, 149–150, 152–156, 159–164, 167, 172, 174–175, 177–178, 182, 188, 192, 196–197, 200, 203–207, 209–210, 212, 218, 221, 223–224, 235, 242, ix, 3, 221, 223–226, 235, 245

prana, xxi, 4, 14, 55, 144, 226, 235, 264

pranayama, (yogic breathwork/energy practices), xxi, 4–6, 17, 27, 39, 115, 130, 144–145, 226, 234–235, 264

prayer, ix–x, xv–xvi, xxi, 4, 7, 15, 19, 24, 29, 36, 50, 52, 61, 94, 111, 120, 129, 136–137, 143–145, 156, 159, 163, 197, 203, 221, 224, ix, 221, 224–226, 231–233, 264

prophecy, 142, 203, 226

Proverbs , 59–60, 74, 126, 156, 207

Psalms, ix, 7, 15, 23–24, 143, 156, 160–161, 195, 201, 218, ix, 226, 232, 264

purity, 64–65, 149, 172, 193, 200–203, 226–227, 234, 263

R

Rabbi Abraham Abulafia, 145, 226

Rabbi Aryeh Kaplan, 145, 203, 226

Rabbi Ebner, 4, 222, 224, 222, 224, 226

Rabbi Joseph Tzayah, 157, 227

Rabbi Mendel Furtefas, 14, 227

Rabbi Moses Maimonides, 20, 163, 227

Rabbi Moshe Chaim Luzzato, 206, 227

Rabbi Nachman of Breslov, 204, 227

Rabbi Shimon Ben Gamliel, 20–21, 51, 125, 181, 235, 227, 233

Rabbi Shlomo Riskin, 155, 227

Rabbi Yitzhak Luria, 94, 145, 227

Rashi, 76, 171, 227, 265

Rav Matis Weinberg, xix, 227

Relationships , 15, 41, 58, 105, 116, 136, 180, 187, 202, 242

Rosh Chodesh, 53–56, 227

Ruach Elohim, 145, 227

S

Samadhi, 130, 217–218, 227, 235

Sameach b'chelko, (rejoicing in your portion), 205, 227

INDEX

santosha, (contentment), 200, 205, 227, 234

Sauca, (Cleanliness), 64, 111, 200–201, 227

Sefirah, xviii, 92, 94, 105, 157, 209, 227

sefirot, 18, 37–38, 93, 157, 173, 227, 231–232, 265

Sfat Emet, 62, 74, 80, 227

Shabbat, xiii–xvii, 3, 15, 17, 24, 27, 39–40, 43, 59, 62, 64, 67–68, 115, 126–127, 129–130, 132–139, 141–144, 146–147, 165, 167–168, 182–183, 223–224, 235, 3, 223–225, 227, 265

Shacharit, 17, 143, 227

Shalom, 133, 142, 165, 176–178, 227

Shalosh Regalim, (the three 'foot' festivals), xviii, 227

shavasana, 40, 141–142, 146, 168, 227

sheker, 182, 227

Shema, 15, 61, 123, 144, 156, 203, 221, 221, 227, 233

Sheva brachot, (seven blessings following marriage), 35, 227

Shiva, (seven days of mourning), 35, 227

Shulchan Aruch, 155, 223, 223, 227

Simchat Bet HaShoevah, 51, 227

Simchat Torah, 47, 49–52, 227

spiritual, xiv–xv, xvii–xviii, xxi, 3, 10–11, 14–17, 20, 23, 27–29, 32, 35–36, 38, 43, 47, 54, 56, 59, 61, 74, 77, 81, 84, 94, 98, 103, 105, 108–110, 114, 116, 120, 123, 130, 132, 134, 146–148, 156, 158, 163–164, 173, 179, 186, 188–189, 191–192, 196–202, 204, 212–214, 216, 227, 235

strength, (see discipline, Gevurah), 16, 18, 37, 98, 107, 137, 165, 209, 225, 227, 231, 265

study, 48, 65, 104, 172, 200, 203, 213–216, 221, 221, 227, 234

Succah, 31–36, 47, 51, 227

Succot, ix, xviii, 23–37, 39–40, 43, 47–48, 50, 52, 57, 68–69, ix, 227–228

Sun Salutes, (see Surya Namaskar*), 19, 25, 32, 85, 123, 138, 227

surrender, 161, 217–218, 227, 234

Surya Namaskar, (see Sun Salutes), xxiii–xxiv, 31, 83–84, 159, 227

svadhyaya, (self-study), 65, 200, 227, 234

T

Tadasana, (Mountain Pose), 15–16, 19, 107, 227

Taharat Mishpaha, (Laws of Family Purity), 193, 227

Tahor, 65, 202, 227

Talmud, 28, 51–52, 57–59, 61–62, 64, 68–69, 76, 81, 83, 104, 114, 116, 118, 129, 142, 175, 177, 182–183, 185, 187, 196, 214, 223, 223, 227 tapas, 43, 74, 200, 209, 211, 227, 234

Temple, xviii, 17, 19, 35, 59, 61–62, 64–65, 67–70, 113–116, 118, 120–121, 123–124, 137, 202, 210, 223, 223, 227, 231, 233

Ten Commandments, 111, 173, 185, 227

Teshuva, (return or repentance), 11, 15, 227, 265

Torah, xiv, xviii, 9–10, 13, 16, 29, 32, 35, 38, 47, 49–52, 54, 73, 80, 94, 107, 109, 111, 113–114, 116, 118, 124, 131, 154, 171, 173, 191, 193, 196, 198, 202–203, 213–215, 222, 235, 242, 222, 226–227, 245

treif, 202, 227

Truth, 4, 179–183, 188, 198–199, 212, 225, 228, 235, 265

U

Uddiyana kriya, 204, 228

Ujiya, (Breath), 153–154, 159, 228

unity, ix, xv, 11, 19, 24–25, 28–29, 60–61, 63, 79–81, 111, 133, 138–139, 144, 158, 160, 201, 214, 221, ix, 221, 228

Ushpizin, (Guests on Succot), 34, 36–37, 228

V

vinyasa, xxi, xxiii, 80, 104, 130, 135, 138, 143–145, 149, 151, 154, 160, 163, 172, 177, 204, 214, 221, 221, 228, 234–235, 265

violence, xxi, 116, 133, 171–172, 175–176, 203, 211, 228, 234, 236, 264

W

war, 4, 27, 59, 76, 175, 178, 228

warrior, 48, 59, 61, 63–64, 67, 69, 228

wealth, 31, 58, 185, 189, 197, 199–200, 205–206, 228, 265

Y

yamas, xxi, 171–172, 228, 234

Yechidah, 17, 35, 228

yichud, 145, 228

Yichudim, ix, 29, ix, 225, 228

Z

Zman Capparah, 56, 228

Zman Simchateinu, (another Biblical name for Succot), 28, 33, 228

Zohar, 36, 38, 50, 85, 104, 114–115, 173, 228, 233, 265

OTHER PUBLICATIONS BY FREEDTHINKER BOOKS

The Kabbalah Sutras:
49 Steps to Enlightenment
by Marcus J Freed
Connect to Kabbalistic wisdom within your body: find deep peace, healing and fulfil your soul's mission. *The Kabbalah Sutras* shares a system to connect with Divine Light and apply it to your body, mind, soul, relationships, business and career. *"Marcus J Freed succeeds in a unique synthesis of traditional Kabbalistic thought, contemplative meditation and bodily expression. Bubbling with fascinating sources and insights, both traditional and modern, this book is a wonderful initiation into a compelling Jewish spirituality for the 21st Century"*.
- Rabbi Dr Raphael Zarum, The London School of Jewish Studies.
8.3 x 10.6, 266 Pages, Paperback,
ISBN 978-0996350600.
Also: Kindle/E-book. $29.99/£19.99

The Kosher Sutras:
The Jewish Way in Yoga & Meditation
by Marcus J Freed
Experience Torah wisdom through the lens of yoga and meditation. *The Kosher Sutras* provide a new framework for learning ancient wisdom with an authentic and refreshing perspective. *"Freed's eloquently written and well-released practice manual unites the Western Jewish ritual, textual, and historical traditions with the philosophy and practice of Hatha Yoga"* - LA Yoga Magazine.
8.3 x 10.6, 210 pages, Paperback,
ISBN 978-162407588.
Also: Kindle/E-book. $29.99/£19.99

www.ingramcontent.com/pod-product-compliance
Lightning Source LLC
LaVergne TN
LVHW051545070426
835507LV00021B/2420